GREENBOOK'S
Fourth Guide To
Department 56
Collectibles

THE ORIGINAL SNOW VILLAGE©

THE HERITAGE VILLAGE COLLECTION™

SNOWBABIES©

GREENBOOK ®

The Most Respected Guides to Popular Collectibles & Their After Market Values

Old Coach at Main, Box 515
East Setauket, New York 11733
516.689.8466
FAX 516.689.8177

ISBN 0-923628-20-7

This paper is recycled, can be recycled, and is made from a renewable resource.

ACKNOWLEDGEMENTS

The GREENBOOK would like to thank -

Department 56 for assisting in the compilation of the factual information contained in this Guide.

The collectors, dealers, exchanges, newsletters and magazines across the country who supply us with information including secondary market status and prices.

NOTE FROM THE PUBLISHER

It's just human nature. Often times I think people purchase the deluxe model of an otherwise practical item to get additional features that are seldom, if ever, used in real life. Take a dishwasher for example. When's the last time you used your dishwasher to warm plates? Or how about the fine china or potscrubber cycles?

With three editions of the Guide under our belt, we're confident the basics are solid (i.e. the dishes are getting clean). So this is our Potscrubber Edition - more data has been added - use it if you're so inclined. Much of the additional information concerns variations. My advice? Don't drive yourself crazy with the variations. In fact, I even hesitated to include them to this degree because I feel very strongly that as the collections grow, and more and more pieces are produced in more than one country, variations are inevitable, and will eventually become something of a non-issue. So, they're here for now. They may be gone tomorrow. Staying in the kitchen for my analogies, I liken it to the day I finally tossed out the gourmet pineapple cutter because it got in the way every time I reached for the slotted spoon.

MEET PETER GEORGE, GREENBOOK DEPARTMENT 56 HISTORIAN

Most collectors naturally assume I'm an avid D56 collector. Actually I'm not. Not by your standards anyway. This year GREENBOOK will publish five guides covering at least fifteen different major collectible lines. You know how much time, energy and money it takes to do what you do. So you've probably figured out I don't - and couldn't - do this all by myself. This is my way of introducing Peter George, the new GREENBOOK Department 56 Historian. In addition to his been-around-the-block collecting anecdotes and Question & Answer section, Peter's contributions to the Fourth Edition have been many. Some were as subtle as, "Hey, the Heritage Village Utility Accessories really don't belong under 'Electrical' since there's nothing electrical about them," to suggesting and thereby confirming something we had been considering - separating the miniatures from the rest of Snowbabies. Then there's the trees. If you own the First Edition of the Guide with the accompanying infamous bookmark, you know that tree is a four letter word at GREENBOOK. Suffice it to say, the Fourth Edition has undergone yet another major review of attached trees.

Rather than being a walking encyclopedia on the Villages or Snowbabies, hopefully my expertise is in the format and presentation of the information contained in the guides. We rely on experts to help us keep you informed. So, it's Peter, not me, you're apt to see giving an informative seminar or attending events.

Peter's day job is publishing a magazine for D56 collectors, *the Village Chronicle*. Just like you don't do your due diligence before buying a stock and then not monitor it on some kind of a regular basis, likewise, you must be aware of when this Guide was published and what's happened since. The magazine's an entertaining way to stay informed throughout the year. You should also be aware GREENBOOK produces an update, designed to function as a bookmark, when anything of major significance happens. Depending on when your Guide was shipped to the retailer, an update may or may not be slipped inside the front cover. In any case, updates are available, free of charge, if you send us a stamped, self-addressed business size envelope with "D56 update" written in the lower left corner.

DISNEY & D56!

As someone who has seriously calculated how many timeshare points it would take to live year-round in Disney's Vacation Club Resort in Orlando, there now exists my first "have-to-have everything" village. As this 4th Edition goes to press, the specific information (Item #s, Names etc.) is public knowledge but not official so we chose to simply reprint the joint press release as it appeared in the *Quarterly*. It's on page 98.

A CHANGE TO THE ITEM HISTORY LIST

D56's Item History Lists are goodies everyone pretty much takes for granted. If D56 is all you collect, you might not realize how unusual it is for a producer to print a list that absolutely, positively defines what pieces are in a Collection and their status, update it every year, and make it available free of charge. I bring this up because this year there's a big change in the History List. Previously the Suggested Retail Price column reflected the *Original* Suggested Retail Price - now it's the *Current* Suggested Retail Price. As you can imagine, using the Original SRP was a big headache for retailers. Take Victoria Station for example. Previously it would have read "CURRENT" and SRP at the original "$100." Now it reads status "CURRENT" and SRP at the current "$110." If you're meticulous in charting the value of your pieces, and have never noticed before the GREENBOOK TRUMARKET Price reflects increases in SRP on current pieces, you might want to take this opportunity to adjust your records.

I'd like to take a moment here to suggest you use the Table Of Contents as your roadmap through the Guide. Notice the inclusion of information on Winter Silhouettes and the new Snowbunnies.

REAL HOUSES ARE LIKE GUIDES ...

Because of the saga in the last edition, I'm often asked about the progress of our house renovations and difficulties with the Hysterical (Historical) Society. I'd sum it up by saying I don't know what the neighborhood is going to do for entertainment when it's completed. Being around the guys working on the house on a regular basis, I've decided some idiosyncrasies are universal no matter what your profession. With them, they leave little things behind unfinished as they move on to bigger hunks of the project. That way we don't have to judge if it's perfect or not. After all, it's not finished.

The same holds true with the Guide. One of the hardest things is to let it go. As the deadline nears, invariably you think of things you'd like to do differently. This year it was doubly hard - ten days or so ago I finally had to ask Peter to go out and get himself a little reporter type notebook and write "Next Year" on the cover ...

... As I tell my 6 year-old, like Mary Poppins, we're only "practically perfect."

Thanks for buying the Guide,

Louise Patterson Langenfeld
Editor & Publisher

TABLE OF CONTENTS

HOW TO USE THIS GUIDE

The GREENBOOK ARTCHART & LISTINGS contain exclusive
GREENBOOK line drawings as well as specific factual information and
GREENBOOK TRUMARKET Prices for each piece.

Factual information includes Title, Description, Year Of Introduction, Item
Number, Material, Is it part of a Set and if so the number of pieces comprising the set, Is it Lighted?, Market Status or specific edition limit, and the
Original Suggested Retail Price.

Secondary Market Prices, as reported by retailers and collectors, are included
as well. Because there are so many factors based on individual judgements,
and because prices can vary depending on time of year or section of the
country, GREENBOOK TRUMARKET Prices are never an absolute number.
Use them as a benchmark.

The Guide is divided into three main sections: The Original Snow Village,
The Heritage Village Collection, and Snowbabies. Within each section,
GREENBOOK Listings are in chronological date of introduction order. It's
important to remember "the year of introduction indicates the year in which
the piece was designed, sculpted, and copyrighted" and the piece is generally
available to collectors the following calendar year.

Within each year the listings are in Department 56 Item Number order.

Each piece has been assigned a GREENBOOK ARTCHART Number comprised of a coded alphabetic prefix (SV = Snow Village, CIC = Christmas In
The City, etc.), followed by year of introduction, and then a sequential
number.

If you know the name of the piece but not the year of introduction, use the
Name/D56 Item #/Page # Index in the back of the Guide to locate the piece.
If you know the D56 Item # but not the name or year of introduction, use the
Item #/Page # Index.

Variations and comments are noted in the shaded area of each listing. And in
most cases there's room for your own notes as well.

DEPARTMENT 56 TIMELINE

1976 • introduces first lighted houses, Snow Village

1979 • retires buildings for first time

1988 • publishes the first of five newsletters

1989 • exhibits for the first time at the International Collectible Exposition in South Bend, IN
• 1-800-LIT-TOWN Consumer Service Line is made available to collectors

1990 • first Bachman's Village Gathering is held in Minneapolis, MN

1991 • doors of One Village Place, D56's headquarters, are opened
• publishes the first issue of the *Quarterly* magazine

1992 • the first event piece, the Gate House, is sold at selected dealers' Open House Events
• six major Gatherings featuring Jeanne-Marie Dickens are scheduled
• Forstmann, Little and Company, an investment firm, purchases Department 56 for a reported $270 million

1993 • exhibits at the International Collectible Exposition in Long Beach, CA for first time
• Forstmann, Little and Company files with the Securities and Exchange Commission to sell 4.6 million public shares of D56 stock
• Ed Bazinet becomes D56's first CEO
• Todd Bachman is promoted to President of D56

1994 • exhibits for the first time at the International Collectible Exposition in Secaucus, NJ
• schedules 13 Gatherings across the country

The Original Snow Village

1976   • D56 introduces the first six Snow Village Houses

1977   • three more SV houses are introduced creating an ongoing collection

1979   • the first pieces, ten of them, are retired
         • first time American flag is featured on a building
         • first accessory, Carolers, is introduced
         • the Meadowland Series, though not originally intended to be part of SV, is introduced

1980   • the first vehicle, the Ceramic Car, makes its debut

1982   • Gabled House and New Stone Church are the first "early release" pieces offered to GCC
         • Snowman with Broom is introduced becoming the first accessory made with another material as well as ceramic

1983   • the word "Original" is added to the Snow Village title

1985   • pieces sold in styrofoam boxes and sleeves for first time

1986   • *Snow Village Traditions*, a small book illustrated by Kristi Jensen, (now known to collectors as Snowbabies artist, Kristi Jensen Pierro) is published to commemorate the 10th Anniversary of SV

1987   • accessory sizes are scaled down

1990   • American Architectural Series is introduced

1993   • the first Limited Edition for Snow Village, Nantucket Renovation, is issued and limited to one year of production

THE ORIGINAL SNOW VILLAGE

SV76-4

COUNTRY CHURCH

Vines and painted welcome on walls, short-spired, door ajar, circular upper windows, painted side windows, snow laden tree shades one wall.

SV76-3

THE INN

Two large brick chimneys, full length covered porch, welcome mat at timbered front doors, snow laden tree on one side, bright yellow door on opposite side.

SV76-2

GABLED COTTAGE

Four-peaked roof with two chimneys, curtained windows, ivy climbs walls to roof, welcome mat, door & several windows have wreath design, snow laden tree with bluebird.

SV76-6

SMALL CHALET

Two-story small gingerbread look home, flower box with snow covered plants set off large windows on upper story, bluebirds decorate corners of flower box, chimney, tree.

SV76-1

MOUNTAIN LODGE

Bright colored skis lean against two-story lodge, upper windows painted to appear as lead panes, sunburst painted above door, snow laden tree at side.

SV76-5

STEEPLED CHURCH

One spire, large circular window over double wood front doors flanked by leaded lattice design windows, side Chapel, snow covered tree, bluebird on steeple.

ART CHART #	NAME	ITEM #	MATERIAL	SET?	♥ MARKET STATUS	ORIGINAL SRP	GREENBOOK TRUMKT PRICE
			VARIATIONS/MISC/COLLECTOR NOTES				
SV76-1	MOUNTAIN LODGE	5001-3	Ceramic	NO	✓ RETIRED 1979	$ 20.00	$ 370.00
SV76-2	GABLED COTTAGE	5002-1	Ceramic	NO	✓ RETIRED 1979	20.00	385.00
SV76-3	THE INN	5003-9	Ceramic	NO	✓ RETIRED 1979	20.00	490.00
SV76-4	COUNTRY CHURCH	5004-7	Ceramic	NO	✓ RETIRED 1979	18.00	375.00
	Also known as "Wayside Chapel."						
SV76-5	STEEPLED CHURCH	5005-4	Ceramic	NO	✓ RETIRED 1979	25.00	640.00
SV76-6	SMALL CHALET	5006-2	Ceramic	NO	✓ RETIRED 1979	15.00	365.00
	Also known as "Gingerbread Chalet." Variation in number of flowers in box and color - tan to dark brown.						

CLIPBOARD
• "Original 6" pieces characterized by simple design, rough construction, and bright colors.
• All have attached snow laden evergreen trees with unique feature – bulb that lights house also lights tree.
• The "Gabled Cottage" and "The Inn" were the first Original Snow Village pieces to put out the welcome mats.

THE ORIGINAL SNOW VILLAGE

1977 | **1977**

SV77-1

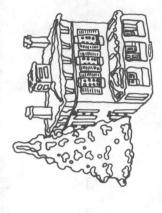

VICTORIAN HOUSE

Textured to portray shingles and clapboard. Steps lead up to front door. Stained glass inserts above windows. Attached snow laden evergreen tree.

SV77-2

MANSION

White brick with porch supported by pillars, windows are shuttered, two chimneys plus cupola on roof. Attached snow laden evergreen tree.

SV77-3

STONE CHURCH

Norman style stone building, steeple with ceramic bell. Double doors with circular window above, snow laden evergreen tree.

ART CHART #	NAME	ITEM #	MATERIAL	SET?	♟☐	MARKET STATUS	ORIGINAL SRP	GREENBOOK TRUMKT PRICE
	VARIATIONS/MISC/COLLECTOR NOTES							
SV77-1	VICTORIAN HOUSE	5007-0	Ceramic	NO	✓	RETIRED 1979	$ 30.00	$ 435.00
	Variations in color, with and without three birds on roof, and with and without attached tree.							
SV77-2	MANSION	5008-8	Ceramic	NO	✓	RETIRED 1979	30.00	550.00
	Variations in roof color.							
SV77-3	STONE CHURCH	5009-6	Ceramic	NO	✓	RETIRED 1979	35.00	725.00
	This is the original Stone Church. Size is 10.5". Ceramic bell is separate, attached by wire. See 1979, #5059-1 (SV79-6) and 1982, #5083-0 (SV82-10).							

CLIPBOARD
- Broader range of architectural styles, moved away from simple country village style.
- New building materials.
- Again, all had attached snow laden evergreen trees.

THE ORIGINAL SNOW VILLAGE

SV78-1 MAD

HOMESTEAD
Old fashioned farmhouse, front porch full length of house. Second floor bay windows. Triple window in front gable. Attached tree.

SV78-2

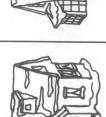

GENERAL STORE
Full length porch supported by pillars. Sign above porch. Christmas tree on porch roof. Store supplied food, postal service, & gas.

SV78-3

CAPE COD
Steep gabled roof with chimney, small dormer, and painted landscaping. Attached snow laden tree.

SV78-4

NANTUCKET
Yellow cottage with green roof. Small front porch, attached greenhouse/sunroom on side, attached snow laden tree.

SV78-5

SKATING RINK/ DUCK POND SET
Snowman, log pile, large snow laden tree.
&
Park bench, birds, large snow laden tree.

SV78-6

SMALL DOUBLE TREES
Small lighted snow laden trees with birds.

ART CHART #	NAME	ITEM #	MATERIAL	SET?	🔔	MARKET STATUS	ORIGINAL SRP	GREENBOOK TRUMKT PRICE
	VARIATIONS/MISC/COLLECTOR NOTES							
SV78-1	HOMESTEAD	5011-2	Ceramic	NO	✓	RETIRED 1984	$ 30.00	$ 240.00
SV78-2	GENERAL STORE	5012-0	Ceramic	NO	✓	RETIRED 1980	25.00	See Below
	Variations in color affect price: white @ $450, tan @ $605, and gold @ $560. Also variation in sign lettering: "Y & L" and "S & L Brothers."							
SV78-3	CAPE COD	5013-8	Ceramic	NO	✓	RETIRED 1980	20.00	360.00
SV78-4	NANTUCKET	5014-6	Ceramic	NO	✓	RETIRED 1986	25.00	315.00
	See "Nantucket Renovation," 1993, #5441-0 (SV93-1).							
SV78-5	SKATING RINK/ DUCK POND SET	5015-3	Ceramic	SET OF 2	✓	RETIRED 1979	16.00	1000.00
	One of first non-house accessory pcs. (Skating Rink is piece with snowman.) Trees were attached directly to pond bases - their size and weight caused frequent breakage, therefore retired in 1979. Revised skating pond in 1982, #5017-2 (SV82-1), with trees molded separately.							
SV78-6	SMALL DOUBLE TREES	5016-1	Ceramic	NO	✓	RETIRED 1989	13.50	52.00
	One of the first non-house accessory pieces. First w/blue birds, then red birds. GREENBOOK TRUMARKET PRICE for blue birds is $175. Mold changes and variations in amount of snow over the years as well.							

CLIPBOARD
• New designs reflected a regional influence (New England).

THE ORIGINAL SNOW VILLAGE

SV79-1

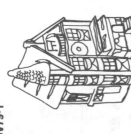

VICTORIAN

Steps lead to covered porch entry, three story turret, small balcony on third floor front room.

SV79-2

KNOB HILL

Three story San Francisco-style Victorian row house, steep steps to entry level.

SV79-3

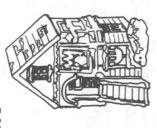

BROWNSTONE

Three stories with wreath trimmed bay windows on all floors, overall flat roof.

SV79-4

LOG CABIN

Rustic log house with stone chimney, roof extends to cover porch, log pile at side, skis by door.

SV79-5

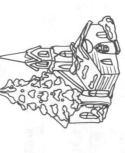

COUNTRYSIDE CHURCH

White clapboard church with central bell steeple, attached tree has all lower branches pruned.

SV79-6

STONE CHURCH

Steeple attached to one side has separate entry. Circular window above front doors.

SV79-7

SCHOOL HOUSE

American flag flies from roof peak above red brick one-room school.

SV79-8

TUDOR HOUSE

Brick chimney and fireplace on simple L-shaped timber trimmed home, split-shingle roof.

ART CHART #	NAME	ITEM #	MATERIAL	SET?	🔔 MARKET STATUS	ORIGINAL SRP	GREENBOOK TRUMKT PRICE
	VARIATIONS/MISC/COLLECTOR NOTES						
SV79-1	VICTORIAN	5054-2	Ceramic	NO	✓ RETIRED 1982	$ 30.00	$ 380.00
	Variations in color and exterior finish. They are - in order of desirability - peach, gold, and gold clapboard.						
SV79-2	KNOB HILL	5055-9	Ceramic	NO	✓ RETIRED 1981	30.00	350.00
	Two color variations: gray and yellow.						
SV79-3	BROWNSTONE	5056-7	Ceramic	NO	✓ RETIRED 1981	36.00	560.00
	Variations in roof color: gray and red. Red most desired.						
SV79-4	LOG CABIN	5057-5	Ceramic	NO	✓ RETIRED 1981	22.00	475.00
SV79-5	COUNTRYSIDE CHURCH	5058-3	Ceramic	NO	✓ RETIRED 1984	27.50	295.00
	For no snow version see MEADOWLAND 1979, #5051-8.						
SV79-6	STONE CHURCH	5059-1	Ceramic	NO	✓ RETIRED 1980	32.00	1000.00
	Height is 8.5". Ceramic bell is separate, attaches with wire. See 1977, #5009-6 (SV77-3) and 1982, #5083-0 (SV82-10).						
SV79-7	SCHOOL HOUSE	5060-9	Ceramic*	NO	✓ RETIRED 1982	30.00	340.00
	First design to feature the American flag. *Removable metal flag.						
SV79-8	TUDOR HOUSE	5061-7	Ceramic	NO	✓ RETIRED 1981	25.00	330.00

THE ORIGINAL SNOW VILLAGE

SV79-9

MISSION CHURCH

Sun dried clay with structural timbers visible at roof line. Small arched bell tower above entry.

SV79-10

MOBILE HOME

Similar to aluminum skinned Airstream mobile home. To be towed by car or truck for travel.

SV79-11

GIANT TREES

Snow covered large evergreen trees. Birds perch on branches.

SV79-12

ADOBE HOUSE

Small sundried clay home. Outside oven on side, chili peppers hang from roof beams.

ART CHART #	NAME	ITEM #	MATERIAL	SET?	🔔	MARKET STATUS	ORIGINAL SRP	GREENBOOK TRUMKT PRICE
	VARIATIONS/MISC/COLLECTOR NOTES							
SV79-9	MISSION CHURCH	5062-5	Ceramic	NO	✓	RETIRED 1980	$ 30.00	$ 1260.00
	Ceramic bell is attached by wire.							
SV79-10	MOBILE HOME	5063-3	Ceramic	NO	✓	RETIRED 1980	18.00	1700.00
SV79-11	GIANT TREES	5065-8	Ceramic	NO	✓	RETIRED 1982	20.00	360.00
SV79-12	ADOBE HOUSE	5066-6	Ceramic	NO	✓	RETIRED 1980	18.00	2495.00

CLIPBOARD
• First year of retirement.

THE ORIGINAL SNOW VILLAGE

SV80-1

CATHEDRAL CHURCH
Central dome with two shorter bell towers.

SV80-2

STONE MILL HOUSE
Waterwheel on dark weathered stone block mill, bag of grain hangs from block and tackle, another bag propped by door.

SV80-3

COLONIAL FARM HOUSE
Wide front porch, two front dormers in attic, symmetrical layout of windows.

SV80-4

TOWN CHURCH
Short bell tower rises from central nave area, attached tree tucks in close to side chapel.

SV80-5

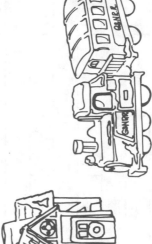

TRAIN STATION WITH 3 TRAIN CARS
Station clock over entry door, two small wings on either side of main room, brick and timbered design.
Train – engine, passenger car, baggage/mail caboose. "G&N RR" on all cars.

ART CHART #	NAME	ITEM #	MATERIAL	SET?	🔔	MARKET STATUS	ORIGINAL SRP	GREENBOOK TRU MKT PRICE
	VARIATIONS/MISC/COLLECTOR NOTES							
SV80-1	CATHEDRAL CHURCH	5067-4	Ceramic*	NO	✓	RETIRED 1981	$ 36.00	$ 1895.00
	Production problems (fragile domes) forced retirement after one year. *Stained glass windows are acrylic. Inspired by St. Paul's Cathedral in St. Paul, MN.							
SV80-2	STONE MILL HOUSE	5068-2	Ceramic	NO	✓	RETIRED 1982	30.00	545.00
	Separate bag of oats hung with wire.							
SV80-3	COLONIAL FARM HOUSE	5070-9	Ceramic	NO	✓	RETIRED 1982	30.00	365.00
SV80-4	TOWN CHURCH	5071-7	Ceramic	NO	✓	RETIRED 1982	33.00	355.00
SV80-5	TRAIN STATION WITH 3 TRAIN CARS	5085-6	Ceramic	SET OF 4	✓	RETIRED 1985	100.00	See Below
	Variation: Original station, smaller in size and had 6 window panes, round window in door. Brick on front, not sides - Market Price $375. Revised had 8 window panes, 2 square windows in door, brick on front and sides - Market Price $325. First Original Snow Village train and station design. All four pieces lit.							

CLIPBOARD
• Few introductions due to large number of ongoing pieces.
• Understamping accompanied adhesive stickers.

THE ORIGINAL SNOW VILLAGE

SV81-1

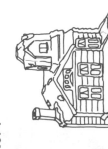

WOODEN CLAPBOARD

White house with green roof and trim and wraparound porch. Red brick chimney.

SV81-2

ENGLISH COTTAGE

Thatched roof and timbered frame, two chimneys. 1 1/2 stories. Roof comes down to meet top of first story.

SV81-3

BARN

Red barn and silo. Grey roof, two vents on roof ridge, root cellar on side, hay loft over animals and equipment.

SV81-4

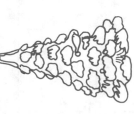

CORNER STORE

Red brick with one large display window, entry door on corner, bay window in family living area, shutters on windows, shingled roof.

SV81-5

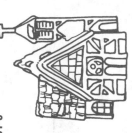

BAKERY

Bakery store beneath family living area, white with green trim, half turret form gives unique angle to front and second story bay window.

SV81-6

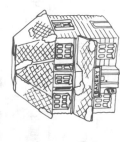

ENGLISH CHURCH

Steep pitched roof, side chapel, steeple topped by gold cross, arched windows, triangular window in gable above entry double doors.

SV81-7

LARGE SINGLE TREE

One snow covered evergreen tree. Birds perch on branches.

ART CHART #	NAME	ITEM #	MATERIAL	SET?	🔔	MARKET STATUS	ORIGINAL SRP	GREENBOOK TRUMKT PRICE
	VARIATIONS/MISC/COLLECTOR NOTES							
SV81-1	WOODEN CLAPBOARD	5072-5	Ceramic	NO	✓	RETIRED 1984	$ 32.00	$ 260.00
SV81-2	ENGLISH COTTAGE	5073-3	Ceramic	NO	✓	RETIRED 1982	25.00	285.00
	Variations in color of thatched roof.							
SV81-3	BARN	5074-1	Ceramic	NO	✓	RETIRED 1984	32.00	460.00
	a/k/a "Original Barn."							
SV81-4	CORNER STORE	5076-8	Ceramic	NO	✓	RETIRED 1983	30.00	260.00
SV81-5	BAKERY	5077-6	Ceramic	NO	✓	RETIRED 1983	30.00	275.00
	This is the original Bakery. Same Item # was used for the 1986 Bakery – a new and different design. Designed after The Scofield Building in Northfield, MN.							
SV81-6	ENGLISH CHURCH	5078-4	Ceramic	NO	✓	RETIRED 1982	30.00	390.00
	The Cross is separate and inserts into the steeple.							
SV81-7	LARGE SINGLE TREE	5080-6	Ceramic	NO	✓	RETIRED 1989	17.00	55.00
	Mold changes and variations in amount of snow over the years.							

THE ORIGINAL SNOW VILLAGE

SV82-1

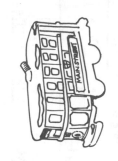

SKATING POND

Snowman on edge of small snow covered skating pond. Tree trunks piled together provide seating. Two evergreen trees complete the set.

SV82-2

STREET CAR

Bright yellow with green "Main Street" sign on side. #2 car, hook-up on top for pole to connect to electric power.

SV82-3

CENTENNIAL HOUSE

Two story clapboard, square tower, carved and curved window frames, "wooden" balcony & porch.

SV82-4

CARRIAGE HOUSE

Bright lamps flank entry to storage area for carriages. Driver has small apartment above.

SV82-5

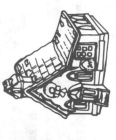

PIONEER CHURCH

Simple design appears to be of wood construction, front notice board sends joy to all who pass, short steeple on front of roof ridge.

SV82-6

SWISS CHALET

Stone base walls support timber upper stories. Upper floor has front balcony with railing and is enclosed by roof overhang. Unusual roof.

SV82-7

BANK

Corner building with entry by revolving door. Outside covered stairway leads to second story. Sign becomes part of corner design.

SV82-8

GABLED HOUSE

Shingled house with four gabled roof, two small covered porches, one lower and one upper window to each side.

ART CHART #	NAME	ITEM #	MATERIAL	SET?	🔔	MARKET STATUS	ORIGINAL SRP	GREENBOOK TRUMKT PRICE
				VARIATIONS/MISC/COLLECTOR NOTES				
SV82-1	SKATING POND	5017-2	Ceramic	SET OF 2	✓	RETIRED 1984	$ 25.00	$ 390.00
	Replaces the Skating Rink/Duck Pond Set (1978, #5015-3, SV78-5). Has two trees. Trees are separate from the pond.							
SV82-2	STREET CAR	5019-9	Ceramic	NO	✓	RETIRED 1984	16.00	368.00
SV82-3	CENTENNIAL HOUSE	5020-2	Ceramic	NO	✓	RETIRED 1984	32.00	350.00
SV82-4	CARRIAGE HOUSE	5021-0	Ceramic	NO	✓	RETIRED 1984	28.00	305.00
SV82-5	PIONEER CHURCH	5022-9	Ceramic	NO	✓	RETIRED 1984	30.00	310.00
SV82-6	SWISS CHALET	5023-7	Ceramic	NO	✓	RETIRED 1984	28.00	415.00
SV82-7	BANK	5024-5	Ceramic	NO	✓	RETIRED 1983	32.00	600.00
SV82-8	GABLED HOUSE	5081-4	Ceramic	NO	✓	RETIRED 1983	30.00	360.00
	Variations in color. Same Item # was used for the 1987 Red Barn (SV87-7). Early release to Gift Creations Concepts.							

THE ORIGINAL SNOW VILLAGE

SV82-9

FLOWER SHOP

Flower boxes rest outside by large display window. Rolled up awnings above front windows.

SV82-10

NEW STONE CHURCH

Long nave with side chapel, stone block construction, steeple rises on side opposite chapel. Front has arched windows and two lamps.

ART CHART #	NAME	ITEM #	MATERIAL	SET?	🔔	MARKET STATUS	ORIGINAL SRP	GREENBOOK TRUMKT PRICE
			VARIATIONS/MISC/COLLECTOR NOTES					
SV82-9	FLOWER SHOP	5082-2	Ceramic	NO	✓	RETIRED 1983	$ 25.00	$ 425.00
	Variations in color. Same Item # was used for the 1987 Jefferson School (SV87-8).							
SV82-10	NEW STONE CHURCH	5083-0	Ceramic	NO	✓	RETIRED 1984	32.00	370.00
	Early release to Gift Creations Concepts.							

THE ORIGINAL SNOW VILLAGE

SV83-1

TOWN HALL

Brick and stone, two corner covered side entries, symmetrical design (window over window), steeple above front main wall.

SV83-2

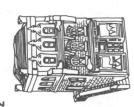

GROCERY

Red brick, full painted display windows, decorative cornice trim above/below front windows. Outside staircase leads to family quarters.

SV83-3

VICTORIAN COTTAGE

Ornate carved woodwork on house front, ornamental arched entry design. First floor French windows separated by pillars.

SV83-4

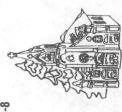

GOVERNOR'S MANSION

Brick, metal ironwork featured on roof cupola, wide entry steps, repetitive design above door, second story, and central attic windows.

SV83-5

TURN OF THE CENTURY

Steps lead to covered entry, front triangular ornate design crowns front gable, squared turret rises from left front corner and ends in highest roof peak.

SV83-6

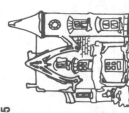

GINGERBREAD HOUSE

Designed like a Christmas edible treat. Cookies trim sides while candy canes and sugar heart decorate roof.

SV83-7

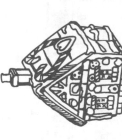

VILLAGE CHURCH

Stone steps lead to double carved doors, design repeats on roof trim. Steeple has long narrow openings. Pointed arch windows are featured.

SV83-8

GOTHIC CHURCH

Stone block, steeple rises straight from large double doors ending in a cross. Bell chamber has ornate grillwork. Smaller entry doors flank central area repeating design.

ART CHART #	NAME	ITEM #	MATERIAL	SET?	🔔	MARKET STATUS	ORIGINAL SRP	GREENBOOK TRU/MKT PRICE
	VARIATIONS/MISC/COLLECTOR NOTES							
SV83-1	TOWN HALL	5000-8	Ceramic*	NO	✓	RETIRED 1984	$ 32.00	$ 330.00
	Ceramic bell in tower. *Stamped metal weathervane is separate.							
SV83-2	GROCERY	5001-6	Ceramic	NO	✓	RETIRED 1985	35.00	300.00
SV83-3	VICTORIAN COTTAGE	5002-4	Ceramic	NO	✓	RETIRED 1984	35.00	360.00
SV83-4	GOVERNOR'S MANSION	5003-2	Ceramic*	NO	✓	RETIRED 1985	32.00	300.00
	*Metal trim on front tower.							
SV83-5	TURN OF THE CENTURY	5004-0	Ceramic	NO	✓	RETIRED 1986	36.00	235.00
SV83-6	GINGERBREAD HOUSE	5025-3	Ceramic	NO		RETIRED 1984	24.00	270.00
	See footnote[1], page 31.							
SV83-7	VILLAGE CHURCH	5026-1	Ceramic	NO	✓	RETIRED 1984	30.00	375.00
	Early release to Gift Creations Concepts.							
SV83-8	GOTHIC CHURCH	5028-8	Ceramic	NO	✓	RETIRED 1986	36.00	275.00

SV83-9

PARSONAGE

Tower rises above entry. Ornate coping on front gable topped by Cross. Coping details repeated around windows, doors, and small balcony. Community rooms on first floor, family lives upstairs.

SV83-10

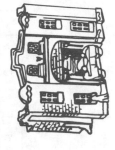

WOODEN CHURCH

White clapboard, crossed timber design repeats over door, roof peak, and steeple. Side chapel has separate entry door.

SV83-11

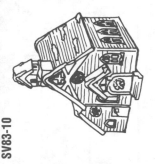

FIRE STATION

Central doors open to reveal red fire truck. Brick columns from base to roof add to sturdy look. Dalmatian sits by entry ready when necessary.

SV83-12

ENGLISH TUDOR

Stucco finish. Brick chimneys. Three front roof peaks create front gable design.

SV83-13

CHATEAU

First story large windows which include front and side bow windows are a feature. Diamond design on roof shingles, stone for walls, cylindrical chimney with domed flue cap. Front dormers and side peaks exhibit ornate carved design.

ART CHART #	NAME	ITEM #	MATERIAL	SET?	💡	MARKET STATUS	ORIGINAL SRP	GREENBOOK TRUMKT PRICE
	VARIATIONS/MISC/COLLECTOR NOTES							
SV83-9	PARSONAGE	5029-6	Ceramic	NO	✓	RETIRED 1985	$ 35.00	$ 380.00
SV83-10	WOODEN CHURCH	5031-8	Ceramic	NO	✓	RETIRED 1985	30.00	375.00
SV83-11	FIRE STATION	5032-6	Ceramic	NO	✓	RETIRED 1984	32.00	650.00
	Variation: without dog.							
SV83-12	ENGLISH TUDOR	5033-4	Ceramic	NO	✓	RETIRED 1985	30.00	260.00
SV83-13	CHATEAU	5084-9	Ceramic	NO	✓	RETIRED 1984	35.00	470.00
	Early release to Gift Creations Concepts.							

[1] In 1983, Department 56 issued the **Gingerbread House** with all intentions of it being a lit house. After realizing it did not fit well with the other Snow Village Houses, Department 56 decided to close the light hole in the back, put in a slot for coins and create a bank! Some of the original lit pieces made their way to consumers through the Bachman's stores, leading to much of the confusion. Adding to the confusion, is the fact that the Gingerbread House is listed as a Snow Village piece in the SV History List. (Note it does not appear in the new Snow Village poster.)

SV84-1

MAIN STREET HOUSE

White and green 1 1/2 story house. Clapboard lower story with timbered upper story, two lamps outside front door.

SV84-2

STRATFORD HOUSE

Vertical ornamental timbers featured, gables all rise to same height.

SV84-3

HAVERSHAM HOUSE

All gables, balconies, porch, decorated with ornately carved woodwork.

SV84-4

GALENA HOUSE

Steps lead to double entry doors of brick home. Bay window fills one side. Second floor incorporated into roof construction.

SV84-5

RIVER ROAD HOUSE

White house, large and grand with many windows, first floor front windows are highlighted with half circle paned glass above them, side bay windows project out from house wall.

SV84-6

DELTA HOUSE

Brick house with balcony above wrap-around porch which is separate from entry. Porch design is repeated where roof and brick meet and on turret.

SV84-7

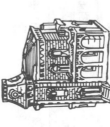

BAYPORT

Corner entry with a turret addition positioned between the two main wings of two story house.

SV84-8

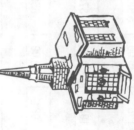

CONGREGATIONAL CHURCH

Brick with fieldstone front. Stone repeated on steeple. Louver vents on belfry.

ART CHART #	NAME	ITEM #	MATERIAL	SET?	🔔	MARKET STATUS	ORIGINAL SRP	GREENBOOK TRUMKT PRICE
	VARIATIONS/MISC/COLLECTOR NOTES							
SV84-1	MAIN STREET HOUSE	5005-9	Ceramic	NO	✓	RETIRED 1986	$ 27.00	$ 250.00
	Early release to Gift Creations Concepts.							
SV84-2	STRATFORD HOUSE	5007-5	Ceramic	NO	✓	RETIRED 1986	28.00	215.00
SV84-3	HAVERSHAM HOUSE	5008-3	Ceramic	NO	✓	RETIRED 1987	37.00	310.00
	Early release to Gift Creations Concepts. Variations in size.							
SV84-4	GALENA HOUSE	5009-1	Ceramic	NO	✓	RETIRED 1985	32.00	330.00
SV84-5	RIVER ROAD HOUSE	5010-5	Ceramic	NO	✓	RETIRED 1987	36.00	220.00
	Early release to Gift Creations Concepts. Variations in window cuts.							
SV84-6	DELTA HOUSE	5012-1	Ceramic*	NO	✓	RETIRED 1986	32.00	345.00
	*"Iron works" atop tower.							
SV84-7	BAYPORT	5015-6	Ceramic	NO	✓	RETIRED 1986	30.00	230.00
SV84-8	CONGREGATIONAL CHURCH	5034-2	Ceramic	NO	✓	RETIRED 1985	28.00	540.00

SV84-9

TRINITY CHURCH

Steeples of different heights, clerestory windows to bring additional light to central nave, two large wreaths by front doors.

SV84-10

SUMMIT HOUSE

Corner house features rounded turret, large entry door with side lights, cornices appear to support roof edge. Each second story window capped by a molded projection.

SV84-11

NEW SCHOOL HOUSE

Two story schoolhouse with bell tower and clock.

SV84-12

PARISH CHURCH

White country church with unique three level steeple. Arched windows, red door, circular window over entry.

ART CHART #	NAME	ITEM #	MATERIAL	SET?	![]	MARKET STATUS	ORIGINAL SRP	GREENBOOK TRU/MKT PRICE
	VARIATIONS/MISC/COLLECTOR NOTES							
SV84-9	TRINITY CHURCH	5035-0	Ceramic	NO	✓	RETIRED 1986	$ 32.00	$ 305.00
SV84-10	SUMMIT HOUSE	5036-9	Ceramic	NO	✓	RETIRED 1985	28.00	385.00
SV84-11	NEW SCHOOL HOUSE	5037-7	Ceramic*	NO	✓	RETIRED 1986	35.00	275.00
	*Separate flag - wooden pole, paper flag (not shown).							
SV84-12	PARISH CHURCH	5039-3	Ceramic	NO	✓	RETIRED 1986	32.00	370.00

THE ORIGINAL SNOW VILLAGE

SV85-1

STUCCO BUNGALOW

Two story small house with one roof dormer as mini tower, second dormer features timbered design. Entry door built into archway under a low roof peak. Wreath and garland decorate door.

SV85-2

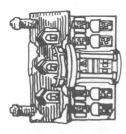

WILLIAMSBURG HOUSE

Traditional two story colonial, all windows shuttered, three dormers, two chimneys, covered entry topped by second floor balcony.

SV85-3

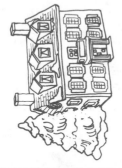

PLANTATION HOUSE

Entry features two story wood columns, three dormers, two chimneys, four first floor front windows have canopies.

SV85-4

CHURCH OF THE OPEN DOOR

Steeple is on side chapel. Design over front entry above circular window has small repeated motif on eaves.

SV85-5

SPRUCE PLACE

Victorian with windowed turret rising above covered porch. Decorative molding above porch, windows, dormer. Circular window over porch decorated with wreath.

SV85-6

DUPLEX

A two-family house with shared entry. Each family had up/down rooms and a bay window. Design has small second story balcony and roof dormers.

SV85-7

DEPOT AND TRAIN WITH 2 TRAIN CARS

Two wings connected by a central area, each wing has its own chimney, corners of building fortified with stone blocks.

SV85-8

RIDGEWOOD

Porches run length of both first and second story. First floor front windows are arched and design is repeated over front door and on attic windows.

ART CHART #	NAME	ITEM #	MATERIAL	SET?	⚡	MARKET STATUS	ORIGINAL SRP	GREENBOOK TRU MKT PRICE
	VARIATIONS/MISC/COLLECTOR NOTES							
SV85-1	STUCCO BUNGALOW	5045-8	Ceramic	NO	✓	RETIRED 1986	$ 30.00	$ 385.00
SV85-2	WILLIAMSBURG HOUSE	5046-6	Ceramic	NO	✓	RETIRED 1988	37.00	145.00
SV85-3	PLANTATION HOUSE	5047-4	Ceramic	NO	✓	RETIRED 1987	37.00	118.00
SV85-4	CHURCH OF THE OPEN DOOR	5048-2	Ceramic	NO	✓	RETIRED 1988	34.00	135.00
SV85-5	SPRUCE PLACE	5049-0	Ceramic	NO	✓	RETIRED 1987	33.00	270.00
SV85-6	DUPLEX	5050-4	Ceramic	NO	✓	RETIRED 1987	35.00	165.00
SV85-7	DEPOT AND TRAIN WITH 2 TRAIN CARS	5051-2	Ceramic	SET OF 4	✓	RETIRED 1988	65.00	135.00
	Train is non-lighting. Variations in color and depot exterior finish. Second Original Snow Village train and station design. Coal car has plastic bag of coal.							
SV85-8	RIDGEWOOD	5052-0	Ceramic	NO	✓	RETIRED 1987	35.00	165.00

SV86-1

WAVERLY PLACE

Ornate Victorian home has two different turret-like window designs. First story capped by molding and roof shingles creating unique bowed window. Second story features half moon window highlights and carved moldings.

SV86-2

TWIN PEAKS

Two matching three story stone turrets, a multitude of windows on each story soften fortress look. Red entry doors reached by wide steps.

SV86-3

2101 MAPLE

Brick two story home. Side of front porch built out from stone turret. Two story bay windows capped by half circle window.

SV86-4

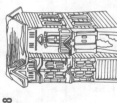

LINCOLN PARK DUPLEX

Two family attached home. Each has two story bay windows and share a front door. Floor plan unique feature is placement of chimneys – as if floor plans reversed, one is at front, other is at rear.

SV86-5

SONOMA HOUSE

Flavor of Southwest. Stucco walls, red roof. Decorative curved front rises up two and a half stories. Square turret adjacent to front door capped by same design which repeats on chimney.

SV86-6

HIGHLAND PARK HOUSE

Brick, timbered, and gabled house brings English Tudor design to cozy home. Rounded arch front door repeats theme in two windows in mid roof gable. Brick chimney on side. Layout of roof shingles add to English flavor.

SV86-7

BEACON HILL HOUSE

A row house, typical of urban Boston, MA neighborhoods. House has a solid compact look. Features bay windows on first and second story highlighted by paneled framing. Balcony on other front window also serves as canopy over oval paned front door.

SV86-8

PACIFIC HEIGHTS HOUSE

A West Coast row house that appears tall and narrow based on repeated vertical theme of front porch/balcony support columns. Motif repeated on windows and reinforced by pointed arch and roof line.

ART CHART #	NAME	ITEM #	MATERIAL	SET?	🐛	MARKET STATUS	ORIGINAL SRP	GREENBOOK TRU MKT PRICE
	VARIATIONS/MISC/COLLECTOR NOTES							
SV86-1	WAVERLY PLACE	5041-5	Ceramic	NO	✓	RETIRED 1986	$ 35.00	$ 300.00
	Early release to Gift Creations Concepts, Fall 1985. Designed after the Gingerbread Mansion in Ferndale, CA.							
SV86-2	TWIN PEAKS	5042-3	Ceramic	NO	✓	RETIRED 1986	32.00	510.00
	Early release to Gift Creations Concepts, Fall 1985.							
SV86-3	2101 MAPLE	5043-1	Ceramic	NO	✓	RETIRED 1986	32.00	360.00
	Early release to Gift Creations Concepts, Fall 1985.							
SV86-4	LINCOLN PARK DUPLEX	5060-1	Ceramic	NO	✓	RETIRED 1988	33.00	125.00
SV86-5	SONOMA HOUSE	5062-8	Ceramic	NO	✓	RETIRED 1988	33.00	118.00
	Early release to Gift Creations Concepts, Fall 1986.							
SV86-6	HIGHLAND PARK HOUSE	5063-6	Ceramic	NO	✓	RETIRED 1988	35.00	150.00
	Early release to Gift Creations Concepts, Fall 1986.							
SV86-7	BEACON HILL HOUSE	5065-2	Ceramic	NO	✓	RETIRED 1988	31.00	165.00
SV86-8	PACIFIC HEIGHTS HOUSE	5066-0	Ceramic	NO	✓	RETIRED 1988	33.00	100.00

THE ORIGINAL SNOW VILLAGE

SV86-9

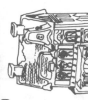

RAMSEY HILL HOUSE
Victorian with double chimneys. Steps to front door, porch is adjacent to entry. Side door also features small porch. Low balustrade fronts second story windows. Handpainting adds detailing to design.

SV86-13

TOY SHOP
Front windows display toys. Roof molding brings focus to teddy bear design under pediment. Three story brick.

SV86-10

SAINT JAMES CHURCH
Long central nave flanked by lower roofed side sections fronted by two towers. Gold main cross reinforced by smaller crosses on each section of tower roof. Smaller round windows repeat central window over entry. Announcement panels copy shape and design of front doors.

SV86-14

APOTHECARY
Two doors flank a central display bow window. Bas-relief of a mortar and pestle symbolizes the profession of owner and is on front panel above second floor family windows.

SV86-11

ALL SAINTS CHURCH
Smaller country church, simple design of long nave with entry door in base of bell tower.

SV86-15

BAKERY
Corner bakery with two large multi-paned display windows protected by ribbed canopy. Greek key designs around roof edging highlight the bas-relief cupcake topped by a cherry that is centrally placed over entry.

SV86-12

CARRIAGE HOUSE
Small home from building used originally for carriages. A second story is achieved with many dormer windows changing the distinctive flat and curved roof. Fieldstone makes up the foundation allowing great weight during original function.

SV86-16

DINER
An eating place based on the railroads famous dining car. Reputation of good, wholesome food. Large windows are a feature. Glass block entry protects diners from weather as customers come in/go out. Diners generally have counter service as well as a dining room.

ART CHART #	NAME	ITEM #	MATERIAL	SET?	🛍	MARKET STATUS	ORIGINAL SRP	GREENBOOK TRU MKT PRICE
			VARIATIONS/MISC/COLLECTOR NOTES					
SV86-9	RAMSEY HILL HOUSE	5067-9	Ceramic	NO	✓	RETIRED 1989	$ 36.00	$ 98.00
	Early release to Gift Creations Concepts, Fall 1986.							
SV86-10	SAINT JAMES CHURCH	5068-7	Ceramic	NO	✓	RETIRED 1988	37.00	160.00
SV86-11	ALL SAINTS CHURCH	5070-9	Ceramic	NO	✓	CURRENT	38.00	45.00
SV86-12	CARRIAGE HOUSE	5071-7	Ceramic	NO	✓	RETIRED 1988	29.00	110.00
SV86-13	TOY SHOP	5073-3	Ceramic	NO	✓	RETIRED 1990	36.00	90.00
	Main Street design.							
SV86-14	APOTHECARY	5076-8	Ceramic	NO	✓	RETIRED 1990	34.00	85.00
	Main Street design. Some sleeves read "Antique Shop."							
SV86-15	BAKERY	5077-6	Ceramic	NO	✓	RETIRED 1991	35.00	80.00
	Main Street design. Same Item # was used for the first Original Snow Village Bakery: 1981 Bakery (SV81-5).							
SV86-16	DINER	5078-4	Ceramic	NO	✓	RETIRED 1987	22.00	530.00
	Also known as "Mickey's." Designed after Mickey's Diner in St. Paul, MN.							

THE ORIGINAL SNOW VILLAGE

SV87-1

ST. ANTHONY HOTEL & POST OFFICE

Three story red brick with green trim. Dated 1886, the address of this hotel is "56 Main Street." American flag flies outside the ground floor P.O. Two chimneys and skylight on roof.

SV87-2

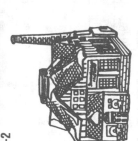

SNOW VILLAGE FACTORY

Wood building rises on stone block base with tall smokestack at rear. Factory products were available in small shop at front.

SV87-3

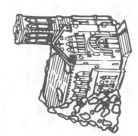

CATHEDRAL

Mosaic "stained glass" decorates the Gothic windows on all sides as well as the large turret.

SV87-4

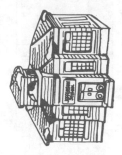

CUMBERLAND HOUSE

Multi-colored curved roof supported by four columns, two chimneys, shuttered windows.

SV87-5

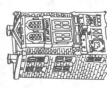

SPRINGFIELD HOUSE

Lower level has two multi-paned bay windows, one is bowed. Upper level windows are shuttered. Roof dormers are half-circle sunbursts. Stone chimney completes this clapboard home.

SV87-6

LIGHTHOUSE

Five story lighthouse beacon rises from sturdy stone slab base and is connected to caretaker's cottage.

SV87-7

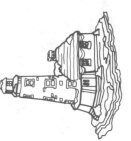

RED BARN

Stone base, wooden barn, double cross-buck doors on long side, hayloft doors above main doors. Three ventilator cupolas on roof ridge. Cat sleeps in hayloft.

SV87-8

JEFFERSON SCHOOL

Two room schoolhouse with large multi-paned windows with top transoms. Short bell tower incorporated into roof.

ART CHART #	NAME	ITEM #	MATERIAL	SET?	🔔	MARKET STATUS	ORIGINAL SRP	GREENBOOK TRUMKT PRICE
	VARIATIONS/MISC/COLLECTOR NOTES							
SV87-1	ST. ANTHONY HOTEL & POST OFFICE	5006-7	Ceramic*	NO	✓	RETIRED 1989	$ 40.00	$ 115.00
	Main Street addition. *Metal flag.							
SV87-2	SNOW VILLAGE FACTORY	5013-0	Ceramic	SET OF 2	✓	RETIRED 1989	45.00	110.00
	Smoke stack is separate.							
SV87-3	CATHEDRAL	5019-9	Ceramic	NO	✓	RETIRED 1990	50.00	110.00
SV87-4	CUMBERLAND HOUSE	5024-5	Ceramic	NO	✓	CURRENT	42.00	45.00
SV87-5	SPRINGFIELD HOUSE	5027-0	Ceramic	NO	✓	RETIRED 1990	40.00	100.00
SV87-6	LIGHTHOUSE	5030-0	Ceramic	NO	✓	RETIRED 1988	36.00	650.00
SV87-7	RED BARN	5081-4	Ceramic	NO	✓	RETIRED 1992	38.00	75.00
	Same Item # was used for the 1982 Gabled House (SV82-8). Early release to Gift Creations Concepts.							
SV87-8	JEFFERSON SCHOOL	5082-2	Ceramic	NO	✓	RETIRED 1991	36.00	115.00
	Same Item # was used for the 1982 Flower Shop (SV82-9). Early release to Gift Creations Concepts.							

THE ORIGINAL SNOW VILLAGE

SV87-9

FARM HOUSE
2 1/2 story wood frame home with front full-length porch. Roof interest is two low, one high peak with attic window in highest peak.

SV87-10

FIRE STATION NO. 2
Large double doors for station housing two engines, side stair leads to living quarters. Brick building with stone arch design at engine doors and front windows.

SV87-11

SNOW VILLAGE RESORT LODGE
Bright yellow with green, scalloped roof, covered porch and side entry. Bay windows on front house section. Back section rises to dormered 3 1/2 stories with louvered ventilator areas directly under roof cap.

ART CHART #	NAME	ITEM #	MATERIAL	SET?	🖐	MARKET STATUS	ORIGINAL SRP	GREENBOOK TRUMKT PRICE
			VARIATIONS/MISC/COLLECTOR NOTES					
SV87-9	FARM HOUSE	5089-0	Ceramic	NO	✓	RETIRED 1992	$ 40.00	$ 75.00
SV87-10	FIRE STATION NO. 2	5091-1	Ceramic	NO	✓	RETIRED 1989	40.00	140.00
	Early release to Gift Creations Concepts.							
SV87-11	SNOW VILLAGE RESORT LODGE	5092-0	Ceramic	NO	✓	RETIRED 1989	55.00	120.00

CLIPBOARD
- Effort to bring the accessories down to scale.

THE ORIGINAL SNOW VILLAGE

SV88-1

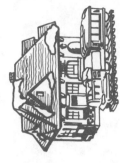

VILLAGE MARKET

Silk-screened "glass" windows detail merchandise available, red and white canopy protects shoppers using in/out doors. Sign over second story windows.

SV88-2

KENWOOD HOUSE

Old-fashioned wrap-around veranda with arched openings on three story home. Front facade features scalloped shingles on third story.

SV88-3

MAPLE RIDGE INN

Replica of Victorian mansion, ornamental roof piece concealed lightning rods.

SV88-4

VILLAGE STATION AND TRAIN

Station features an outside ticket window, soft drink vending machine, and outside benches, with a three car train.

SV88-5

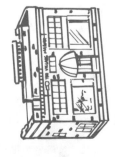

COBBLESTONE ANTIQUE SHOP

Silk-screened front windows display antiques for sale, bay window fills second story width, building date of 1881 on arched cornice.

SV88-6

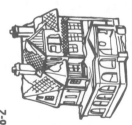

CORNER CAFE

"Pie" and "Coffee" silkscreen on windows of corner restaurant with red, white, and blue striped awnings on main windows. Corner double door entrance. Building date of 1875 inscribed on corner turret design.

SV88-7

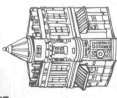

SINGLE CAR GARAGE

Double doors open to house car, two outside lights for convenience, designed to look like house, windows have shutters, roof has dormers, roof projects over wood pile.

SV88-8

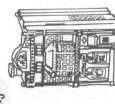

HOME SWEET HOME/ HOUSE & WINDMILL

Based on landmark historic home, saltbox with asymmetrical arrangement of windows. Doors for root cellar are at front corner, one central brick chimney. Four bladed windmill.

ART CHART #	NAME	ITEM #	MATERIAL	SET?	♺	MARKET STATUS	ORIGINAL SRP	GREENBOOK TRUMKT PRICE
	VARIATIONS/MISC/COLLECTOR NOTES							
SV88-1	VILLAGE MARKET	5044-0	Ceramic	NO	✓	RETIRED 1991	$ 39.00	$ 75.00
	Early release to Gift Creations Concepts.							
SV88-2	KENWOOD HOUSE	5054-7	Ceramic	NO	✓	RETIRED 1990	50.00	100.00
	Early release to Gift Creations Concepts.							
SV88-3	MAPLE RIDGE INN	5121-7	Ceramic	NO	✓	RETIRED 1990	55.00	75.00
	Interpretation of an American landmark in Cambridge, New York. 1991 GCC Catalog Exclusive @ $75.00.							
SV88-4	VILLAGE STATION AND TRAIN	5122-5	Ceramic	SET OF 4	✓	RETIRED 1992	65.00	105.00
	Third Original Snow Village train and station design.							
SV88-5	COBBLESTONE ANTIQUE SHOP	5123-3	Ceramic	NO	✓	RETIRED 1992	36.00	70.00
SV88-6	CORNER CAFE	5124-1	Ceramic	NO	✓	RETIRED 1991	37.00	80.00
SV88-7	SINGLE CAR GARAGE	5125-0	Ceramic	NO	✓	RETIRED 1990	22.00	65.00
SV88-8	HOME SWEET HOME/HOUSE & WINDMILL	5126-8	Ceramic*	SET OF 2	✓	RETIRED 1991	60.00	110.00
	* Metal blades of windmill are separate. Inspired by the home of John Howard Payne, composer of "Home Sweet Home," in East Hampton, NY.							

THE ORIGINAL SNOW VILLAGE

SV88-9

REDEEMER CHURCH

Stone corners add strength and support to church and bell tower. Arched windows, heavy wooden double doors.

SV88-10

SERVICE STATION

Two gas pumps, candy machine, restroom, work area and office. White building blue roof, red trim.

SV88-11

STONEHURST HOUSE

Red brick punctuated with black and white painted bricks. Half circle sunburst design second story dormers restate the arch shape of first floor windows. Shutters repeat arch design.

SV88-12

PALOS VERDES

Spanish style with green tiled roof, covered entry porch, stucco finish, second floor has shuttered windows. Coming forward from main wing is two story round turret and ground floor window alcove.

ART CHART #	NAME	ITEM #	MATERIAL	SET?	☎ MARKET STATUS	ORIGINAL SRP	GREENBOOK TRU MKT PRICE
			VARIATIONS/MISC/COLLECTOR NOTES				
SV88-9	REDEEMER CHURCH	5127-6	Ceramic	NO	✓ RETIRED 1992	$ 42.00	$ 75.00
SV88-10	SERVICE STATION	5128-4	Ceramic	SET OF 2	✓ RETIRED 1991	37.50	165.00
	Pumps included. a/k/a "Bill's Service Station."						
SV88-11	STONEHURST HOUSE	5140-3	Ceramic	NO	✓ CURRENT	37.50	37.50
SV88-12	PALOS VERDES	5141-1	Ceramic*	NO	✓ RETIRED 1990	37.50	75.00
	*Potted sisal miniature tree on porch - separate.						

THE ORIGINAL SNOW VILLAGE

SV89-1

JINGLE BELLE HOUSEBOAT

Floating house sports a Christmas tree on wheelhouse roof and rear deck. Name is stenciled on bow and life preservers. Gray, blue, offset by red trim and white rails.

SV89-2

COLONIAL CHURCH

Front entry with four floor to roof columns supporting roof over porch. Front facade repeats design with four half columns set into wall. Circular windows ring upper part and are incorporated as upper half of side windows. Cross on three tier steeple bell tower.

SV89-4

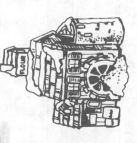

PARAMOUNT THEATER

Spanish theme Art Deco building, double marques. Ticket booth in center flanked by two double doors. Corner billboards display scenes from movie.

SV89-3

NORTH CREEK COTTAGE

Cape cod style with colonial columned front porch. Attached garage with deck on top, front dormer, stone chimney.

SV89-8

J. YOUNG'S GRANARY

Central waterwheel for grinding grain, stone silo on one side, and small storage/store on other side.

SV89-5

DOCTOR'S HOUSE

Home and office within house. Rounded turret completes front. Three story home has arched windows, porthole windows, and bay windows to add to Victorian charm. Yellow with light brown roof, white porch columns and molding decorate and highlight.

SV89-6

COURTHOUSE

Four corner roof turrets with central clock tower, windows with half circle sunbursts, decorative molding on second story with two front windows being clear half-circles for light. Greek key molding circles entire top. Basement visible via front windows.

SV89-7

VILLAGE WARMING HOUSE

Used by skaters to warm up from the chill, small red house has steep front roof. Bench at side for a brief rest.

ART CHART #	NAME	ITEM #	MATERIAL	SET?	♬ MARKET STATUS	ORIGINAL SRP	GREENBOOK TRUMKT PRICE
	VARIATIONS/MISC/COLLECTOR NOTES						
SV89-1	JINGLE BELLE HOUSEBOAT	5114-4	Ceramic*	NO	✓ RETIRED 1991	$ 42.00	$ 80.00
	*Stamped metal bell is separate.						
SV89-2	COLONIAL CHURCH	5119-5	Ceramic*	NO	✓ RETIRED 1992	60.00	75.00
	Early release to Gift Creations Concepts. *Metal cross.						
SV89-3	NORTH CREEK COTTAGE	5120-9	Ceramic	NO	✓ RETIRED 1992	45.00	65.00
	Early release to Gift Creations Concepts.						
SV89-4	PARAMOUNT THEATER	5142-0	Ceramic	NO	✓ RETIRED 1993	42.00	78.00
SV89-5	DOCTOR'S HOUSE	5143-8	Ceramic	NO	✓ RETIRED 1992	56.00	85.00
SV89-6	COURTHOUSE	5144-6	Ceramic	NO	✓ RETIRED 1993	65.00	110.00
	Design based on Gibson County Courthouse in Princeton, IN.						
SV89-7	VILLAGE WARMING HOUSE	5145-4	Ceramic	NO	✓ RETIRED 1992	42.00	60.00
	Trees detach.						
SV89-8	J. YOUNG'S GRANARY	5149-7	Ceramic	NO	✓ RETIRED 1992	45.00	75.00

SV89/9

PINEWOOD LOG CABIN

Log construction with two fireplaces for heating/cooking, tree trunk porch pillars, firewood stack, bucket for water, red roof, house name on sign above porch, attached tree.

ART CHART #	NAME	ITEM #	MATERIAL	SET?		MARKET STATUS	ORIGINAL SRP	GREENBOOK TRUMKT PRICE
			VARIATIONS/MISC/COLLECTOR NOTES					
SV89-9	PINEWOOD LOG CABIN	5150-0	Ceramic	NO	✓	CURRENT	$ 37.50	$ 37.50
	Early release to Gift Creations Concepts, Fall 1990.							

THE ORIGINAL SNOW VILLAGE

SV90-1

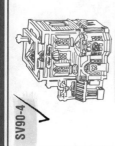

56 FLAVORS ICE CREAM PARLOR

Decorated like a sundae, peppermint pillars flank door, sugar cone roof with a cherry on peak, window boxes hold ice cream cones.

SV90-2

MORNINGSIDE HOUSE

Pink/coral split level house with one car garage. Fieldstone chimney, curved front steps, terraced landscaping with movable trees.

SV90-3

MAINSTREET HARDWARE STORE

Three story building with store on ground level. Rental rooms on second and third story with access by outside staircase. Awning covers store display window and front rooms on second floor.

SV90-4

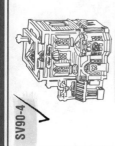

VILLAGE REALTY

Two story main building houses real estate office. Front bay display window for available properties. Shutters that follow curve of second story windows can open/close. Adjacent building houses small Italian dining place with colorful striped awning.

SV90-5

SPANISH MISSION CHURCH

Sun dried clay Spanish style, arcade along one side gives protected access.

SV90-6

PRAIRIE HOUSE

Two story home with upper floor set in and back atop first story. Large windows to maximize light. Balcony area off one upper room. Large chimney rises up through first story. Two large pillars support covered entry.

SV90-7

QUEEN ANNE VICTORIAN

Broad steps lead up to pillared porch with unique corner gazebo style sitting area. Ornate turret on corner of second story decorated with scalloped shingles.

ART CHART #	NAME	ITEM #	MATERIAL	SET?		MARKET STATUS	ORIGINAL SRP	GREENBOOK TRUMKT PRICE
	VARIATIONS/MISC/COLLECTOR NOTES							
SV90-1	56 FLAVORS ICE CREAM PARLOR	5151-9	Ceramic	NO	✓	RETIRED 1992	$ 42.00	$ 80.00
	Early release to Gift Creations Concepts.							
SV90-2	MORNINGSIDE HOUSE	5152-7	Ceramic*	NO	✓	RETIRED 1992	45.00	50.00
	Early release to Showcase Dealers and the National Association of Limited Edition Dealers. *Sisal trees detach.							
SV90-3	MAINSTREET HARDWARE STORE	5153-5	Ceramic	NO	✓	RETIRED 1993	42.00	55.00
SV90-4	VILLAGE REALTY	5154-3	Ceramic	NO	✓	RETIRED 1993	42.00	60.00
	"J. Saraceno" over door is a tribute to D56's former National Sales Manager.							
SV90-5	SPANISH MISSION CHURCH	5155-1	Ceramic*	NO	✓	RETIRED 1992	42.00	72.00
	*Three metal crosses for cemetery. Designed after Enga Memorial Chapel in Minneapolis, MN.							
SV90-6	PRAIRIE HOUSE	5156-0	Ceramic	NO	✓	RETIRED 1993	42.00	50.00
	American Architecture Series.							
SV90-7	QUEEN ANNE VICTORIAN	5157-8	Ceramic	NO	✓	CURRENT ✓	48.00	50.00
	American Architecture Series.							

THE ORIGINAL SNOW VILLAGE

SV91-4

VILLAGE GREENHOUSE

Plant growing area has bricked bottom and "glass" roof to allow sunlight in. Attached small store sells accessories. It has brick chimney, shingled roof, and covered entry.

SV91-3

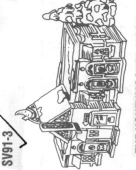

THE HONEYMOONER MOTEL

Moon and stars sign above office door is advertisement for motel. White building with blue awnings & doors. Windows and trim in red. Soda and ice machine by office door.

SV91-6

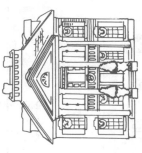

GOTHIC FARMHOUSE

Columned front porch and entry. First floor large bay window with second story rising to a gable with carved molding which is repeated on two dormer windows over porch. Clapboard home with roof shingles in diamond pattern.

SV91-2

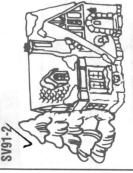

OAK GROVE TUDOR

Red brick base with stucco and timbered second story. Fireplace of brick and stone by entry door. Rough stone frames door. Bay window with flower boxes.

SV91-1

THE CHRISTMAS SHOP

Pediment on brick building advertises the holiday by the French "NOEL." Striped awning over door. Large Teddy Bear by front window.

SV91-5

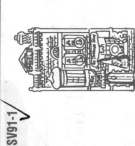

SOUTHERN COLONIAL

Four columns rise from ground to roof with second story veranda across front. Double chimneys surrounded by a balustrade. Shutters by each window both decorate and shut out heat of sun. Two urns flank steps of entryway.

ART CHART #	NAME	ITEM #	MATERIAL	SET?	🛒	MARKET STATUS	ORIGINAL SRP	GREENBOOK TRUMKT PRICE
			VARIATIONS/MISC/COLLECTOR NOTES					
SV91-1	THE CHRISTMAS SHOP	5097-0	Ceramic	NO	✓	CURRENT ✓	$ 37.50	$ 37.50
	Early release to Gift Creations Concepts and Showcase Dealers.							
SV91-2	OAK GROVE TUDOR	5400-3	Ceramic	NO	✓	CURRENT	42.00	42.00
	Early release to Showcase Dealers.							
SV91-3	THE HONEYMOONER MOTEL	5401-1	Ceramic	NO	✓	RETIRED 1993	42.00	75.00
	Early release to Showcase Dealers.							
SV91-4	VILLAGE GREENHOUSE	5402-0	Ceramic*	NO	✓	CURRENT	35.00	36.00
	*Acrylic panels.							
SV91-5	SOUTHERN COLONIAL	5403-8	Ceramic*	NO	✓	CURRENT	48.00	50.00
	American Architecture Series. *Sisal trees detach.							
SV91-6	GOTHIC FARMHOUSE	5404-6	Ceramic	NO	✓	CURRENT	48.00	48.00
	American Architecture Series.							

THE ORIGINAL SNOW VILLAGE

SV91-7

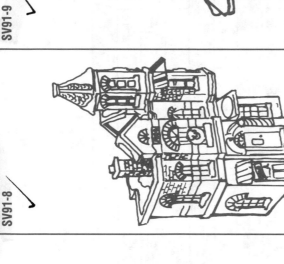

FINKLEA'S FINERY COSTUME SHOP

Pediment over front door repeated in roof design. Red awnings over 1st floor display windows. Dressed stone trims the facade of the three story brick building. Hood projects over third floor windows - an area used by piano teacher. Attached side setback is two stories w/decorated rental return door and awning on upper window.

SV91-8

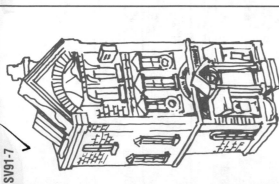

JACK'S CORNER BARBER SHOP

Also houses M. Schmitt Photography Studio and second floor Tailor Shop. Two story turret separates two identical wings of brick building. Fantail window design repeated on doors and on roof peaks.

SV91-9

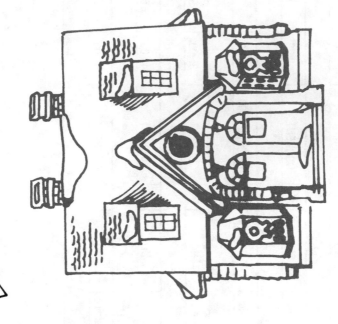

DOUBLE BUNGALOW

Early two family home - double entry doors, each side has bow window downstairs, a roof dormer, and own chimney. A brick facade dresses up clapboard house.

ART CHART #	NAME	ITEM #	MATERIAL	SET?	♥	MARKET STATUS	ORIGINAL SRP	GREENBOOK TRUMKT PRICE
			VARIATIONS/MISC/COLLECTOR NOTES					
SV91-7	FINKLEA'S FINERY COSTUME SHOP	5405-4	Ceramic	NO	✓	RETIRED 1993	$ 45.00	$ 70.00
SV91-8	JACK'S CORNER BARBER SHOP	5406-2	Ceramic	NO	✓	CURRENT	42.00	42.00
	"M. Schmitt Studio" is in honor of Matthew Schmitt, the photographer for D56's Quarterly, brochures, etc.							
SV91-9	DOUBLE BUNGALOW	5407-0	Ceramic	NO	✓	CURRENT	45.00	45.00

THE ORIGINAL SNOW VILLAGE

SV92-1

GRANDMA'S COTTAGE

Small porch nestled between two identical house sections. Hooded double windows, front side sections with evergreens flanking each area. Double chimneys rise off main roof. White clapboard with carved fan-like design on each gable.

SV92-5

GOOD SHEPHERD CHAPEL & CHURCH SCHOOL

White chapel w/red roof rises on stone base. Steeple at front entry. School has double doors w/tall windows and small bell tower bisects roof. Stone chimney on side. Church side door meets school side door. Holiday pageant banner on school wall.

SV92-2

ST. LUKE'S CHURCH

Brick church features three square based steeples w/the central one rising off nave roof. Other two are front corners of church w/doors at base & trefoil design on the front/side repeated on main entry doors. Ribbing on side walls between windows.

SV92-6

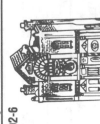

PRINT SHOP & VILLAGE NEWS

Stone in front pediment notes 1893 construction. Symmetrical building design emphasized by double chimneys, matching windows, and columns that flank doors and corners. Brick building also houses Muffin Shop.

SV92-3

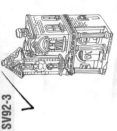

VILLAGE POST OFFICE

Doric columns support porch to double entry doors. Two story brick with two story turret rising above sign. Greek key and incised design separate stories. Door and windows repeat arched design. Molding accents roof.

SV92-7

HARTFORD HOUSE

Steeply pitched roof with ornate front covered entry pediment design, repeated in steep front gable. Molding surrounds windows, is present on porch columns and under eaves.

SV92-4

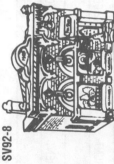

AL'S TV SHOP

TV antenna on roof. Red awnings on upper windows and red canopy over lower display window. Store entry on corner of building.

SV92-8

VILLAGE VET AND PET SHOP

Arched crescents over picture windows that are screened designs depicting dogs, kittens, fish, and birds. Ornamental molding outlines roof edge, where 1920 date is prominent. Dog sits on front steps entry to Vet's office.

ART CHART #	NAME	ITEM #	MATERIAL	SET?	🔔	MARKET STATUS	ORIGINAL SRP	GREENBOOK TRUMKT PRICE
	VARIATIONS/MISC/COLLECTOR NOTES							
SV92-1	GRANDMA'S COTTAGE	5420-8	Ceramic	NO	✓	CURRENT ⟲	$ 42.00	$ 45.00
	Early release to Gift Creations Concepts.							
SV92-2	ST. LUKE'S CHURCH	5421-6	Ceramic	NO	✓	CURRENT	45.00	45.00
	Early release to Gift Creations Concepts.							
SV92-3	VILLAGE POST OFFICE	5422-4	Ceramic	NO	✓	CURRENT	35.00	37.50
	Early release to Showcase Dealers.							
SV92-4	AL'S TV SHOP	5423-2	Ceramic	NO	✓	CURRENT	40.00	40.00
SV92-5	GOOD SHEPHERD CHAPEL & CHURCH SCHOOL	5424-0	Ceramic	SET OF 2	✓	CURRENT ⟲	72.00	72.00
SV92-6	PRINT SHOP & VILLAGE NEWS	5425-9	Ceramic	NO	✓	CURRENT	37.50	37.50
SV92-7	HARTFORD HOUSE	5426-7	Ceramic	NO	✓	CURRENT	55.00	55.00
SV92-8	VILLAGE VET AND PET SHOP	5427-5	Ceramic	NO	✓	CURRENT	32.00	32.00

THE ORIGINAL SNOW VILLAGE

SV92-9

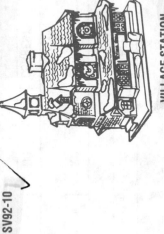

CRAFTSMAN COTTAGE

Stone based porch extends across front of house ending in stone chimney.
Large squared pillars are part of support for second story room above entryway.
Small dormer by chimney.

SV92-10

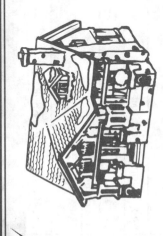

VILLAGE STATION

Clock tower rises on one side of two story red brick station.
Platform sign behind a stack of luggage announces arrivals and departures.
Many windowed waiting room for travelers extends length of station.

SV92-11

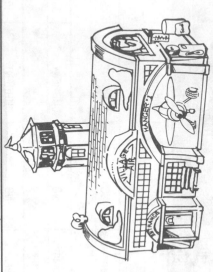

AIRPORT

Semicircular vaulted roof extends length of plane hangar,
with control tower rising off central rear of building.
One engine prop plane sits in hangar entrance.
Fuel tank pump at corner, plus thermometer, and crop dusting schedule.
Door at opposite front corner for passenger and freight business.

ART CHART #	NAME	ITEM #	MATERIAL	SET?	![]	MARKET STATUS	ORIGINAL SRP	GREENBOOK TRUMKT PRICE
			VARIATIONS/MISC/COLLECTOR NOTES					
SV92-9	CRAFTSMAN COTTAGE	5437-2	Ceramic	NO	✓	CURRENT	$ 55.00	$ 55.00
	American Architecture Series							
SV92-10	VILLAGE STATION	5438-0	Ceramic	NO	✓	CURRENT	65.00	65.00
SV92-11	AIRPORT	5439-9	Ceramic	NO	✓	CURRENT 尺	60.00	60.00

THE ORIGINAL SNOW VILLAGE

SV93-1

NANTUCKET RENOVATION

Matching gabled wing has been added to the original design & greenhouse has been moved to front of house. Front porch columns are now milled. Small evergreens now at front & large tree moved to rear corner, exposing side bay window. House remains bright yellow shingle with green roof.

SV93-2

MOUNT OLIVET CHURCH

Brick church with large stained glass window above double door entry. Square bell tower with steeple roof.

SV93-3

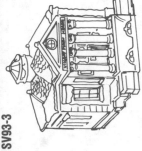

VILLAGE PUBLIC LIBRARY

Brick and stone building with four Greek columns supporting front portico. Entry from side steps to double doors. Brick cupola rises from center of roof.

SV93-4

WOODBURY HOUSE

Turned spindle posts support front porch of clapboard home. Double gable design with lower gable featuring 2 story bow windows. Brick chimney extends through roof line from central heating system.

SV93-5

HUNTING LODGE

Rustic log structure on stone foundtion and with stone fireplace. Antlers decorate front gable above porch entry.

SV93-6

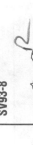

DAIRY BARN

Cow barn with attached silo. Tin mansard roof. Cow weathervane.

SV93-7

DINAH'S DRIVE-IN

Burger in bun and bubbly soda top circular fast food drive-in.

SV93-8

SNOWY HILLS HOSPITAL

Brick hospital, steps lead to double main doors with emergency entry drive-up on side.

65

ART CHART #	NAME	ITEM #	MATERIAL	SET?	🔔 MARKET STATUS	ORIGINAL SRP	GREENBOOK TRUMKT PRICE
			VARIATIONS/MISC/COLLECTOR NOTES				
SV93-1	NANTUCKET RENOVATION	5441-0	Ceramic	NO	✓ 1993 ANNUAL	$ 55.00	$ 105.00
	Available only through retailers who carried Snow Village in 1986, Showcase Dealers, and select buying groups. For the original Nantucket see 1978, Item # 5014-6, (SV78-4), page 15. Special box and hang tag. Blueprints of renovation included.						
SV93-2	MOUNT OLIVET CHURCH	5442-9	Ceramic	NO	✓ CURRENT	65.00	65.00
SV93-3	VILLAGE PUBLIC LIBRARY	5443-7	Ceramic	NO	✓ CURRENT	55.00	55.00
SV93-4	WOODBURY HOUSE	5444-5	Ceramic	NO	✓ CURRENT	45.00	45.00
SV93-5	HUNTING LODGE	5445-3	Ceramic	NO	✓ CURRENT	50.00	50.00
SV93-6	DAIRY BARN	5446-1	Ceramic	NO	✓ CURRENT	55.00	55.00
SV93-7	DINAH'S DRIVE-IN	5447-0	Ceramic	NO	✓ CURRENT	45.00	45.00
SV93-8	SNOWY HILLS HOSPITAL	5448-8	Ceramic	NO	✓ CURRENT	48.00	48.00
	Portion of proceeds from sale of piece will be donated to AmFAR through the Gift For Life Foundation.						

66

THE ORIGINAL SNOW VILLAGE

1994

1994

SV94-1

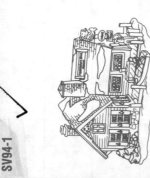

FISHERMAN'S NOOK RESORT
Office/store for cabin rental, bait, and gas for boats, plus places for boats to tie up.

SV94-2

FISHERMAN'S NOOK CABINS:

FISHERMAN'S NOOK BASS CABIN

FISHERMAN'S NOOK TROUT CABIN

SV94-3

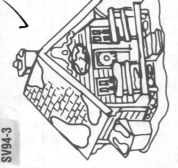

FISHERMAN'S NOOK BASS CABIN | FISHERMAN'S NOOK TROUT CABIN
Each cabin named for fish – rustic wood cabin with wood pile and fireplace for heat.

SV94-4

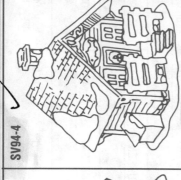

SV94-5

THE ORIGINAL SNOW VILLAGE STARTER SET
- Shady Oak Church
- Sunday School Serenade accessory
- three assorted "bottle-brush" sisal trees
- a bag of "Real Plastic Snow"

SHADY OAK CHURCH
Steeple rises above side entry to simple clapboard country church. Windows have pointed arch topped by trefoil design.

SUNDAY SCHOOL SERENADE
Choir boys sing carols.

ART CHART #	NAME	ITEM #	MATERIAL	SET?	⚕	MARKET STATUS	ORIGINAL SRP	GREENBOOK TRUMKT PRICE
			VARIATIONS/MISC/COLLECTOR NOTES					
SV94-1	FISHERMAN'S NOOK RESORT	5460-7	Ceramic	NO	✓	CURRENT	$75.00	$75.00
SV94-2	**FISHERMAN'S NOOK CABINS**	**5461-5**	Ceramic	**SET OF 2**	✓	**CURRENT**	**50.00**	**50.00**
SV94-3	*FISHERMAN'S NOOK BASS CABIN*	5461-5	Ceramic	1 of a 2 pc set	✓	CURRENT	----	----
SV94-4	*FISHERMAN'S NOOK TROUT CABIN*	5461-5	Ceramic	1 of a 2 pc set	✓	CURRENT	----	----
SV94-5	THE ORIGINAL SNOW VILLAGE STARTER SET	5462-3	Ceramic	SET OF 6	✓	CURRENT ↺	49.99	49.99

Featured at D56 National Open Houses hosted by participating GCC retailers the first weekend in November 1994.

new 94 Smoky Mntn Retreat
Bus Station
Police Dept
Boulder Spring House

Beacon Hill House
Gas Station - Garage
Ice Palace

Bus

Nick Tree Farm
Just married

ACCESSORIES . . .

THE ORIGINAL SNOW VILLAGE

ACCESSORIES . . .

SVA79-1

CAROLERS
Couple, girl, garlanded lamppost, snowman.

SVA80-2

CERAMIC CAR
Open roadster holds lap rugs, Christmas tree, and wrapped presents.

SVA81-3

CERAMIC SLEIGH
Patterned after old fashioned wood sleigh, holds Christmas tree and wrapped presents.

SVA82-4

SNOWMAN WITH BROOM
Top hat, red nose, snowman holds straw broom.

SVA83-5

MONKS-A-CAROLING
Four friars singing carols.

SVA84-6

SCOTTIE WITH TREE
Black dog waits by snow covered tree with star at top.

SVA84-7

Original, #6460-2, was actually giftware - not SV. It wasn't glazed, had paper song books and cord for sashes. It was adopted as a SV piece by collectors.

MONKS-A-CAROLING
Four friars singing carols.

SVA85-8

SINGING NUNS
Four nuns in habits, sing carols.

ART CHART #	NAME	ITEM #	MATERIAL	SET?	MARKET STATUS	ORIGINAL SRP	GREENBOOK TRUMKT PRICE
	VARIATIONS/MISC/COLLECTOR NOTES						
SVA79-1	CAROLERS (1979)	5064-1	Ceramic	SET OF 4	RETIRED 1986	$ 12.00	$ 125.00
	First non-lit accessory.						
SVA80-2	CERAMIC CAR (1980)	5069-0	Ceramic	NO	RETIRED 1986	5.00	52.00
	First vehicle, no other cars available until 1985. Did not come in a box.						
SVA81-3	CERAMIC SLEIGH (1981)	5079-2	Ceramic	NO	RETIRED 1986	5.00	55.00
	Did not come in a box.						
SVA82-4	SNOWMAN WITH BROOM (1982)	5018-0	Ceramic*	NO	RETIRED 1990	3.00	15.00
	*Straw broom.						
SVA83-5	MONKS-A-CAROLING (1983)	6459-9	Ceramic	NO	RETIRED 1984	6.00	75.00
	Retired after just one year due to maker being unable to supply. On this piece, Monks have a diffused rosy blush. Re-introduced in 1984 as #5040-7 (SVA84-7) from another supplier. On later piece, Monks have a distinct red circle to give cheeks blush. For color photo, see Second Edition, pg 225.						
SVA84-6	SCOTTIE WITH TREE (1984)	5038-5	Ceramic	NO	RETIRED 1985	3.00	140.00
SVA84-7	MONKS-A-CAROLING (1984)	5040-7	Ceramic	NO	RETIRED 1988	6.00	38.00
	Replaced 1983 Monks-A-Caroling #6459-9 (SVA83-5). For color photo, see Second Edition, page 225.						
SVA85-8	SINGING NUNS (1985)	5053-9	Ceramic	NO	RETIRED 1987	6.00	105.00

70

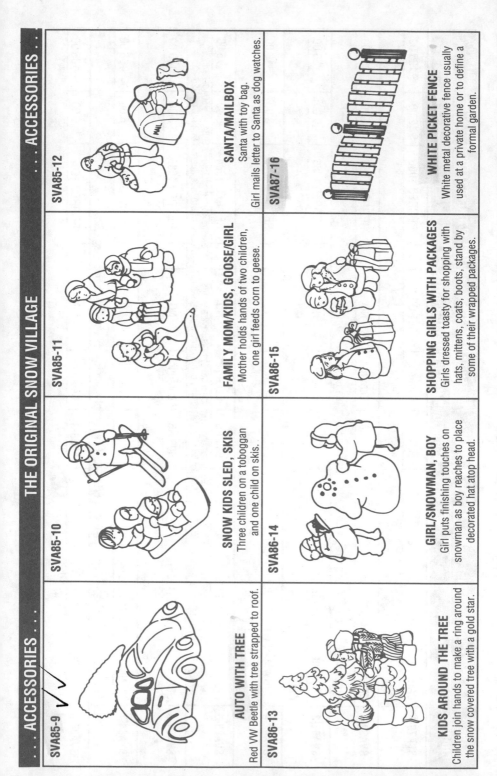

SVA85-9

AUTO WITH TREE
Red VW Beetle with tree strapped to roof.

SVA86-13

KIDS AROUND THE TREE
Children join hands to make a ring around the snow covered tree with a gold star.

SVA85-10

SNOW KIDS SLED, SKIS
Three children on a toboggan and one child on skis.

SVA86-14

GIRL/SNOWMAN, BOY
Girl puts finishing touches on snowman as boy reaches to place decorated hat atop head.

SVA85-11

FAMILY MOM/KIDS, GOOSE/GIRL
Mother holds hands of two children, one girl feeds corn to geese.

SVA86-15

SHOPPING GIRLS WITH PACKAGES
Girls dressed toasty for shopping with hats, mittens, coats, boots, stand by some of their wrapped packages.

SVA85-12

SANTA/MAILBOX
Santa with toy bag.
Girl mails letter to Santa as dog watches.

SVA87-16

WHITE PICKET FENCE
White metal decorative fence usually used at a private home or to define a formal garden.

ART CHART #	NAME	ITEM #	MATERIAL	SET?	☎ MARKET STATUS	ORIGINAL SRP	GREENBOOK TRUMKT PRICE
	VARIATIONS/MISC/COLLECTOR NOTES						
SVA85-9	AUTO WITH TREE (1985)	5055-5	Ceramic/Sisal	NO	CURRENT	$ 5.00	$ 6.50
	Sisal tree attached. Did not come in a box. 1st issue looks as if the tree's weight crushed the car.						
SVA85-10	SNOW KIDS SLED, SKIS (1985)	5056-3	Ceramic	SET OF 2	RETIRED 1987	11.00	50.00
	See "Snow Kids," 1987, #5113-6 (SVA87-25).						
SVA85-11	FAMILY MOM/KIDS, GOOSE/GIRL (1985)	5057-1	Ceramic	SET OF 2	RETIRED 1988	11.00	45.00
	Variations in size.						
SVA85-12	SANTA/MAILBOX (1985)	5059-8	Ceramic	SET OF 2	RETIRED 1988	11.00	48.00
	Variations in size - larger Santa before downscaled was 3.2", new Santa with trimmer silhouette is 3".						
SVA86-13	KIDS AROUND THE TREE (1986)	5094-6	Ceramic	NO	RETIRED 1990	15.00	40.00
	Variations in size. Dramatically scaled down 5.75" to 4.5". GREENBOOK TRUMARKET Price for larger, pre-1987 piece, is $70.00.						
SVA86-14	GIRL/SNOWMAN, BOY (1986)	5095-4	Ceramic	SET OF 2	RETIRED 1987	11.00	70.00
	See "Snow Kids," 1987, #5113-6 (SVA87-25).						
SVA86-15	SHOPPING GIRLS WITH PACKAGES (1986)	5096-2	Ceramic	SET OF 2	RETIRED 1988	11.00	44.00
	Variations in size - 3" vs. 2.75", pre-1987 pieces are larger.						
SVA87-16	WHITE PICKET FENCE (1987)	5100-4	Metal	NO	CURRENT	3.00	3.00
	Size is 6" x 1.75". One of the first metal accessories (other was Park Bench). Also available in a set of 4, Item #5101-2, @ $12.00 SRP.						

. . . ACCESSORIES . . .   THE ORIGINAL SNOW VILLAGE   . . . ACCESSORIES . . .

SVA87-17

3 NUNS WITH SONGBOOKS
Three nuns in habits carry songbooks to sing carols.

SVA87-18

PRAYING MONKS
Three monks, standing side-by-side, praying.

SVA87-19

CHILDREN IN BAND
One child conducts three band players: horn, drum, and tuba.

SVA87-20

CAROLING FAMILY
Father holds baby, mother and son, and girl with pup.

SVA87-21

TAXI CAB
Yellow Checker cab.

SVA87-22

CHRISTMAS CHILDREN
Children at outdoor activities: girl and pup on sled pulled by boy, girl holding wreath, girl feeding carrot to bunny.

SVA87-23

FOR SALE SIGN
Holly decorates a house for sale sign. Usually sign post inserted at edge of property to be seen by drivers and people passing by.

SVA87-24

VILLAGE PARK BENCH
Green metal bench usually found on a Village Green, park, or at a public building.

ART CHART #	NAME	ITEM #	MATERIAL	SET?	🔔	MARKET STATUS	ORIGINAL SRP	GREENBOOK TRUMKT PRICE
	VARIATIONS/MISC/COLLECTOR NOTES							
SVA87-17	3 NUNS WITH SONGBOOKS (1987)	5102-0	Ceramic	NO		RETIRED 1988	$ 6.00	$ 115.00
SVA87-18	PRAYING MONKS (1987)	5103-9	Ceramic	NO		RETIRED°1988	6.00	42.00
SVA87-19	CHILDREN IN BAND (1987)	5104-7	Ceramic	NO		RETIRED 1989	15.00	24.00
SVA87-20	CAROLING FAMILY (1987)	5105-5	Ceramic	SET OF 3		RETIRED 1990	20.00	32.00
SVA87-21	TAXI CAB (1987)	5106-3	Ceramic	NO		CURRENT	6.00	6.50
SVA87-22	CHRISTMAS CHILDREN (1987)	5107-1	Ceramic	SET OF 4		RETIRED 1990	20.00	30.00
SVA87-23	FOR SALE SIGN (1987)	5108-0	Ceramic	NO		RETIRED 1989	3.50	10.00
	Variation: blank sign for personalization, #581-9, Gift Creations Concepts 1989 Christmas Catalog Exclusive, free w/$100 Dept. 56 purchase.							
SVA87-24	VILLAGE PARK BENCH (1987)	5109-8	Metal	NO		RETIRED 1993	3.00	6.00
	Size is 2.5". One of the first metal accessories (other was Picket Fence). Also considered to be a Heritage Village Accessory.							

SVA87-25

SNOW KIDS
Three kids on toboggan, child on skis, boy and girl putting finishing touches on snowman.

SVA88-26

TOWN CLOCK
Free standing large faced clock on a pedestal base usually on display on a business street, train station, or public building.

SVA88-27

MAN ON LADDER HANGING GARLAND
Man carries garland up ladder to decorate eaves of house.

SVA88-28

HAYRIDE
Farmer guides horse-drawn hay-filled sleigh with children as riders.

SVA88-29

SCHOOL CHILDREN
Three children carrying school books.

SVA88-30

APPLE GIRL/NEWSPAPER BOY
Girl holds wood tray carrier selling apples for 5¢, newsboy sells the Village News.

SVA88-31

WOODSMAN AND BOY
Man chops and splits logs and boy prepares to carry supply to fireplace.

SVA88-32

DOGHOUSE/CAT IN GARBAGE CAN
Dog sits outside doghouse decorated with wreath; cat looks at empty boxes and wrappings in garbage can.

ART CHART #	NAME	ITEM #	MATERIAL	SET?	💡	MARKET STATUS	ORIGINAL SRP	GREENBOOK TRUMKT PRICE
	VARIATIONS/MISC/COLLECTOR NOTES							
SVA87-25	SNOW KIDS (1987)	5113-6	Ceramic	SET OF 4		RETIRED 1990	$ 20.00	$ 48.00
	Set of 4 incorporates 1985 #5056-3 (SVA85-10) and 1986 #5095-4 (SVA86-14), re-scaled to the smaller size.							
SVA88-26	TOWN CLOCK (1988)	5110-1	Metal	NO		CURRENT	2.70	3.00
	Size is 3.5". Choice of green or black. Also considered to be a Heritage Village Accessory.							
SVA88-27	MAN ON LADDER HANGING GARLAND (1988)	5116-0	See Below*	NO		RETIRED 1992	7.50	16.00
	*Ladder is wooden, garland is fiber, man is ceramic.							
SVA88-28	HAYRIDE (1988)	5117-9	Ceramic	NO		RETIRED 1990	30.00	65.00
SVA88-29	SCHOOL CHILDREN (1988)	5118-7	Ceramic	SET OF 3		RETIRED 1990	15.00	28.00
SVA88-30	APPLE GIRL/NEWSPAPER BOY (1988)	5129-2	Ceramic	SET OF 2		RETIRED 1990	11.00	22.00
SVA88-31	WOODSMAN AND BOY (1988)	5130-6	Ceramic	SET OF 2		RETIRED 1991	13.00	25.00
SVA88-32	DOGHOUSE/CAT IN GARBAGE CAN (1988)	5131-4	Ceramic	SET OF 2		RETIRED 1992	15.00	30.00

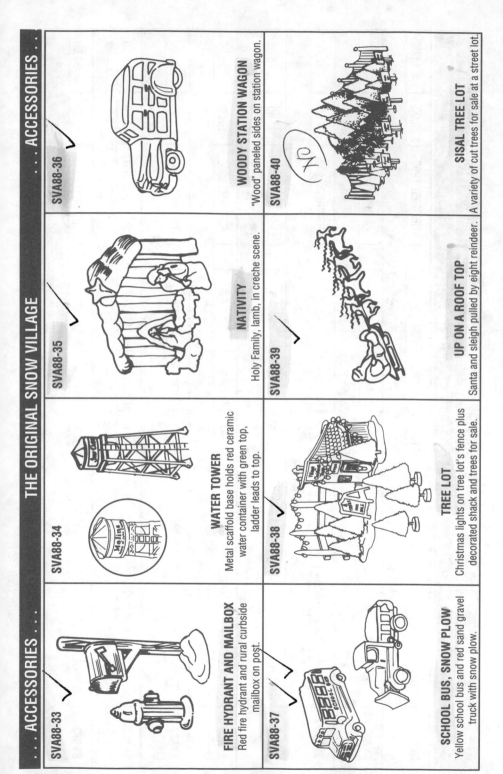

SVA88-33

FIRE HYDRANT AND MAILBOX
Red fire hydrant and rural curbside mailbox on post.

SVA88-37

SCHOOL BUS, SNOW PLOW
Yellow school bus and red sand gravel truck with snow plow.

SVA88-34

WATER TOWER
Metal scaffold base holds red ceramic water container with green top, ladder leads to top.

SVA88-38

TREE LOT
Christmas lights on tree lot's fence plus decorated shack and trees for sale.

SVA88-35

NATIVITY
Holy Family, lamb, in creche scene.

SVA88-39

UP ON A ROOF TOP
Santa and sleigh pulled by eight reindeer.

SVA88-36

WOODY STATION WAGON
"Wood" paneled sides on station wagon.

SVA88-40

SISAL TREE LOT
A variety of cut trees for sale at a street lot.

ART CHART #	NAME	ITEM #	MATERIAL	SET?	♥ MARKET STATUS	ORIGINAL SRP	GREENBOOK TRUMKT PRICE
	VARIATIONS/MISC/COLLECTOR NOTES						
SVA88-33	FIRE HYDRANT AND MAILBOX (1988)	5132-2	Metal	SET OF 2	CURRENT	$ 6.00	$ 6.00
	Sizes are 1.5" and 2.75", respectively.						
SVA88-34	WATER TOWER (1988)	5133-0	Metal/Ceramic	2 PIECES	RETIRED 1991	20.00	52.00
	"John Deere Co." Water Tower (1989), #2510-4, Original SRP was $24.00 + Shipping. GREENBOOK TRUMARKET Price is $395.00.						
SVA88-35	NATIVITY (1988)	5135-7	Ceramic	NO	CURRENT	7.50	7.50
	Size is 2.25".						
SVA88-36	WOODY STATION WAGON (1988)	5136-5	Ceramic	NO	RETIRED 1990	6.50	30.00
SVA88-37	SCHOOL BUS, SNOW PLOW (1988)	5137-3	Ceramic	SET OF 2	RETIRED 1991	16.00	55.00
SVA88-38	TREE LOT (1988)	5138-1	See Below*	NO	CURRENT	33.50	37.50
	*Sisal trees, wood fence, ceramic shack.						
SVA88-39	UP ON A ROOF TOP (1988)	5139-0	Pewter	2 PIECES	CURRENT	6.50	6.50
	Size is 4" long. Also considered to be a Heritage Village Accessory.						
SVA88-40	SISAL TREE LOT (1988)	8183-3	Sisal	NO	RETIRED 1991	45.00	85.00

SVA89-41

VILLAGE GAZEBO

Small, open, red roofed garden structure that will protect folks from rain/snow, or be a private place to sit.

SVA89-45

STREET SIGN

Green street signs can be personalized to give each village street a unique name.

SVA89-42

CHOIR KIDS

Four kids in white and red robes with green songbooks caroling.

SVA89-46

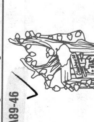

KIDS TREE HOUSE

Decorated club house built on an old dead tree. Steps lead up to hideaway.

SVA89-43

SPECIAL DELIVERY

Mailman and mailbag with his mail truck in USPO colors red, white, and blue with the eagle logo.

SVA89-47

BRINGING HOME THE TREE

Man pulls sled holding tree as girl watches to make sure it doesn't fall off.

SVA89-44

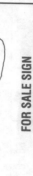

FOR SALE SIGN

Enameled metal sign can be "For Sale" or "SOLD." Birds decorate and add color.

SVA89-48

SKATE FASTER MOM

Two children sit in sleigh as skating Mom pushes them across the ice.

ART CHART #	NAME	ITEM #	MATERIAL	SET?	🔔 MARKET STATUS	ORIGINAL SRP	GREENBOOK TRUMKT PRICE
	VARIATIONS/MISC/COLLECTOR NOTES						
SVA89-41	VILLAGE GAZEBO (1989)	5146-2	Ceramic	NO	CURRENT	$ 27.00	$ 30.00
SVA89-42	CHOIR KIDS (1989)	5147-0	Ceramic	NO	RETIRED 1992	15.00	28.00
SVA89-43	SPECIAL DELIVERY (1989)	5148-9	Ceramic	SET OF 2	RETIRED 1990	16.00	42.00
	Discontinued due to licensing problems with the U.S. Postal Service. Replaced with 1990 Special Delivery #5197-7 (SVA90-68).						
SVA89-44	FOR SALE SIGN (1989)	5166-7	Metal	NO	CURRENT	4.50	4.50
	Size is 3" tall. Insert illustrates #539-8, Bachman's exclusive Village Gathering 1990 "For Sale" sign.						
SVA89-45	STREET SIGN (1989)	5167-5	Metal	6 PCS/PKG	DISCONTINUED	7.50	8.00
	Use street names provided (Lake St., Maple Dr., Park Ave., River Rd., Elm St., Ivy Lane.....) or personalize. Size is 4.25" tall.						
SVA89-46	KIDS TREE HOUSE (1989)	5168-3	Resin	NO	RETIRED 1991	25.00	45.00
SVA89-47	BRINGING HOME THE TREE (1989)	5169-1	Ceramic/Sisal	NO	RETIRED 1992	15.00	22.00
SVA89-48	SKATE FASTER MOM (1989)	5170-5	Ceramic	NO	RETIRED 1991	13.00	24.00

SVA89-49

CRACK THE WHIP

Fast moving line of skaters hold tightly to person in front of them. First person does slow patterns but as line snakes out, last people are racing to keep up and they whip out.

SVA89-50

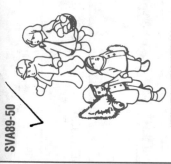

THROUGH THE WOODS

Children bring tree and basket of goodies to Grandma.

SVA89-51

STATUE OF MARK TWAIN

Tribute to author who wrote about lives of American folk.

SVA89-52

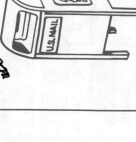

CALLING ALL CARS

Police car and patrolman directing traffic.

SVA89-53

STOP SIGN

Octagonal sign, placed on a corner or dangerous entry/exit to cause vehicles to come to a complete stop.

SVA89-54

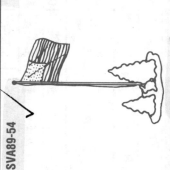

FLAG POLE

Pole with American flag to display in public.

SVA89-55

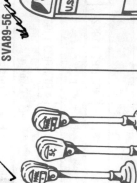

PARKING METER

You can still park for 5¢ in the Snow Village.

SVA89-56

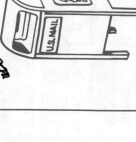

MAILBOX

Freestanding public mailbox in USPO colors red, white, and blue with logo.

ART CHART #	NAME	ITEM #	MATERIAL	SET?	☎	MARKET STATUS	ORIGINAL SRP	GREENBOOK TRUMKT PRICE
		VARIATIONS/MISC/COLLECTOR NOTES						
SVA89-49	CRACK THE WHIP (1989)	5171-3	Ceramic	SET OF 3		CURRENT	$ 25.00	$ 25.00
SVA89-50	THROUGH THE WOODS (1989)	5172-1	Ceramic/Sisal	SET OF 2		RETIRED 1991	18.00	22.00
SVA89-51	STATUE OF MARK TWAIN (1989)	5173-0	Ceramic	NO		RETIRED 1991	15.00	30.00
SVA89-52	CALLING ALL CARS (1989)	5174-8	Ceramic	SET OF 2		RETIRED 1991	15.00	30.00
SVA89-53	STOP SIGN (1989) Size is 3" tall.	5176-4	Metal	2 PCS/PKG		CURRENT	5.00	5.00
SVA89-54	FLAG POLE (1989) *Resin base, metal pole, cloth flag, thread rope. Size is 7" tall.	5177-2	See Below*	NO		CURRENT	8.50	8.50
SVA89-55	PARKING METER (1989) Size is 2" tall.	5178-0	Metal	4 PCS/PKG		CURRENT	6.00	6.00
SVA89-56	MAILBOX (1989) Red, white & blue version. Discontinued due to licensing problems w/the USPO. Replaced with 1990 Mailbox #5198-5 (SVA90-69).	5179-9	Metal	NO		RETIRED 1990	3.50	20.00

. . . ACCESSORIES . . .   THE ORIGINAL SNOW VILLAGE   . . . ACCESSORIES . . .

SVA89-57

METAL BIRDS
Small red and blue sitting birds for use in decorating and as accessories.

SVA89-58

VILLAGE POTTED TOPIARY PAIR
Sisal evergreen trees in large planters, pruned in size and shape for formal garden and/or display.

SVA90-59

KIDS DECORATING THE VILLAGE SIGN
Two children place garland on Snow Village Sign.

SVA90-60

DOWN THE CHIMNEY HE GOES
Santa with bag of toys enters chimney to make delivery on Christmas Eve.

SVA90-61

SNO-JET SNOWMOBILE
Snowmobile, red with silver trim, front ski runners and rear caterpillar treads.

SVA90-62

SLEIGHRIDE
Family rides in open old fashioned green sleigh pulled by one horse.

SVA90-63

HERE WE COME A CAROLING
Children and pet dog sing carols.

SVA90-64

HOME DELIVERY
Milkman and milk truck.

ART CHART #	NAME	ITEM #	MATERIAL	SET?	🔔	MARKET STATUS	ORIGINAL SRP	GREENBOOK TRUMKT PRICE
	VARIATIONS/MISC/COLLECTOR NOTES							
SVA89-57	METAL BIRDS (1989)	5180-2	Metal	6 PCS/PKG		CURRENT	$ 3.50	$ 3.50
	Also considered to be a Heritage Village Accessory.							
SVA89-58	VILLAGE POTTED TOPIARY PAIR (1989)	5192-6	Sisal/Resin	PAIR		CURRENT	5.00	5.00
	Size is 4.75" tall. Also considered to be a Heritage Village Accessory.							
SVA90-59	KIDS DECORATING THE VILLAGE SIGN (1990)	5134-9	Ceramic	NO		RETIRED 1993	12.50	21.00
SVA90-60	DOWN THE CHIMNEY HE GOES (1990)	5158-6	Ceramic	NO		RETIRED 1993	6.50	14.00
SVA90-61	SNO-JET SNOWMOBILE (1990)	5159-4	Ceramic	NO		RETIRED 1993	15.00	24.00
SVA90-62	SLEIGHRIDE (1990)	5160-8	Ceramic	NO		RETIRED 1992	30.00	54.00
SVA90-63	HERE WE COME A CAROLING (1990)	5161-6	Ceramic	SET OF 3		RETIRED 1992	18.00	25.00
SVA90-64	HOME DELIVERY (1990)	5162-4	Ceramic	SET OF 2		RETIRED 1992	16.00	30.00

SVA90-65

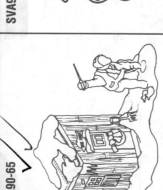

FRESH FROZEN FISH
Ice Fisherman, Ice House.

SVA90-69

VILLAGE MAIL BOX
Snow Village mail receptacle in red and green Snow Village Mail Service colors.

SVA90-66

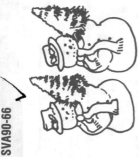

A TREE FOR ME
Snowman with top hat, corn cob pipe, and red muffler carries his own small snow covered tree.

SVA90-70

CHRISTMAS TRASH CANS
Two galvanized refuse cans filled with holiday wrappings and garbage.

SVA90-67

A HOME FOR THE HOLIDAYS
Red and yellow birdhouse on a pole with blue bird sitting on roof. Pole decorated with garland and small snow covered evergreen.

SVA91-71

WREATHS FOR SALE
Girl holds for sale sign, boy holds up wreaths, child pulls sled to carry wreaths. Fence holds wreaths.

SVA90-68

SPECIAL DELIVERY
Snow Village postman and truck in red and green Snow Village Mail Service colors.

SVA91-72

WINTER FOUNTAIN
Angel holds sea shell with water frozen as it flowed.

ART CHART #	NAME	ITEM #	MATERIAL	SET?	✏️	MARKET STATUS	ORIGINAL SRP	GREENBOOK TRUMKT PRICE
	VARIATIONS/MISC/COLLECTOR NOTES							
SVA90-65	FRESH FROZEN FISH (1990)	5163-2	Ceramic	SET OF 2		RETIRED 1993	$ 20.00	$ 35.00
SVA90-66	A TREE FOR ME (1990)	5164-0	Ceramic/Sisal	2 PCS/PKG		CURRENT	7.50	8.00
SVA90-67	A HOME FOR THE HOLIDAYS (1990)	5165-9	Ceramic	NO		CURRENT	6.50	7.00
SVA90-68	SPECIAL DELIVERY (1990)	5197-7	Ceramic	SET OF 2		RETIRED 1992	16.00	38.00
	"S.V. Mail" Service. Replaces discontinued 1985 Special Delivery #5148-9 (SVA89-43).							
SVA90-69	VILLAGE MAIL BOX (1990)	5198-5	Metal	NO		CURRENT	3.50	3.50
	Size is 2". "S.V. Mail" Service. Replaces discontinued 1985 Mailbox #5179-9 (SVA89-56).							
SVA90-70	CHRISTMAS TRASH CANS (1990)	5209-4	See Below*	SET OF 2		CURRENT	6.50	7.00
	Size is 1.5". *Metal/Plastic/Paper. Tops come off.							
SVA91-71	WREATHS FOR SALE (1991)	5408-9	See Below*	SET OF 4		CURRENT	27.50	27.50
	*Ceramic/Wood/Sisal.							
SVA91-72	WINTER FOUNTAIN (1991)	5409-7	See Below*	NO		RETIRED 1993	25.00	45.00
	*Ceramic/Acrylic.							

SVA91-73

COLD WEATHER SPORTS
Three children play ice hockey.

SVA91-74

COME JOIN THE PARADE
Two children carry parade banner.

SVA91-75

VILLAGE MARCHING BAND
Drum Major, two horn players, and two drummers.

SVA91-76

CHRISTMAS CADILLAC
Pink car holds tree and presents.

SVA91-77

SNOWBALL FORT
One boy behind wall, one hides behind tree, one in open clearing - all with snowballs to throw.

SVA91-78

COUNTRY HARVEST
Farm folk with market basket and pitchfork. (Reminiscent of American Gothic painting...)

SVA91-79

VILLAGE GREETINGS
Holiday banners to hang on side of buildings.

SVA92-80

VILLAGE USED CAR LOT
Small wooden office on a stone base with stone chimney. Attached tree. Free standing sign plus office sign advertises used cars and good terms. Three cars sit in lot. Electric pole holds banners and is perch for bird.

ART CHART #	NAME	ITEM #	MATERIAL	SET?	🔔 MARKET STATUS	ORIGINAL SRP	GREENBOOK TRUMKT PRICE
	VARIATIONS/MISC/COLLECTOR NOTES						
SVA91-73	COLD WEATHER SPORTS (1991)	5410-0	Ceramic	SET OF 4	CURRENT	$ 27.50	$ 27.50
SVA91-74	COME JOIN THE PARADE (1991)	5411-9	Ceramic	NO	RETIRED 1992	12.50	18.00
SVA91-75	VILLAGE MARCHING BAND (1991)	5412-7	Ceramic	SET OF 3	RETIRED 1992	30.00	45.00
SVA91-76	CHRISTMAS CADILLAC (1991)	5413-5	Ceramic/Sisal	NO	CURRENT	9.00	9.00
SVA91-77	SNOWBALL FORT (1991)	5414-3	Ceramic	SET OF 3	RETIRED 1993	27.50	40.00
SVA91-78	COUNTRY HARVEST (1991)	5415-1	Ceramic	NO	RETIRED 1993	13.00	25.00
SVA91-79	VILLAGE GREETINGS (1991)	5418-6	Metal	SET OF 3	CURRENT	5.00	5.00
SVA92-80	VILLAGE USED CAR LOT (1992)	5428-3	Ceramic	SET OF 5	CURRENT	45.00	45.00

THE ORIGINAL SNOW VILLAGE

SVA92-81

VILLAGE PHONE BOOTH
Silver and red outdoor phone booth with accordion open/close doors.

SVA92-85

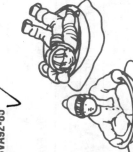

ROUND & ROUND WE GO!
Two kids go sledding on round saucer sleds.

SVA92-82

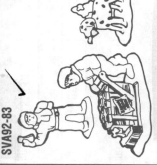

NANNY AND THE PRESCHOOLERS
Two girls and boy hold onto Nanny's shopping basket as she pushes carriage with baby.

SVA92-86

A HEAVY SNOWFALL
Girl stops to look at bird perched on handle of her shovel as boy shovels snow off the walkway.

SVA92-83

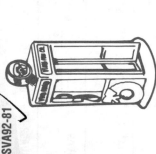

EARLY MORNING DELIVERY
Village kids deliver morning newspaper, one tosses to house, one pushes sled, and Dalmatian dog holds next paper in mouth.

SVA92-87

WE'RE GOING TO A CHRISTMAS PAGEANT
Children wear costumes of Santa, a decorated tree and a golden star.

SVA92-84

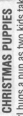

CHRISTMAS PUPPIES
One girl hugs a pup as two kids take box of pups for a ride in red wagon.

SVA92-88

WINTER PLAYGROUND
Two swings and a playground slide. Two trees and two birds complete piece.

ART CHART #	NAME	ITEM #	MATERIAL	SET?	🕯 MARKET STATUS	ORIGINAL SRP	GREENBOOK TRU/MKT PRICE
				VARIATIONS/MISC/COLLECTOR NOTES			
SVA92-81	VILLAGE PHONE BOOTH (1992)	5429-1	Ceramic	NO	CURRENT	$ 7.50	$ 7.50
SVA92-82	NANNY AND THE PRESCHOOLERS (1992)	5430-5	Ceramic	SET OF 2	CURRENT	27.50	27.50
SVA92-83	EARLY MORNING DELIVERY (1992)	5431-3	Ceramic	SET OF 3	CURRENT	27.50	27.50
SVA92-84	CHRISTMAS PUPPIES (1992)	5432-1	Ceramic	SET OF 2	CURRENT ℞	27.50	27.50
SVA92-85	ROUND & ROUND WE GO! (1992)	5433-0	Ceramic	SET OF 2	CURRENT	18.00	18.00
SVA92-86	A HEAVY SNOWFALL (1992)	5434-8	Ceramic	SET OF 2	CURRENT	16.00	16.00
SVA92-87	WE'RE GOING TO A CHRISTMAS PAGEANT (1992)	5435-6	Ceramic	NO	CURRENT	15.00	15.00
SVA92-88	WINTER PLAYGROUND (1992)	5436-4	Ceramic	NO	CURRENT	20.00	20.00

SVA92-89

SPIRIT OF SNOW VILLAGE AIRPLANE

Red prop plane with set of double wings. Metal strap spring on three tree base allows positioning.

SVA93-90

VILLAGE ANIMATED SKATING POND

Skaters move alone or as pair in set patterns on ice pond surface.

SVA93-91

SAFETY PATROL

Older children are safety guards at street crossing for 2 younger children.

SVA93-92

CHRISTMAS AT THE FARM

Calf and lamb greet girl carrying a pail of feed.

SVA93-93

CHECK IT OUT BOOKMOBILE

Bookmobile van carries stories to children in villages and farms. Boys and girls select books to borrow.

SVA93-94

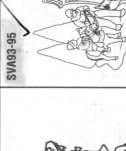

TOUR THE VILLAGE

Tourist information booth with clerk to assist visitors new to the village.

SVA93-95

PINT-SIZE PONY RIDES

One child waits to buy a pony ride as another rides and one offers carrot to pony. Stable building and bench for man with pony ride and 3 children.

SVA93-96

PICK-UP AND DELIVERY

Pickup truck carries Christmas tree.

ART CHART #	NAME	ITEM #	MATERIAL	SET?		MARKET STATUS	ORIGINAL SRP	GREENBOOK TRU MKT PRICE
				VARIATIONS/MISC/COLLECTOR NOTES				
SVA92-89	SPIRIT OF SNOW VILLAGE AIRPLANE (1992)	5440-2	Ceramic/Metal	NO		CURRENT ↲	$ 32.50	$ 32.50
SVA93-90	VILLAGE ANIMATED SKATING POND (1993)	5229-9	-------	SET OF 15		CURRENT	60.00	60.00
SVA93-91	SAFETY PATROL (1993)	5449-6	Ceramic	SET OF 4		CURRENT	27.50	27.50
SVA93-92	CHRISTMAS AT THE FARM (1993)	5450-0	Ceramic	SET OF 2		CURRENT ↲	16.00	16.00
SVA93-93	CHECK IT OUT BOOKMOBILE (1993)	5451-8	Ceramic	SET OF 3		CURRENT	25.00	25.00
SVA93-94	TOUR THE VILLAGE (1993)	5452-6	Ceramic	NO		CURRENT	12.50	12.50
SVA93-95	PINT-SIZE PONY RIDES (1993)	5453-4	Ceramic	SET OF 3		CURRENT	37.50	37.50
SVA93-96	PICK-UP AND DELIVERY (1993)	5454-2	Ceramic	NO		CURRENT	10.00	10.00

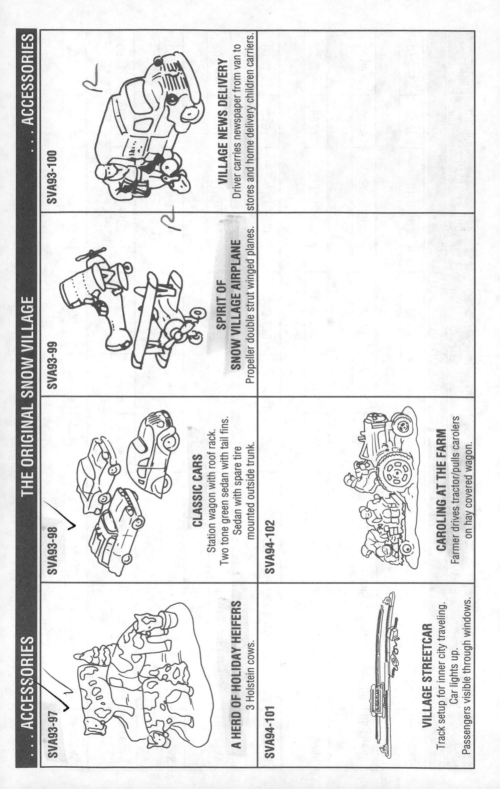

SVA93-100

VILLAGE NEWS DELIVERY
Driver carries newspaper from van to
stores and home delivery children carriers.

SVA93-99

**SPIRIT OF
SNOW VILLAGE AIRPLANE**
Propeller double strut winged planes.

SVA93-98

CLASSIC CARS
Station wagon with roof rack.
Two tone green sedan with tail fins.
Sedan with spare tire
mounted outside trunk.

SVA94-102

CAROLING AT THE FARM
Farmer drives tractor/pulls carolers
on hay covered wagon.

SVA93-97

A HERD OF HOLIDAY HEIFERS
3 Holstein cows.

SVA94-101

VILLAGE STREETCAR
Track setup for inner city traveling.
Car lights up.
Passengers visible through windows.

ART CHART #	NAME	ITEM #	MATERIAL	SET?	♥ MARKET STATUS	ORIGINAL SRP	GREENBOOK TRUMKT PRICE
	VARIATIONS/MISC/COLLECTOR NOTES						
SVA93-97	A HERD OF HOLIDAY HEIFERS (1993)	5455-0	Ceramic	SET OF 3	CURRENT	$ 18.00	$ 18.00
SVA93-98	CLASSIC CARS (1993)	5457-7	Ceramic	SET OF 3	CURRENT	22.50	22.50
SVA93-99	SPIRIT OF SNOW VILLAGE AIRPLANE (1993) *2 Assorted: Blue, Yellow.	5458-5	Ceramic	2 ASST.*	CURRENT	12.50	12.50
SVA93-100	VILLAGE NEWS DELIVERY (1993)	5459-3	Ceramic	SET OF 2	CURRENT	15.00	15.00
SVA94-101	VILLAGE STREETCAR (1994) Passenger's silhouettes on windows.	5240-0	---------	SET OF 10	CURRENT	65.00	65.00
SVA94-102	CAROLING AT THE FARM (1994)	5463-1	Ceramic	NO	CURRENT	35.00	35.00

MEADOWLAND

MDW79-1

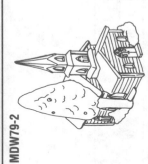

THATCHED COTTAGE

Small thatched cottage with attached tree. Chimney at rear of stucco and timber trim.

MDW79-2

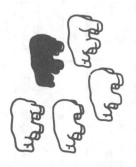

COUNTRYSIDE CHURCH

Countryside Church in a springtime setting. Large green tree against a simple white wood church with steeple rising from entry to nave.

MDW79-3

ASPEN TREES

The trees that shiver and tremble in the wind. Small leaves on a hardwood tree.

MDW79-4

SHEEP

Grazing white and black sheep make up this flock.

MEADOWLAND (COMPOSITE)

ART CHART #	NAME	ITEM #	MATERIAL	SET?	♘	MARKET STATUS	ORIGINAL SRP	GREENBOOK TRUMKT PRICE
	VARIATIONS/MISC/COLLECTOR NOTES							
MDW79-1	THATCHED COTTAGE	5050-0	Ceramic	NO	✓	RETIRED 1980	$ 30.00	$ 600.00
MDW79-2	COUNTRYSIDE CHURCH	5051-8	Ceramic	NO	✓	RETIRED 1980	25.00	NE
	For snow version see 1979 Countryside Church #5058-3 (SV79-5).							
MDW79-3	ASPEN TREES (ACCESSORY)	5052-6	Ceramic	NO		RETIRED 1980	16.00	NE
MDW79-4	SHEEP (ACCESSORY)	5053-4	Ceramic	SET OF 12		RETIRED 1980	12.00	NE
	9 white, 3 black.							

CLIPBOARD
• Technically not part of the Original Snow Village. Limited distribution.

NE = Not Established

BACHMAN'S

BCH87-1

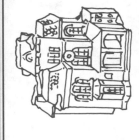

HOME TOWN BOARDINGHOUSE

Three story brick building with rented rooms above main floor parlor and dining room. Ground floor has front bay window adjacent to covered entry porch which extends around side to windowed area. Second story features arched windows. Brick turret-like structures appear attached to rectangular design. Taller turret has windows on all four sides of roof with attic used for rental or storage.

BCH88-1

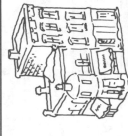

HOME TOWN DRUGSTORE

Drugstore is corner store in a two attached buildings structure. Taller three story building houses barber shop on main level and eye glass shop above. Entry to drugstore is at corner of shorter building with three support columns providing an open area to entry and for support of upper windowed turret design. Garlands decorate the awnings over display windows.

BCH87-2

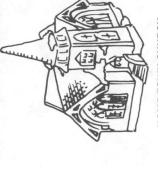

HOME TOWN CHURCH

Cross-shaped floor plan with spire rising from one side of transept. Simple entry door at base of spire in contrast to large arched windows that fill end walls.

ART CHART #	NAME	ITEM #	MATERIAL	SET?	♥	MARKET STATUS	ORIGINAL SRP	GREENBOOK TRUMKT PRICE
	VARIATIONS/MISC/COLLECTOR NOTES							
BCH87-1	HOME TOWN BOARDING HOUSE (1987 - 1988)	670-0	Porcelain	NO	✓	DISCONTINUED	$ 34.00	$ 330.00
	Inspired by Sprague House in Red Wing, MN.							
BCH87-2	HOME TOWN CHURCH (1987 - 1988)	671-8	Porcelain	NO	✓	DISCONTINUED	40.00	300.00
	Designed after a St. Paul, MN church.							
BCH88-1	HOME TOWN DRUGSTORE (1988 - 1989)	672-6	Porcelain	NO	✓	DISCONTINUED	40.00	675.00
	Same mold as the Christmas In The City Variety Store. Inspired by a store in Stillwater, MN.							

CLIPBOARD
• Pieces were available in stores as a "Purchase With Purchase."
• Fourth piece, a Bookstore, was created to fit snugly against the Drugstore but was never produced.

Department 56, Inc. has entered into a licensing agreement with The Walt Disney Company to design a new village.

The following is the text of their joint press release:

Department 56 signs licensing agreement with the Walt Disney Company. Will introduce "Disney Parks Village Series" based on Disney theme park scenes.

Minneapolis, May 23, 1994 - Department 56, Inc. (NYSE:DFS), a leading specialty giftware company, announced today that it has entered into a licensing agreement with The Walt Disney Company to create "Disney Parks Village Series," a set of classic Disney characters and theme park buildings that will be part of Department 56's Heritage Village Collection. The license runs through 1996. Other terms of the agreement were not disclosed.

Department 56 said the Disney Parks Village Series will initially consist of four lit, hand-painted porcelain replicas of Disney theme park buildings and coordinating accessories. The new series will preview at the Disneyana Convention to be held at the Contemporary Resort Hotel at Walt Disney World in Lake Buena Vista, Florida, in early September 1994. The products will first be available at Walt Disney theme parks and resorts starting in September, and then will also be available at selected Department 56 retailers starting in December.

"We are extremely pleased that Walt Disney has selected Department 56 to create a unique line of products based on its most well-known and beloved images and characters. We share Disney's continuing commitment to detail, design, and quality," said Ed Bazinet, Chairman and Chief Executive Officer. "We believe the Disney Parks Village Series could become an important dimension of our business in future years."

The Heritage Village Collection

1984 • D56 announces its first porcelain village, Dickens' Village

1985 • the first limited edition, the Village Mill - limited to 2,500 pieces, is introduced

1986 • New England Village becomes the second porcelain village
  • Alpine Village makes it debut, becoming the third porcelain village
  • Christmas Carol Collection is introduced, the first grouping pertaining to the works of Charles Dickens

1987 • sleeves began to support the Heritage Village logo
  • Christmas in the City is added to Heritage Village
  • Little Town of Bethlehem is announced and is the only village to date not to have any retirements or additions
  • Cold Cast Porcelain replicas of Dickens' Village and New England Village pieces are introduced
  • Lite-Ups, miniature versions of Dickens' Village and New England Village pieces, are introduced

1988 • first Dickens' Village pieces are retired

1990 • the North Pole Collection is introduced bringing the number of Heritage Villages to six

1992 • the first Charles Dickens' Signature Series piece, the Crown & Cricket Inn, is introduced
  • the Gate House, D56's first Event piece, is made available at selected dealers' Open House Events

1993 • D56 announces that it will cease production of the limited edition Cathedral Of St. Mark due to production problems - only 3,024 of the planned 17,500 are produced

1994 • seventh village in the Heritage Village Collection, Disney Parks Village Series, is announced
  • Dickens' Village 10th Year Anniversary piece, Postern, is issued

DV84-1

THE ORIGINAL SHOPS OF DICKENS' VILLAGE:

CROWNTREE INN

CANDLE SHOP

GREEN GROCER

GOLDEN SWAN BAKER

BEAN AND SON SMITHY SHOP

ABEL BEESLEY BUTCHER

JONES & CO.

BRUSH & BASKET SHOP

DV84-2

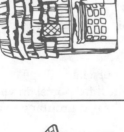

CROWNTREE INN

Large multi-paned windows run length of front of Inn with entry door decorated by wreath, second story stone, attic dormer.

DV84-3

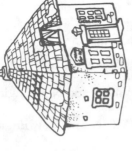

CANDLE SHOP

Timber framed windows, plaster over stone small house/store. Rental rooms in attic, light over open front door.

DV84-4

GREEN GROCER

Thatched roof over timbered two story grocery/provisions store. Bay window for display. Attached storage room on side of store.

DV84-5

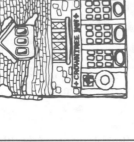

GOLDEN SWAN BAKER

Painted sign with gold swan hangs above large bay window for display. Timbered building, brick chimney, light above entry door.

DV84-6

BEAN AND SON SMITHY SHOP

Double wood door, stone first story, second story set upon stone with overhang. Steep curved roof with one brick chimney.

DV84-7

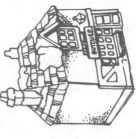

ABEL BEESLEY BUTCHER

Timbered bottom half, second story plaster over stone, two chimneys.

DV84-8

JONES & CO. BRUSH & BASKET SHOP

Cellar shop is a cobbler with small sign by his door to advertise, rest of building is for basketry, mats, and brush. Narrow staircase leads to entry. House rises 2 1/2 stories plus cellar at ground level.

ART CHART #	NAME	ITEM #	MATERIAL	SET?	🖐	MARKET STATUS	ORIGINAL SRP	GREENBOOK TRUMKT PRICE
				VARIATIONS/MISC/COLLECTOR NOTES				
DV84-1	THE ORIGINAL SHOPS OF DICKENS' VILLAGE	6515-3	Porcelain	SET OF 7	✓	RETIRED 1988	$175.00	$1325.00
DV84-2	CROWNTREE INN	6515-3	Porcelain	1 of a 7 pc set	✓	RETIRED 1988	25.00	320.00
DV84-3	CANDLE SHOP	6515-3	Porcelain	1 of a 7 pc set	✓	RETIRED 1988	25.00	190.00
	Variations in roof color - gray was first release, blue was subsequent.							
DV84-4	GREEN GROCER	6515-3	Porcelain	1 of a 7 pc set	✓	RETIRED 1988	25.00	185.00
DV84-5	GOLDEN SWAN BAKER	6515-3	Porcelain	1 of a 7 pc set	✓	RETIRED 1988	25.00	180.00
DV84-6	BEAN AND SON SMITHY SHOP	6515-3	Porcelain	1 of a 7 pc set	✓	RETIRED 1988	25.00	190.00
DV84-7	ABEL BEESLEY BUTCHER	6515-3	Porcelain	1 of a 7 pc set	✓	RETIRED 1988	25.00	120.00
DV84-8	JONES & CO. BRUSH & BASKET SHOP	6515-3	Porcelain	1 of a 7 pc set	✓	RETIRED 1988	25.00	335.00

THE HERITAGE VILLAGE COLLECTION – DICKENS' VILLAGE

1985

1985

DV85-1

DICKENS' VILLAGE CHURCH

Stone church with entry at base of massive turret. Nave has exposed stone base with timber/plaster upper walls. Irregular shingled roof. Turret bell chamber has rounded arches. Entry door and nave windows demonstrate a more pointed arch shape.

DV85-2

DICKENS' COTTAGES:

THATCHED COTTAGE

STONE COTTAGE

TUDOR COTTAGE

DV85-3

THATCHED COTTAGE

Double chimneys rise from thatched roof, second story plastered/timbered home with second story extending out on sides.

DV85-4

STONE COTTAGE

Varigated fieldstone walls crowned with rough-hewn shingle roof. House has two wings each with own chimney.

DICKENS' VILLAGE MILL

DICKENS' VILLAGE MILL

Rough-hewn stone makes up 3 section mill with large wooden millwheel. Two sets double doors – one large set to allow carriage to be brought directly into building, smaller doors open into silo area Pronounced roof ridges on two sections.

DV85-5

DV85-6

TUDOR COTTAGE

Stone foundation with timbered/plastered walls forming a small house. Two chimneys for heating/cooking.

ART CHART #	NAME	ITEM #	MATERIAL	SET?	🔔 MARKET STATUS	ORIGINAL SRP	GREENBOOK TRUMKT PRICE
				VARIATIONS/MISC/COLLECTOR NOTES			
DV85-1	DICKENS' VILLAGE CHURCH	6516-1	Porcelain	NO	RETIRED 1989	$ 35.00	See Below
	Variations in color affect TRUMARKET Price; see footnote[1] below.						
DV85-2	**DICKENS' COTTAGES**	**6518-8**	**Porcelain**	**SET OF 3**	**RETIRED 1988**	**75.00**	**$ 1050.00**
	Early release to Gift Creations Concepts.						
DV85-3	*THATCHED COTTAGE*	6518-8	Porcelain	1 of a 3 pc set	RETIRED 1988	25.00	200.00
	Early release to Gift Creations Concepts.						
DV85-4	*STONE COTTAGE*	6518-8	Porcelain	1 of a 3 pc set	RETIRED 1988	25.00	425.00
	Variations in color: "early tan" and "pea green."						
DV85-5	*TUDOR COTTAGE*	6518-8	Porcelain	1 of a 3 pc set	RETIRED 1988	25.00	450.00
	Early release to Gift Creations Concepts.						
DV85-6	DICKENS' VILLAGE MILL	6519-6	Porcelain	NO	LTD. ED. 2,500	35.00	5150.00
	Early release to Gift Creations Concepts.						

[1] There are five variations of the **Village Church**:
  a) *Winter White*: off white to cream walls, brown roof matches brown cornerstones - $425.00.
  b) *Yellow or Cream*: cream walls with light yellow coloring in mortar between stones, buttercream roof - $295.00.
  c) *Green*: very light green tone on walls, butterscotch roof - $350.00.
  d) *Tan*: tan walls, butterscotch roof - $205.00.
  e) *"Dark" or Butterscotch*: walls are same color or nearly the same as roof - $155.00.
      (Only sleeve to read "Village Church." All others read "Shops Of Dickens' Village.")

THE HERITAGE VILLAGE COLLECTION – DICKENS' VILLAGE

DV86-1

CHRISTMAS CAROL COTTAGES:

FEZZIWIG'S WAREHOUSE

SCROOGE & MARLEY
COUNTING HOUSE

THE COTTAGE OF
BOB CRATCHIT & TINY TIM

DV86-2

FEZZIWIG'S WAREHOUSE
Squared brick two story building
with two brick chimneys. Second story
front face is plaster over brick.
Entire front is windowed.

DV86-3

SCROOGE & MARLEY
COUNTING HOUSE
Simple rectangular shape.
Bottom brick, second story plastered
with shuttered windows. Bay window
major decorative design.

DV86-4

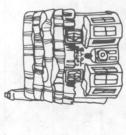

THE COTTAGE OF
BOB CRATCHIT & TINY TIM
Small four room house, main room
has fireplace for heat/cooking.
Half of house rises two stories to provide
sleeping area. Neatly thatched roof.

DV86-5

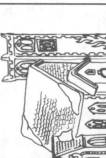

NORMAN CHURCH
Solid four-sided tower used as both
watch and bell tower. Doors and windows
reflect the Romanesque rounded arches.

DV86-6

DICKENS' LANE SHOPS:

THOMAS KERSEY COFFEE HOUSE

COTTAGE TOY SHOP

TUTTLE'S PUB

DV86-7

THOMAS KERSEY COFFEE HOUSE
Unique roof set upon simple rectangular
building rises up to central chimney with
four flue pipes. Brick, plaster, and timber
with tile or slate roof. Large multi-paned
windows predominate front walls.

DV86-8

COTTAGE TOY SHOP
Small thatched roof cottage.
Shop has large bay windows
for light and display. Outside side
stair/entry for family to living quarters.

ART CHART #	NAME	ITEM #	MATERIAL	SET?	🔔	MARKET STATUS	ORIGINAL SRP	GREENBOOK TRUMKT PRICE
			VARIATIONS/MISC/COLLECTOR NOTES					
DV86-1	CHRISTMAS CAROL COTTAGES	6500-5	Porcelain	SET OF 3	✓	CURRENT	$ 75.00	$ 90.00
DV86-2	FEZZIWIG'S WAREHOUSE	6500-5	Porcelain	1 of 3 pc set	✓	CURRENT	25.00	30.00
DV86-3	SCROOGE & MARLEY COUNTING HOUSE	6500-5	Porcelain	1 of a 3 pc set	✓	CURRENT	25.00	30.00
DV86-4	THE COTTAGE OF BOB CRATCHIT & TINY TIM	6500-5	Porcelain	1 of a 3 pc set	✓	CURRENT	25.00	30.00
DV86-5	NORMAN CHURCH	6502-1	Porcelain	NO	✓	LTD. ED. 3,500	40.00	3600.00
	Early release to Gift Creations Concepts. Color variations: light to dark gray.							
DV86-6	DICKENS' LANE SHOPS	6507-2	Porcelain	SET OF 3	✓	RETIRED 1989	80.00	650.00
DV86-7	THOMAS KERSEY COFFEE HOUSE	6507-2	Porcelain	1 of a 3 pc set	✓	RETIRED 1989	27.00	165.00
DV86-8	COTTAGE TOY SHOP	6507-2	Porcelain	1 of a 3 pc set	✓	RETIRED 1989	27.00	250.00

THE HERITAGE VILLAGE COLLECTION – DICKENS' VILLAGE

DV86-9

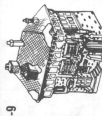

TUTTLE'S PUB

Building rises three stories, ground level has pub for refreshments plus stable area for horse and carriages, second and third story jut out in step fashion. Travelers could rent rooms. Third floor had additional attic rooms. Stone, plaster, and timber, three chimneys.

DV86-10

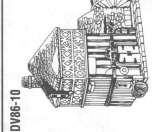

BLYTHE POND MILL HOUSE

Three story timbered house, rough stone wing connects water wheel. Grinding wheels rest alongside house, open front door.

DV86-11

CHADBURY STATION AND TRAIN

Three car train (engine, coal or wood car, and passenger car) and station built of irregularly shaped stone foundation and fieldstone. Columns support overhang keeping passengers dry. Indoor waiting area warmed by fireplace. Wooden benches provide rest area.

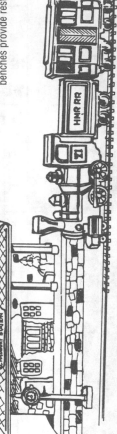

ART CHART #	NAME	ITEM #	MATERIAL	SET?	✿	MARKET STATUS	ORIGINAL SRP	GREENBOOK TRUMKT PRICE
			VARIATIONS/MISC/COLLECTOR NOTES					
DV86-9	*TUTTLE'S PUB*	6507-2	Porcelain	1 of a 3 pc set	✓	RETIRED 1989	$ 27.00	$ 245.00
DV86-10	BLYTHE POND MILL HOUSE	6508-0	Porcelain	NO	✓	RETIRED 1990	37.00	305.00
	Variation: "By The Pond" error on bottom @ $135.00. (Variation is more common than the correct piece.)							
DV86-11	CHADBURY STATION AND TRAIN	6528-5	Porcelain	SET OF 4	✓	RETIRED 1989	65.00	385.00
	Variations in size.							

THE HERITAGE VILLAGE COLLECTION – DICKENS' VILLAGE

DV87-1

BARLEY BREE:

FARMHOUSE

BARN

DV87-2

FARMHOUSE

Thatched roof on small farmhouse with centralized chimney. Second story tucked into steeply pitched roof.

DV87-3

BARN

Stone foundation, thatched roof, for livestock.

DV87-4

THE OLD CURIOSITY SHOP

Corner shop for antiques is adjacent to rare book store. Curiosity building has large windows for display. Two chimneys. Book building is taller but narrower. Upper story window and roof dormer supported by wood ribs. In front corner a drain pipe collects from roof and diverts water from doorway.

DV87-5

KENILWORTH CASTLE

Stronghold for Kings and Lords, began as a fortress and converted to Medieval Palace. Stone, thick walled, compact. Battlements surround all turrets.

DV87-6

BRICK ABBEY

Two spires flank front doors, rose window above entry oak doors. Example of a stage of Gothic architecture.

DV87-7

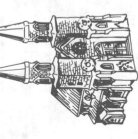

CHESTERTON MANOR HOUSE

Known as a Great House, set into countryside on acres of estate land. Stone facade, slate roof, area of plaster and half timber, open pediment above wood entry doors. Double roof peaks above central hall.

ART CHART #	NAME	ITEM #	MATERIAL	SET?	🔔	MARKET STATUS	ORIGINAL SRP	GREENBOOK TRUMKT PRICE
DV87-1	**BARLEY BREE**	**5900-5**	**Porcelain**	**SET OF 2**	✓	**RETIRED 1989**	**$ 60.00**	**$ 395.00**
	VARIATIONS/MISC/COLLECTOR NOTES							
DV87-2	*FARMHOUSE*	5900-5	Porcelain	1 of 2 pc set	✓	RETIRED 1989	30.00	NE
DV87-3	*BARN*	5900-5	Porcelain	1 of a 2 pc set	✓	RETIRED 1989	30.00	NE
DV87-4	THE OLD CURIOSITY SHOP	5905-6	Porcelain	NO	✓	CURRENT	32.00	40.00
	Designed after the Old Curiosity Shop on Portsmouth Street in London.							
DV87-5	KENILWORTH CASTLE	5916-1	Porcelain	NO	✓	RETIRED 1988	70.00	540.00
	Inspired by the remains of Kenilworth Castle in Warwickshire, England.							
DV87-6	BRICK ABBEY	6549-8	Porcelain	NO	✓	RETIRED 1989	33.00	405.00
	Variation: slight size changes over two years.							
DV87-7	CHESTERTON MANOR HOUSE	6568-4	Porcelain	NO	✓	LTD. ED. 7,500	45.00	1725.00
	Variations in color. Early release to Gift Creations Concepts.							

NE = NOT ESTABLISHED

THE HERITAGE VILLAGE COLLECTION – DICKENS' VILLAGE

1988 . . . **1988 . . .**

DV88-1

COUNTING HOUSE & SILAS THIMBLETON BARRISTER

Square, tall, 3 story, 3 chimney, offices. Double size windows, w/shutters. 4 equal gables create 4 section pitched roof. Attached plaster/timbered 3 story office is smaller and narrower. Ground floor corner wood lattice-work windows.

DV88-2

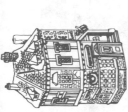

C. FLETCHER PUBLIC HOUSE

5 windows shape corner of unique pub. 2nd story wider/longer, supported by wood ribs. Sweet Shop tucked in alongside pub is plaster/timbered design. Both share roof but have separate chimneys.

DV88-3

COBBLESTONE SHOPS:

THE WOOL SHOP

BOOTER AND COBBLER

T. WELLS FRUIT & SPICE SHOP

DV88-4

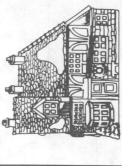

THE WOOL SHOP

Low turret rounds out one front corner of shop. Wood framing of three front windows and lattice design. Light by front door.

DV88-5

BOOTER AND COBBLER

Shoes made and repaired in this stone building with entry via Tannery where leather is cured and dyed. Outdoor light by main display window, wood hatch on roof opening, mansard roof.

DV88-6

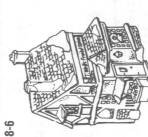

T. WELLS FRUIT & SPICE SHOP

White washed brick and timbered building. Front window has stone ledge. Outdoor covered produce bin for food.

DV88-7

NICHOLAS NICKLEBY:

NICHOLAS NICKLEBY COTTAGE

WACKFORD SQUEERS BOARDING SCHOOL

DV88-8

NICHOLAS NICKLEBY COTTAGE

Brick, stone, and slate roofed home. Three chimneys, curved timbers decorate second floor. Bay window on front room. Two roof dormers.

ART CHART #	NAME	ITEM #	MATERIAL	SET?	⚲	MARKET STATUS	ORIGINAL SRP	GREENBOOK TRUMKT PRICE
	VARIATIONS/MISC/COLLECTOR NOTES							
DV88-1	COUNTING HOUSE & SILAS THIMBLETON BARRISTER	5902-1	Porcelain	NO	✓	RETIRED 1990	$ 32.00	$ 90.00
DV88-2	C. FLETCHER PUBLIC HOUSE	5904-8	Porcelain	NO	✓	LTD. ED. 12,500*	35.00	590.00
	*Plus Proof Editions. Market Price for Proofs is not established. Early release to Gift Creations Concepts.							
DV88-3	COBBLESTONE SHOPS	5924-2	Porcelain	SET OF 3	✓	RETIRED 1990	95.00	355.00
DV88-4	THE WOOL SHOP	5924-2	Porcelain	1 of a 3 pc set	✓	RETIRED 1990	32.00	170.00
DV88-5	BOOTER AND COBBLER	5924-2	Porcelain	1 of a 3 pc set	✓	RETIRED 1990	32.00	105.00
DV88-6	T. WELLS FRUIT & SPICE SHOP	5924-2	Porcelain	1 of a 3 pc set	✓	RETIRED 1990	32.00	95.00
DV88-7	NICHOLAS NICKLEBY	5925-0	Porcelain	SET OF 2	✓	RETIRED 1991	72.00	155.00
	Variation: Set with Nic"k"olas Error @ $195.00.							
DV88-8	NICHOLAS NICKLEBY COTTAGE	5925-0	Porcelain	1 of a 2 pc set	✓	RETIRED 1991	36.00	80.00
	Variation: Nic"k"olas Error @ $120.00.							

DV88-9

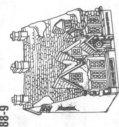

WACKFORD SQUEERS BOARDING SCHOOL

Three chimneys along ridge of steeply pitched roof w/many gables. Classrooms downstairs with student rooms above. Attic windows are shuttered.

DV88-10

MERCHANT SHOPS:

POULTERER

GEO. WEETON WATCHMAKER

THE MERMAID FISH SHOPPE

WHITE HORSE BAKERY

WALPOLE TAILORS

DV88-11

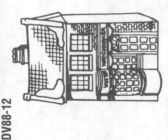

POULTERER

Three story stone block and timber, fresh geese hang outside front door.

DV88-12

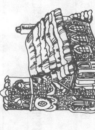

GEO. WEETON WATCHMAKER

All brick, rounded bay window, slate roof, fan light window in oak front door.

DV88-13

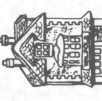

THE MERMAID FISH SHOPPE

Roadside fish bins, bay windows, angled doors and walls, wooden trap door in roof.

DV88-14

WHITE HORSE BAKERY

Two large windows to display baked goods, roof is hipped and gabled with scalloped shingles.

DV88-15

WALPOLE TAILORS

Stone and brick covered by stucco. Large first floor windows have wood panels under sills. 2nd floor has bow window.

DV88-16

IVY GLEN CHURCH

Square-toothed parapet tops stone turret by front entry of a thatched roof church. Curved timber design above door is repeated on bell chamber of turret. Arched windows. This church has a chimney.

ART CHART #	NAME	ITEM #	MATERIAL	SET?	🔔	MARKET STATUS	ORIGINAL SRP	GREENBOOK TRUMKT PRICE
	VARIATIONS/MISC/COLLECTOR NOTES							
DV88-9	WACKFORD SQUEERS BOARDING SCHOOL	5925-0	Porcelain	1 of a 2 pc set	✓	RETIRED 1991	$ 36.00	$ 85.00
DV88-10	MERCHANT SHOPS	5926-9	Porcelain	SET OF 5	✓	RETIRED 1993	150.00	230.00
DV88-11	POULTERER	5926-9	Porcelain	1 of a 5 pc set	✓	RETIRED 1993	32.50	60.00
DV88-12	GEO. WEETON WATCHMAKER	5926-9	Porcelain	1 of a 5 pc set	✓	RETIRED 1993	32.50	60.00
DV88-13	THE MERMAID FISH SHOPPE	5926-9	Porcelain	1 of a 5 pc set	✓	RETIRED 1993	32.50	70.00
DV88-14	WHITE HORSE BAKERY	5926-9	Porcelain	1 of a 5 pc set	✓	RETIRED 1993	32.50	55.00
DV88-15	WALPOLE TAILORS	5926-9	Porcelain	1 of a 5 pc set	✓	RETIRED 1993	32.50	55.00
DV88-16	IVY GLEN CHURCH	5927-7	Porcelain	NO	✓	RETIRED 1991	35.00	80.00

DV89-1

DAVID COPPERFIELD:

MR. WICKFIELD SOLICITOR

BETSY TROTWOOD'S COTTAGE

PEGGOTTY'S SEASIDE COTTAGE

DV89-2

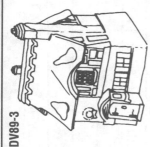

MR. WICKFIELD SOLICITOR

Well-to-do legal practice and home. Second story has two balcony areas defined by low balustrades. 3 small dormers. Side door for family entry.

DV89-3

BETSY TROTWOOD'S COTTAGE

Country home – brick, timbered, whitewash. Two chimneys. Known for variations of wall angles. Roof ridge has unique dogtooth design.

DV89-4

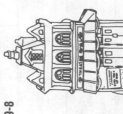

PEGGOTTY'S SEASIDE COTTAGE

Up-side-down boat into a house, iron funnel as chimney, captains bridge, crows nest, barrels, boxes, ropes, and boots near entry.

DV89-5

VICTORIA STATION

Brownstone with granite pillars and facings – central section with domed red tile roof, two side wings, covered front drive-through, gold clock above entry.

DV89-6

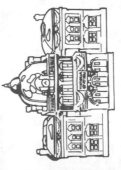

KNOTTINGHILL CHURCH

Beige/honey stone with gray slate roof, arched windows. Turret bell chamber rises where church wings intersect.

DV89-7

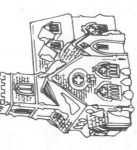

COBLES POLICE STATION

Two story brick, stone outlines front entry and upper windows. Two watch turrets on 2nd story corners.

DV89-8

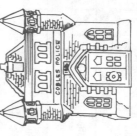

THEATRE ROYAL

Double set of doors and the bulletin board fill the theatre frontage. Garlands and gold bells add festive touch. Second floor rounded arch windows are separated by pilasters.

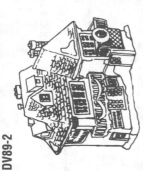

115

ART CHART #	NAME	ITEM #	MATERIAL	SET?	☝	MARKET STATUS	ORIGINAL SRP	GREENBOOK TRUMKT PRICE
	VARIATIONS/MISC/COLLECTOR NOTES							
DV89-1	DAVID COPPERFIELD	5550-6	Porcelain	SET OF 3	✓	RETIRED 1992	$125.00	$190.00
	Variation: with "original tan" Peggotty's @ $250.00. For color photo, see 2nd Ed. page 228. Early release to Showcase Dealers, 1990.							
DV89-2	MR. WICKFIELD SOLICITOR	5550-6	Porcelain	1 of a 3 pc set	✓	RETIRED 1992	42.50	96.00
	Early release to Showcase Dealers, 1990.							
DV89-3	BETSY TROTWOOD'S COTTAGE	5550-6	Porcelain	1 of a 3 pc set	✓	RETIRED 1992	42.50	65.00
	Early release to Showcase Dealers, 1990.							
DV89-4	PEGGOTTY'S SEASIDE COTTAGE	5550-6	Porcelain	1 of a 3 pc set	✓	RETIRED 1992	42.50	60.00
	Variation: "original tan" @ $150.00. For color photo, see 2nd Ed. page 228. Early release to Showcase Dealers, 1990.							
DV89-5	VICTORIA STATION	5574-3	Porcelain	NO	✓	CURRENT	100.00	110.00
	Early release to Showcase Dealers and National Association Of Limited Edition Dealers, 1990. Designed after Victoria Station in London.							
DV89-6	KNOTTINGHILL CHURCH	5582-4	Porcelain	NO	✓	CURRENT	50.00	52.00
DV89-7	COBLES POLICE STATION	5583-2	Porcelain	NO	✓	RETIRED 1991	37.50	90.00
DV89-8	THEATRE ROYAL	5584-0	Porcelain	NO	✓	RETIRED 1992	45.00	80.00
	Inspired by the Theatre Royal in Rochester, England where Charles Dickens saw his first Shakespeare play.							

THE HERITAGE VILLAGE COLLECTION – DICKENS' VILLAGE

DV89-9

DV89-10

DV89-11

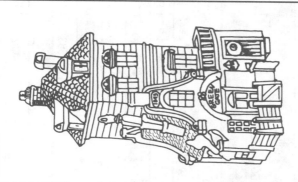

RUTH MARION SCOTCH WOOLENS

Herringbone brick design between timbers decorates front of one and a half story shops and home. Small flower shop tucked onto one side. Bay windows repeat diamond and hexagon panes.

GREEN GATE COTTAGE

Three story home. Repeated vault design on chimney, dormers, and third story windows. Balcony above door. Fenced courtyard and two doors give impression of two homes. Small part has steep roof, crooked chimney, and ornamental molding.

THE FLAT OF EBENEZER SCROOGE

Four stories, broken balustrades and shutters, front door padlocked and chained, ghostly face on door knocker.

ART CHART #	NAME	ITEM #	MATERIAL	SET?	♥ ■ MARKET STATUS	ORIGINAL SRP	GREENBOOK TRUMKT PRICE
	VARIATIONS/MISC/COLLECTOR NOTES						
DV89-9	RUTH MARION SCOTCH WOOLENS	5585-9	Porcelain	NO	✓ LTD. ED. 17,500*	$ 65.00	$ 405.00
	*Plus Proof Editions. Market Price for Proofs is generally 10 to 20% less. Early release to GCC. Named for the wife of D56 artist, Neilan Lund.						
DV89-10	GREEN GATE COTTAGE	5586-7	Porcelain	NO	✓ LTD. ED. 22,500*	65.00	275.00
	*Plus Proof Editions. Market Price for Proofs is generally 10 to 20% less.						
DV89-11	THE FLAT OF EBENEZER SCROOGE	5587-5	Porcelain	NO	✓ CURRENT	37.50	See Below[1]
	Early release to National Association Of Limited Edition Dealers, 1989. Addition to "Christmas Carol" grouping. Variations affect TRUMARKET Price.						

[1] There are four variations of **The Flat Of Ebenezer Scrooge:**
 a) 1st issue: made in Taiwan, has yellow panes in windows, far left shutter on 4th floor is slightly open to allow light to shine through - $135.00.
 b) 2nd issue: made in Taiwan, no panes in windows - $85.00.
 c) 3rd issue: made in Philippines, has yellow panes in windows, far left shutter on 4th floor is sealed - SRP @ $37.50.
 d) 4th issue: made in China, has yellow panes in windows - SRP @ $37.50.

THE HERITAGE VILLAGE COLLECTION – DICKENS' VILLAGE

1990

1990

DV90-1

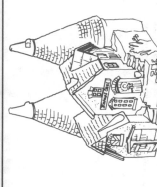

BISHOPS OAST HOUSE

Large attached barn, round cobblestone oasts contain a kiln for drying malt or hops to produce ale. Exterior finished as a rough-cast surface over brick.

DV90-2

KINGS ROAD:

TUTBURY PRINTER

C.H. WATT PHYSICIAN

DV90-3

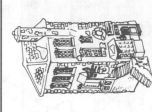

TUTBURY PRINTER

Timbered/plaster design with decorative molding between first and second story. Ground floor bay window with smaller bays on second floor. Steeply pitched roof with a dormer.

DV90-4

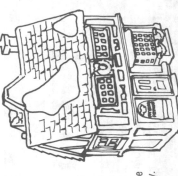

C.H. WATT PHYSICIAN

Doctor's office on ground floor, outside staircase leads to family residence, bricks used above most windows as decorative arch, exposed stone edges on four corners of house walls.

ART CHART #	NAME	ITEM #	MATERIAL	SET?	♥	MARKET STATUS	ORIGINAL SRP	GREENBOOK TRUMKT PRICE
				VARIATIONS/MISC/COLLECTOR NOTES				
DV90-1	BISHOPS OAST HOUSE	5567-0	Porcelain	NO	✓	RETIRED 1992	$ 45.00	$ 85.00
DV90-2	KINGS ROAD	5568-9	Porcelain	SET OF 2	✓	CURRENT	72.00	80.00
DV90-3	TUTBURY PRINTER	5568-9	Porcelain	1 of a 2 pc set	✓	CURRENT	36.00	40.00
DV90-4	C.H. WATT PHYSICIAN	5568-9	Porcelain	1 of a 2 pc set	✓	CURRENT	36.00	40.00

THE HERITAGE VILLAGE COLLECTION – DICKENS' VILLAGE

DV91-4

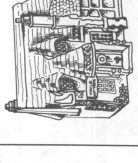

MAYLIE COTTAGE

Pronounced roof ridge. Curved cone roof shape repeated on dormers and front door. One chimney rises up front facade, second chimney on side of house.

DV91-3

BROWNLOW HOUSE

Two story stone house with two brick chimneys and three front gables. Double doors.

OLIVER TWIST:

BROWNLOW HOUSE
MAYLIE COTTAGE

DV91-6

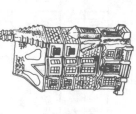

NEPHEW FRED'S FLAT

Four story home with bow windows rising from second floor to roof like a turret. Planters flank front door. Side door with projecting window overhead and crowstepped coping in gable rising to two chimneys. Ivy grows up corner area – garlands, wreaths, and Christmas greetings decorate facade.

DV91-2

DV91-1

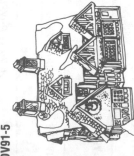

FAGIN'S HIDE-A-WAY

Two attached buildings in disrepair. Broken shutters, cracks in wall. Barrel warehouse with steep roof, gate across doors.

DV91-5

ASHBURY INN

Tudor timbered Inn for coach travelers. Food, lodging, and drink. Double chimneys, two roof dormers, and double peaks over multi-paned windows by entry.

ART CHART #	NAME	ITEM #	MATERIAL	SET?	☞ MARKET STATUS	ORIGINAL SRP	GREENBOOK TRUMKT PRICE
				VARIATIONS/MISC/COLLECTOR NOTES			
DV91-1	FAGIN'S HIDE-A-WAY	5552-2	Porcelain	NO	✓ CURRENT	$ 68.00	$ 72.00
DV91-2	OLIVER TWIST	5553-0	Porcelain	SET OF 2	✓ RETIRED 1993	75.00	140.00
DV91-3	BROWNLOW HOUSE	5553-0	Porcelain	1 of a 2 pc set	✓ RETIRED 1993	37.50	75.00
DV91-4	MAYLIE COTTAGE	5553-0	Porcelain	1 of a 2 pc set	✓ RETIRED 1993	37.50	75.00
DV91-5	ASHBURY INN	5555-7	Porcelain	NO	✓ CURRENT	55.00	60.00
DV91-6	NEPHEW FRED'S FLAT	5557-3	Porcelain	NO	✓ CURRENT	35.00	36.00
	Addition to "Christmas Carol" grouping.						

DV92-1

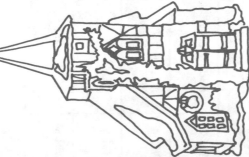

OLD MICHAELCHURCH

Stone base with lath and plaster filling space between timbered upper portion. Tower rises up front facade with heavy solid look, a simple four sided structure. Double wood doors at tower base. Chimney at rear of church.

DV92-2

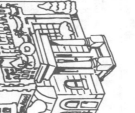

CROWN & CRICKET INN

Three story brick and stone Inn. Pillars flank covered entry. Curved hood extends over Golden Lion Arms Pub on side. Wrought iron balustrade outlines front triple window on second floor. Dressed stone edges walls. Mansard roof with decorative edge trim and molding.

DV92-3

HEMBLETON PEWTERER

Timber framed with plasterwork panels in Elizabethan style. Bay windows frame out half the front facade. Chimney Sweep establishment with steeply roofed building hugs one side of the pewterer.

DV92-4

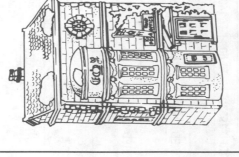

KING'S ROAD POST OFFICE

Simple four-sided stone three story building with semi circular turret-like two story rise out of window area. Entrance door surmounted by pediment just below post office sign. Triple flue chimney rises off back of building.

ART CHART #	NAME	ITEM #	MATERIAL	SET?		MARKET STATUS	ORIGINAL SRP	GREENBOOK TRUMKT PRICE
			VARIATIONS/MISC/COLLECTOR NOTES					
DV92-1	OLD MICHAELCHURCH	5562-0	Porcelain	NO	✓	CURRENT	$42.00	$46.00
	Early release to Showcase Dealers and Gift Creations Concepts.							
DV92-2	CROWN & CRICKET INN	5750-9	Porcelain	NO	✓	1992 ANNUAL	100.00	175.00
	1st Edition Charles Dickens' Signature Series©. Special collector box and hang tag. Variation: light to dark trim.							
DV92-3	HEMBLETON PEWTERER	5800-9	Porcelain	NO	✓	CURRENT	72.00	72.00
DV92-4	KING'S ROAD POST OFFICE	5801-7	Porcelain	NO	✓	CURRENT	45.00	45.00

THE HERITAGE VILLAGE COLLECTION – DICKENS' VILLAGE

DV93-4

LOMAS LTD. MOLASSES

Steps lead up to store above stone lower level where molasses and treacles refined and stored. Double chimneys rise above thatched roof.

DV93-8

GREAT DENTON MILL

Both grinding of grain for baking and animal feed as well as preparation of wool combed into yarn took place at Mill. Narrow 3 story wood structure with water wheel for power to turn wheels.

DV93-3

BUMPSTEAD NYE CLOAKS & CANES

Tall narrow shop with timbered 2nd story. Front gable has design etched into trim. Shop was noted for cloaks and capes as well as canes and walking sticks.

DV93-7

KINGSFORD'S BREW HOUSE

Stone 3 story building with slate roof processed grain into ales by fermentation. Chimneys rise from both sides from ovens & vats where the beverages were brewed. Banner of Tankard hangs outside.

DV93-2

PUMP LANE SHOPPES:

BUMPSTEAD NYE CLOAKS & CANES
LOMAS LTD. MOLASSES
W.M. WHEAT CAKES & PUDDINGS

DV93-6

BOARDING & LODGING SCHOOL

Attended by a young Scrooge, this red brick building combines a fortress-like solidity and elegant appearance based on total symmetry of gables, coping, matching chimneys and rooftop balustrade cupola, and formal front entry with pediment and molding.

DV93-1

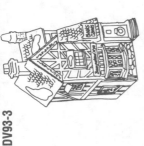

THE PIED BULL INN

Elizabethan style with wood and plaster upper stories canterlevered out from stone and brick lower levels. Front entry at side of Inn allows public rooms to be of good size to service guests and local folk.

DV93-5

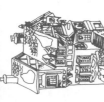

W.M. WHEAT CAKES & PUDDINGS

Baking chimney rises from center of main shop roof. 2nd story rooms are dormered with additional chimney at rear. Wreath hangs above curved front door and arched design is repeated above front windows.

ART CHART #	NAME	ITEM #	MATERIAL	SET?	🔧 MARKET STATUS	ORIGINAL SRP	GREENBOOK TRU/MKT PRICE
	VARIATIONS/MISC/COLLECTOR NOTES						
DV93-1	THE PIED BULL INN	5751-7	Porcelain	NO	1993 ANNUAL	$100.00	$ 160.00
	2nd Edition Charles Dickens' Signature Series©. Special collector box and hang tag.						
DV93-2	PUMP LANE SHOPPES	5808-4	Porcelain	SET OF 3	CURRENT	112.00	112.00
DV93-3	BUMPSTEAD NYE CLOAKS & CANES	5808-4	Porcelain	1 of a 3 pc set	CURRENT	37.50	37.50
DV93-4	LOMAS LTD. MOLASSES	5808-4	Porcelain	1 of a 3 pc set	CURRENT	37.50	37.50
DV93-5	W.M. WHEAT CAKES & PUDDINGS	5808-4	Porcelain	1 of a 3 pc set	CURRENT	37.50	37.50
DV93-6	BOARDING & LODGING SCHOOL	5809-2	Porcelain	NO	1993 ANNUAL*	48.00	200.00
	*With Bottom Stamp of the Charles Dickens Heritage Foundation commemorating the 150 Year Anniversary of *A Christmas Carol*. Features #18 as address. Special box & hang tag. This piece is available in 1994, as Item # 5810-6, but does not have the commemorative stamp. Early release to Showcase Dealers and select buying groups.						
DV93-7	KINGFORD'S BREW HOUSE	5811-4	Porcelain	NO	CURRENT	45.00	45.00
DV93-8	GREAT DENTON MILL	5812-2	Porcelain	NO	CURRENT	50.00	50.00

THE HERITAGE VILLAGE COLLECTION – DICKENS' VILLAGE

DV94-1

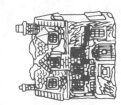

DEDLOCK ARMS

Stone wall courtyard has metal gate and 2 lanterns. 3 story Inn is brightly lit with Inn sign above front window and brass banner designating Inn as part of Signature Series.

DV94-2

DEDLOCK ARMS ORNAMENT

Miniature version of the 1994 annual piece. Packaged in a special keepsake box.

DV94-3

BOARDING & LODGING SCHOOL

Attended by a young Scrooge, this red brick building combines a fortress-like solidity and elegant appearance based on total symmetry of gables, coping, matching chimneys and rooftop balustrade cupola, and formal front entry with pediment and molding.

DV94-4

WHITTLESBOURNE CHURCH

Stone church with a single fortress-like tower rising off front left side. A masonry brace built against right side supports massive stone wall and provides a walkway. Double front doors outlined by stone arch.

DV94-5

GIGGELSWICK MUTTON & HAM

Butcher shop concentrates on meats from sheep and pigs. Smokehouse on side cures meat and adds special flavoring. Shop has corner wraparound windows. Family lives upstairs from shop.

ART CHART #	NAME	ITEM #	MATERIAL	SET?	🎁 MARKET STATUS	ORIGINAL SRP	GREENBOOK TRUMKT PRICE
			VARIATIONS/MISC/COLLECTOR NOTES				
DV94-1	DEDLOCK ARMS	5752-5	Porcelain	NO	✓ 1994 ANNUAL	$100.00	$ 100.00
	3rd Edition Charles Dickens' Signature Series©. Special collector box and hang tag.						
DV94-2	DEDLOCK ARMS ORNAMENT	9872-8	Porcelain	NO	✓ 1994 ANNUAL	12.50	12.50
	Miniature version of the 1994 Annual above, packaged in a special keepsake box.						
DV94-3	BOARDING & LODGING SCHOOL	5810-6	Porcelain	NO	✓ CURRENT	48.00	48.00
	Features #43 as address. See 1993, #5809-2.						
DV94-4	WHITTLESBOURNE CHURCH	5821-1	Porcelain	NO	✓ CURRENT	85.00	85.00
DV94-5	GIGGELSWICK MUTTON & HAM	5822-0	Porcelain	NO	✓ CURRENT	48.00	48.00
	Named after a town in North Yorkshire, England.						

THE HERITAGE VILLAGE COLLECTION – NEW ENGLAND VILLAGE

NE86-1

NEW ENGLAND VILLAGE:

APOTHECARY SHOP

GENERAL STORE

NATHANIEL BINGHAM FABRICS

LIVERY STABLE & BOOT SHOP

STEEPLE CHURCH

BRICK TOWN HALL

RED SCHOOLHOUSE

NE86-2

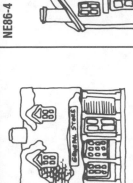

APOTHECARY SHOP
Varigated fieldstone with white wood bay window. Gable and lean-to are blue clapboard.

NE86-3

GENERAL STORE
Round columns support full length covered porch. Large multi-paned window allows one to see the goods for sale. Two small dormers on roof with central chimney.

NE86-4

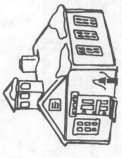

NATHANIEL BINGHAM FABRICS
Clapboard saltbox design fabric store and Post Office. Each shop has own chimney. Living quarters above larger fabric store.

NE86-5

LIVERY STABLE & BOOT SHOP
Two story painted clapboard house with wood planked wing contains tannery and livery stable. Stable has stone chimney, double doors.

NE86-6

STEEPLE CHURCH
White clapboard church w/tier 2 steeple. Windows have molding above and below. Simple design characteristic of area.

NE86-7

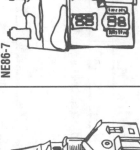

BRICK TOWN HALL
Mansard roof over two story Town Hall. Cupola is centered on roof ridge between two brick chimneys. Windows trimmed with ornamental molding.

NE86-8

RED SCHOOLHOUSE
Red wood school with stone chimney and open belfry. Hand powered water pump by front door.

ART CHART #	NAME	ITEM #	MATERIAL	SET?	‼	MARKET STATUS	ORIGINAL SRP	GREENBOOK TRUMKT PRICE
	VARIATIONS/MISC/COLLECTOR NOTES							
NE86-1	**NEW ENGLAND VILLAGE**	**6530-7**	**Porcelain**	**SET OF 7**	✓	**RETIRED 1989**	**$170.00**	**See Below***
	*Set of 7 can be purchased for approximately 15% less than the sum of the individual TRUMARKET Prices.							
NE86-2	APOTHECARY SHOP	6530-7	Porcelain	1 of a 7 pc set	✓	RETIRED 1989	25.00	92.00
NE86-3	GENERAL STORE	6530-7	Porcelain	1 of a 7 pc set	✓	RETIRED 1989	25.00	360.00
NE86-4	NATHANIEL BINGHAM FABRICS	6530-7	Porcelain	1 of a 7 pc set	✓	RETIRED 1989	25.00	150.00
NE86-5	LIVERY STABLE & BOOT SHOP	6530-7	Porcelain	1 of a 7 pc set	✓	RETIRED 1989	25.00	142.00
NE86-6	STEEPLE CHURCH	6530-7	Porcelain	1 of a 7 pc set	✓	RETIRED 1989	25.00	See Below*
	Re-issued in 1989 as #6539-0 (NE89-4) when #6530-7 retired along with the other pieces of the NEV set. *For TRUMARKET Prices, see footnote[1] pg 131.							
NE86-7	BRICK TOWN HALL	6530-7	Porcelain	1 of a 7 pc set	✓	RETIRED 1989	25.00	215.00
NE86-8	RED SCHOOLHOUSE	6530-7	Porcelain	1 of a 7 pc set	✓	RETIRED 1989	25.00	270.00

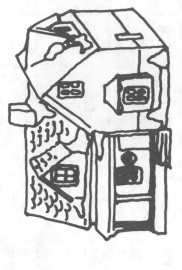

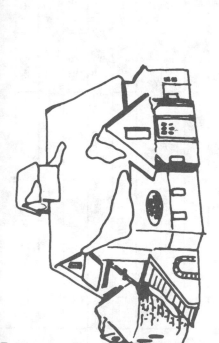

JACOB ADAMS FARMHOUSE AND BARN

Red multi-level wood barn atop a stone foundation.
Stone silo attached.

Home features front porch, small front bay window, butter churn by door, simple design.

ART CHART #	NAME	ITEM #	MATERIAL	SET?	🕯	MARKET STATUS	ORIGINAL SRP	GREENBOOK TRU/MKT PRICE
		VARIATIONS/MISC/COLLECTOR NOTES						
NE86-9	JACOB ADAMS FARMHOUSE AND BARN	6538-2	Porcelain	SET OF 5	✓	RETIRED 1989	$ 65.00	$ 575.00

[1] Steeple Church:
  a) 1st issue: part of NEV Original 7, #6530-7, tree attached with porcelain slip - $175.00.
  b) 2nd issue: #6530-7, tree attached with glue - $100.00.
  c) 3rd issue: Re-issue of church when Set of 7 retired, #6539-0, tree attached with glue - $85.00.
(For color photo, see Second Edition, pg. 229.)

THE HERITAGE VILLAGE COLLECTION – NEW ENGLAND VILLAGE

NE87-1

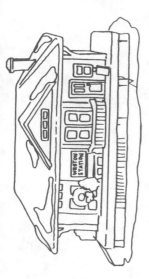

CRAGGY COVE LIGHTHOUSE

Keeper lives in small white clapboard home attached to lighthouse.
Front porch of home features holiday decorated columns.
Stone house foundation, whitewashed brick light tower.

NE87-2

WESTON TRAIN STATION

Luggage ramps lead to platform where you puchase tickets
and wait inside or on benches outside. Wheeled luggage cart stands on
side of building. White with blue trim and red roof.

NE87-3

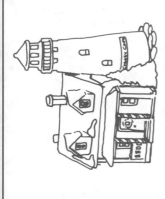

SMYTHE WOOLEN MILL

Fabric woven for manufacture into clothing, yard goods.
Hydro powered by water wheel. Stone base with wood upper stories.
Bales of wool stacked outside office door. Lower windows each with shutter.

NE87-4

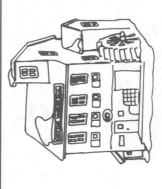

TIMBER KNOLL LOG CABIN

Two stone chimneys and fireplace provide heat and cooking facilities
for rustic log cabin, wood shakes comprise roof. One wing rises two stories.

ART CHART #	NAME	ITEM #	MATERIAL	SET?		MARKET STATUS	ORIGINAL SRP	GREENBOOK TRUMKT PRICE
	VARIATIONS/MISC/COLLECTOR NOTES							
NE87-1	CRAGGY COVE LIGHTHOUSE	5930-7	Porcelain	NO	✓	CURRENT	$ 35.00	$ 45.00
	Early issue has drain hole directly below light tower, later issue does not.							
NE87-2	WESTON TRAIN STATION	5931-5	Porcelain	NO	✓	RETIRED 1989	42.00	265.00
NE87-3	SMYTHE WOOLEN MILL	6543-9	Porcelain	NO	✓	LTD. ED. 7,500	42.00	1255.00
NE87-4	TIMBER KNOLL LOG CABIN	6544-7	Porcelain	NO	✓	RETIRED 1990	28.00	150.00

THE HERITAGE VILLAGE COLLECTION – NEW ENGLAND VILLAGE

NE88-4

OTIS HAYES BUTCHER SHOP

Dutch door entry, stone side walls, brick front with painted sign over front door on gable. Small size and thick walls plus river/lake ice helped keep meat fresh.

NE88-3

BEN'S BARBERSHOP

A barber pole hangs from front house corner next to a bench for customers. Blue half-window coverings provide some privacy. Water tower on roof supplies the shop's needs. Upstairs office used by a lawyer who has separate entry.

NE88-2

CHERRY LANE SHOPS:

BEN'S BARBERSHOP

OTIS HAYES BUTCHER SHOP

ANNE SHAW TOYS

NE88-6

ADA'S BED AND BOARDING HOUSE

Large family home becomes a bed and breakfast for travelers. Double chimneys. Central cupola and wrap-around front porch.

NE88-1

OLD NORTH CHURCH

Red brick church. First and second floor windows feature sunburst and/or spoke tops. Steeple rises from main entry. Belfry has tiered design.

NE88-5

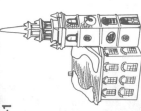

ANNE SHAW TOYS

Large front windows with window boxes allow a look at toys for sale. Chimney rises from center of roof. Molding beneath roof edge and squared shape give roof a turret look/feel. Rest of windows are shuttered.

ART CHART #	NAME	ITEM #	MATERIAL	SET?	● MARKET STATUS	ORIGINAL SRP	GREENBOOK TRUMKT PRICE
	VARIATIONS/MISC/COLLECTOR NOTES						
NE88-1	OLD NORTH CHURCH	5932-3	Porcelain	NO	✓ CURRENT	$ 40.00	$ 45.00
	Based on Historic Landmark re: American Revolution and Paul Revere.						
NE88-2	CHERRY LANE SHOPS	5939-0	Porcelain	SET OF 3	✓ RETIRED 1990	80.00	NE
NE88-3	BEN'S BARBERSHOP	5939-0	Porcelain	1 of a 3 pc set	✓ RETIRED 1990	27.00	85.00
NE88-4	OTIS HAYES BUTCHER SHOP	5939-0	Porcelain	1 of a 3 pc set	✓ RETIRED 1990	27.00	75.00
NE88-5	ANNE SHAW TOYS	5939-0	Porcelain	1 of a 3 pc set	✓ RETIRED 1990	27.00	150.00
NE88-6	ADA'S BED AND BOARDING HOUSE	5940-4	Porcelain	NO	✓ RETIRED 1991	36.00	See Below
	Color and mold variations affect TRUMARKET Price. See footnote[1] below. For color photo, see Second Edition, page 230.						

[1]Ada's Bed And Boarding House:
   a) 1st issue: lemon yellow color, rear steps are part of building's mold, alternating yellow panes are in 2nd floor windows - $300.00.
   b) 2nd issue: paler yellow, same mold - $195.00.
   c) 3rd issue: pale yellow, stairs are added on, 2nd floor windows have yellow panes in top half of window only - $125.00.

THE HERITAGE VILLAGE COLLECTION – NEW ENGLAND VILLAGE

NE89-1

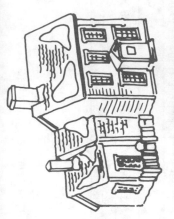

BERKSHIRE HOUSE
Blue dutch colonial inn, two front entries, half porch, five dormered windows on front, second story mansard roof.

NE89-2

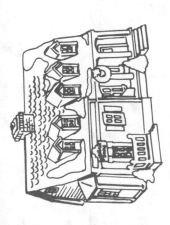

JANNES MULLET AMISH FARM HOUSE
White frame house, fenced yard on side, two chimneys, gutter and leader to barrel to collect rain water.

NE89-3

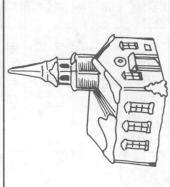

JANNES MULLET AMISH BARN
Wood and fieldstone with attached sheds and silo, Amish family black buggy stands at barn entrance.

NE89-4

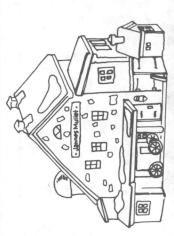

STEEPLE CHURCH
White clapboard church with steeple.
Windows have molding above and below. Simple design characteristic of area.

ART CHART #	NAME	ITEM #	MATERIAL	SET?	🐦	MARKET STATUS	ORIGINAL SRP	GREENBOOK TRUMKT PRICE
	VARIATIONS/MISC/COLLECTOR NOTES							
NE89-1	BERKSHIRE HOUSE	5942-0	Porcelain	NO	✓	RETIRED 1991	$ 40.00	See Below*
	*Variations in color affect TRUMARKET Price: "original blue" @ $150, "teal" @ $95. For color photo, see Second Edition, page 231.							
NE89-2	JANNES MULLET AMISH FARM HOUSE	5943-9	Porcelain	NO	✓	RETIRED 1992	32.00	100.00
NE89-3	JANNES MULLET AMISH BARN	5944-7	Porcelain	NO	✓	RETIRED 1992	48.00	98.00
NE89-4	STEEPLE CHURCH	6539-0	Porcelain	NO	✓	RETIRED 1990	30.00	85.00
	Re-issue of 1986 Steeple Church #6530-7 (NE86-6). See footnote on page 131. For color photo, see Second Edition, page 229.							

THE HERITAGE VILLAGE COLLECTION – NEW ENGLAND VILLAGE

NE90-1

SHINGLE CREEK HOUSE

Saltbox design with chimney rising from mid-roof. Windows have shutters and molding on top and base. Attached shed on one side, with storm cellar doors and fenced side entrance.

NE90-2

CAPTAIN'S COTTAGE

2 1/2 story has balcony full length of 2nd story. Enclosed staircase on house side to second floor. Columns that support balcony create porch for entry. A connected double dormer is centered on front roof between two ridge chimneys.

NE90-3

SLEEPY HOLLOW:

SLEEPY HOLLOW SCHOOL

VAN TASSEL MANOR

ICHABOD CRANE'S COTTAGE

NE90-4

SLEEPY HOLLOW SCHOOL

Framed stone chimney warms log cabin school. Brick and wood belfry houses bell. Wood pile and bench with bucket near front door.

NE90-5

VAN TASSEL MANOR

Yellow house with mansard roof with two front dormers. Wood corner posts support porch. Stone lean-to one side. Double chimneys rise off roof ridge. Four ears of corn decorate front entry.

NE90-6

ICHABOD CRANE'S COTTAGE

Stone first story topped by wood second story. Rough shingled roof with dip in the middle between two brick chimneys.

NE90-7

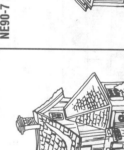

SLEEPY HOLLOW CHURCH

Wood church with steeple rising off front. Arched windows with prominent sills. Front steps lead to double doors with ornate hinges and molding.

ART CHART #	NAME	ITEM #	MATERIAL	SET?	♻	MARKET STATUS	ORIGINAL SRP	GREENBOOK TRU$MKT PRICE
	VARIATIONS/MISC/COLLECTOR NOTES							
NE90-1	SHINGLE CREEK HOUSE	5946-3	Porcelain	NO	✓	CURRENT	$ 37.50	$ 40.00
	Early release to Showcase Dealers and the National Association Of Limited Edition Dealers.							
NE90-2	CAPTAIN'S COTTAGE	5947-1	Porcelain	NO	✓	CURRENT	40.00	42.00
NE90-3	**SLEEPY HOLLOW**	**5954-4**	**Porcelain**	**SET OF 3**	✓	**RETIRED 1993**	**96.00**	**180.00**
NE90-4	*SLEEPY HOLLOW SCHOOL*	5954-4	Porcelain	1 of a 3 pc set	✓	RETIRED 1993	32.00	78.00
NE90-5	*VAN TASSEL MANOR*	5954-4	Porcelain	1 of a 3 pc set	✓	RETIRED 1993	32.00	65.00
NE90-6	*ICHABOD CRANE'S COTTAGE*	5954-4	Porcelain	1 of a 3 pc set	✓	RETIRED 1993	32.00	60.00
NE90-7	SLEEPY HOLLOW CHURCH	5955-2	Porcelain	NO	✓	RETIRED 1993	36.00	65.00

THE HERITAGE VILLAGE COLLECTION – NEW ENGLAND VILLAGE

NE91-1

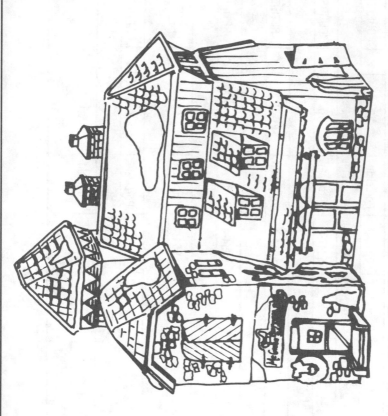

MCGREBE-CUTTERS & SLEIGHS

Builders of carriages, sleighs, and sleds to move people and goods in snowy New England. Stone and wood building. Large doors in front and side to allow movement of vehicles. Stone half has short tower atop roof. Large loft doors above entry.

141

ART CHART #	NAME	ITEM #	MATERIAL	SET?	♥	MARKET STATUS	ORIGINAL SRP	GREENBOOK TRUMKT PRICE
			VARIATIONS/MISC/COLLECTOR NOTES					
NE91-1	MCGREBE-CUTTERS & SLEIGHS	5640-5	Porcelain	NO	✓	CURRENT	$ 45.00	$ 48.00

NE92-1

BLUEBIRD SEED AND BULB

Covered storage area near entry door has open storage bins.
Small shuttered arched window adjacent to door.
Outside stairs lead to other storage areas.
Two stories with stone block lower level and fieldstone chimney.

NE92-2

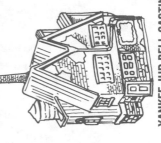

YANKEE JUD BELL CASTING

Red brick foundry with steeply pitched gable roof.
Projecting side doors on second and third story for lifting heavy, large castings.
Tall circular brick chimney rises off rear of foundry.

NE92-3

STONEY BROOK TOWN HALL

Rectangular brick building serves as meeting hall for town governance.
Side entry with a latch gate, cellar windows with shutters, roof dormers and
two chimneys, and many windows on long sides of building complete structure.

ART CHART #	NAME	ITEM #	MATERIAL	SET?	↕	MARKET STATUS	ORIGINAL SRP	GREENBOOK TRUMKT PRICE
			VARIATIONS/MISC/COLLECTOR NOTES					
NE92-1	BLUEBIRD SEED AND BULB	5642-1	Porcelain	NO	✓	CURRENT	$ 48.00	$ 48.00
NE92-2	YANKEE JUD BELL CASTING	5643-0	Porcelain	NO	✓	CURRENT	44.00	44.00
NE92-3	STONEY BROOK TOWN HALL	5644-8	Porcelain	NO	✓	CURRENT	42.00	42.00

NE93-1

BLUE STAR ICE CO.

Stone 1st story with insulated wood upper storage level. Wooden chute enabled ice blocks to be pulled up where sawdust or salt hay insulated each block.

NE93-2

A. BIELER FARM

PENNSYLVANIA DUTCH FARMHOUSE
PENNSYLVANIA DUTCH BARN

NE93-3

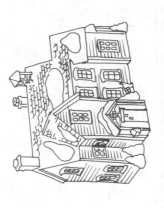

PENNSYLVANIA DUTCH FARMHOUSE

Two story clapboard home.
Many windowed to let in light, colorful trim on all windows, roof and wall moldings.

NE93-4

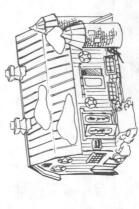

PENNSYLVANIA DUTCH BARN

Red barn with green mansard roof.
Two stone silos on one corner.
Double door entry reached by stone supported ramp.
Hex signs hung on barn outer walls.

ART CHART #	NAME	ITEM #	MATERIAL	SET?	♥	MARKET STATUS	ORIGINAL SRP	GREENBOOK TRUMKT PRICE
				VARIATIONS/MISC/COLLECTOR NOTES				
NE93-1	BLUE STAR ICE CO.	5647-2	Porcelain	NO	✓	CURRENT	$ 45.00	$ 45.00
NE93-2	A. BIELER FARM	5648-0	Porcelain	SET OF 2	✓	CURRENT	92.00	92.00
NE93-3	PENNSYLVANIA DUTCH FARMHOUSE	5648-0	Porcelain	1 of a 2 pc set	✓	CURRENT	42.00	42.00
NE93-4	PENNSYLVANIA DUTCH BARN	5648-0	Porcelain	1 of a 2 pc set	✓	CURRENT	50.00	50.00

146

NE94-1

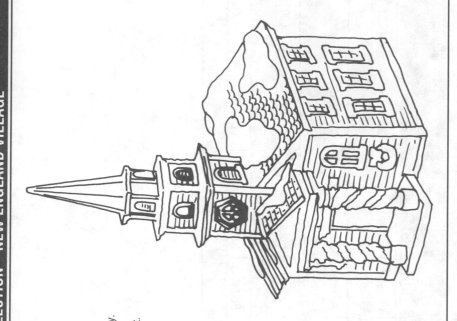

ARLINGTON FALLS CHURCH
Wood church with steeple rising in tiers above from entry.
Pillars at front doors are wrapped in garlands.
Double tiers of windows on side of church let in daylight.
Simple structure with a country look.

147

ART CHART #	NAME	ITEM #	MATERIAL	SET?	⚑	MARKET STATUS	ORIGINAL SRP	GREENBOOK TRUMKT PRICE
			VARIATIONS/MISC/COLLECTOR NOTES					
NE94-1	ARLINGTON FALLS CHURCH	5651-0	Porcelain	NO	✓	CURRENT	$ 40.00	$ 40.00

THE HERITAGE VILLAGE COLLECTION – ALPINE VILLAGE

ALP86-1

ALPINE VILLAGE:

BESSOR BIERKELLER

GASTHOF EISL

APOTHEKE

E. STAUBR BACKER

MILCH-KASE

ALP86-2

BESSOR BIERKELLER
(BEER CELLAR)
Window boxes on second story hung with colorful banners. Third story rustic timbered enclosed balcony has garland decoration.

ALP86-3

GASTHOF EISL
(GUEST HOUSE)
Rustic inn, fieldstone first floor with two stories of stucco topped by orange/red roof. A third story balcony is decorated with greenery and banners. Window boxes also decorate other rooms.

ALP86-4

APOTHEKE
(APOTHECARY)
Cream walls topped by blue roof. Banners flying from attic window. Prescriptions and drugstore supplies available from store on ground floor. Building shares with tobacconist.

ALP86-5

E. STAUBR BACKER
(BAKERY)
Three story building with bakery on ground level. Third story has some timbering design and an oriel window. Tiled roof and two chimneys.

ALP86-6

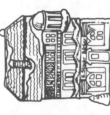

MILCH-KASE
(MILK & CHEESE SHOP)
Milk cans by door denotes shop that sells milk and cheese. Rough slate roof tops blue walls and wood planking exterior. Window box with greenery on second story side wall. Double wood doors allow wagons to bring supplies in/out.

149

ART CHART #	NAME	ITEM #	MATERIAL	SET?		MARKET STATUS	ORIGINAL SRP	GREENBOOK TRUMKT PRICE
	VARIATIONS/MISC/COLLECTOR NOTES							
ALP86-1	ALPINE VILLAGE	6540-4	Porcelain	SET OF 5	✓	CURRENT	$150.00	$185.00
	Early release to National Association Of Limited Edition Dealers, 1987.							
ALP86-2	BESSOR BIERKELLER (BEER CELLAR)	6540-4	Porcelain	1 of a 5 pc set	✓	CURRENT	25.00	37.00
ALP86-3	GASTHOF EISL (GUEST HOUSE)	6540-4	Porcelain	1 of a 5 pc set	✓	CURRENT	25.00	37.00
ALP86-4	APOTHEKE (APOTHECARY)	6540-4	Porcelain	1 of a 5 pc set	✓	CURRENT	25.00	37.00
ALP86-5	E. STAUBR BACKER (BAKERY)	6540-4	Porcelain	1 of a 5 pc set	✓	CURRENT	25.00	37.00
ALP86-6	MILCH-KASE (MILK & CHEESE SHOP)	6540-4	Porcelain	1 of a 5 pc set	✓	CURRENT	25.00	37.00

1987

ALP87-1

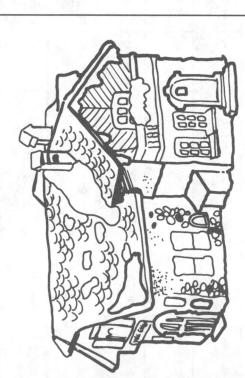

JOSEF ENGEL FARMHOUSE

House and barn are connected. Stucco over stone. Barn has hay loft
above animal and equipment area. Shutters swing overhead.
Home has balcony above front entry with herringbone planking.
Red roof, capped chimneys.

1987

ALP87-2

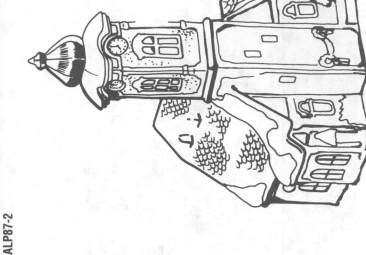

ALPINE CHURCH

Onion dome tops steeple which also features a clock on all sides of the tower.

ART CHART #	NAME	ITEM #	MATERIAL	SET?	🌓	MARKET STATUS	ORIGINAL SRP	GREENBOOK TRUMKT PRICE
VARIATIONS/MISC/COLLECTOR NOTES								
ALP87-1	JOSEF ENGEL FARMHOUSE	5952-8	Porcelain	NO	✓	RETIRED 1989	$ 33.00	$ 960.00
ALP87-2	ALPINE CHURCH	6541-2	Porcelain	NO	✓	RETIRED 1991	32.00	155.00
Variation: dark trim or white trim.								

THE HERITAGE VILLAGE COLLECTION – ALPINE VILLAGE

1988	1990	1991

ALP88-1

GRIST MILL

Irregular shingle roofing tops the mill that grinds corn and wheat into meal and flour.

ALP90-1

BAHNHOF
(TRAIN STATION)

Stucco upper wall atop tiled lower wall. Ticket window in base of tower rises through roof and repeats tile design. Clock featured.

ALP91-1

ST. NIKOLAUS KIRCHE

Bell tower rises above front entry, topped by onion dome. Set-in rounded arched windows accent nave sides. Pebble-dash finish on surface walls. The home of the Christmas hymn "Silent Night, Holy Night."

ART CHART #	NAME	ITEM #	MATERIAL	SET?	🕯	MARKET STATUS	ORIGINAL SRP	GREENBOOK TRU/MKT PRICE
	VARIATIONS/MISC/COLLECTOR NOTES							

1988

ART CHART #	NAME	ITEM #	MATERIAL	SET?	🕯	MARKET STATUS	ORIGINAL SRP	GREENBOOK TRU/MKT PRICE
ALP88-1	GRIST MILL	5953-6	Porcelain	NO	✓	CURRENT	$ 42.00	$ 45.00

1990

ART CHART #	NAME	ITEM #	MATERIAL	SET?	🕯	MARKET STATUS	ORIGINAL SRP	GREENBOOK TRU/MKT PRICE
ALP90-1	BAHNHOF (TRAIN STATION)	5615-4	Porcelain	NO	✓	RETIRED 1993	$ 42.00	$ 85.00
	Variation: some have gilded trim, others have dull gold trim.							

1991

ART CHART #	NAME	ITEM #	MATERIAL	SET?	🕯	MARKET STATUS	ORIGINAL SRP	GREENBOOK TRU/MKT PRICE
ALP91-1	ST. NIKOLAUS KIRCHE	5617-0	Porcelain	NO	✓	CURRENT	$ 37.50	$ 37.50
	Designed after Church Of St. Nikola in Oberndorf, Austria.							

THE HERITAGE VILLAGE COLLECTION – ALPINE VILLAGE

1992

ALP92-1

ALPINE SHOPS:

METTERNICHE WURST

KUKUCK UHREN

ALP92-2

KUKUCK UHREN
(CLOCK SHOP)
Franc Schiller displays his trademark clock on shop sign above recessed entry door. Small shop has cone shaped turret as design on peak of facade gable. Wood timbers outline the stone, brick and stucco exterior.

ALP92-3

METTERNICHE WURST
(SAUSAGE SHOP)
Stucco over stone and brick with steeply pitched roof coming down to first floor on sides. Front facade framed by ornamentally curved coping. Balcony runs width of second story. On side of shop several smoking areas denoted by chimneys.

1993

ALP93-1

SPORT LADEN
Shop for skiing and winter sports equipment. Chalet style open balconies on front 2nd and 3rd stories. Small shop tucked away on one side. Roof overhangs protect facade and chimneys are capped to keep out snow, ice and rain.

ART CHART #	NAME	ITEM #	MATERIAL	SET?	☝	MARKET STATUS	ORIGINAL SRP	GREENBOOK TRU/MKT PRICE
	VARIATIONS/MISC/COLLECTOR NOTES							

1992

ART CHART #	NAME	ITEM #	MATERIAL	SET?	☝	MARKET STATUS	ORIGINAL SRP	GREENBOOK TRU/MKT PRICE
ALP92-1	ALPINE SHOPS	5618-9	Porcelain	SET OF 2	✓	CURRENT	$ 75.00	$ 75.00
ALP92-2	METTERNICHE WURST (SAUSAGE SHOP)	5818-9	Porcelain	1 of a 2 pc set	✓	CURRENT	37.50	37.50
ALP92-3	KUKUCK UHREN (CLOCK SHOP)	5818-9	Porcelain	1 of a 2 pc set	✓	CURRENT	37.50	37.50

1993

ART CHART #	NAME	ITEM #	MATERIAL	SET?	☝	MARKET STATUS	ORIGINAL SRP	GREENBOOK TRU/MKT PRICE
ALP93-1	SPORT LADEN	5612-0	Porcelain	NO	✓	CURRENT	50.00	50.00

THE HERITAGE VILLAGE COLLECTION – CHRISTMAS IN THE CITY

CIC87-1

SUTTON PLACE BROWNSTONES
Three multi-storied homes - attached via shared common walls. Three shops occupy semi-below ground level space. Attic dormer windows have iron grillwork as safety feature. Second story attic windows have ornamental pediments and columns.

CIC87-2

THE CATHEDRAL
Twin spires, early Gothic design, and decorated windows set this Cathedral apart. Stone church incorporates a fortress-like solidness with soaring spires.

CIC87-3

PALACE THEATRE
Mask of Comedy & Tragedy are bas-reliefs on brick building featuring Christmas Show of Nutcracker. Stage entrance on side of building. Flanking double entry doors are display case for Theatre information.

CIC87-4

CHRISTMAS IN THE CITY:

TOY SHOP AND PET STORE

BAKERY

TOWER RESTAURANT

CIC87-5

TOY SHOP AND PET STORE
Width of building occupied by pet shop and toy shop. Ground floor is double high ceilings with half circle windows above store entries. Double chimneys. Tucked in at side is small shop, The Town Tailors.

CIC87-6

BAKERY
Four story building with Bakery on first two levels. Awning over entry and sign above second floor multi-paned windows. Iron grill work for safety and decor on smaller windows. Two different height chimneys.

CIC87-7

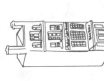

TOWER RESTAURANT
Multi-sided tower structure is integral part of residential building. Double door entry to restaurant/cafe. Iron grillwork for safety and decoration on upper tower windows.

ART CHART #	NAME	ITEM #	MATERIAL	SET?	🔔 MARKET STATUS	ORIGINAL SRP	GREENBOOK TRUMKT PRICE
		VARIATIONS/MISC/COLLECTOR NOTES					
CIC87-1	SUTTON PLACE BROWNSTONES	5961-7	Porcelain	NO	✓ RETIRED 1989	$ 80.00	$ 825.00
CIC87-2	THE CATHEDRAL	5962-5	Porcelain	NO	✓ RETIRED 1990	60.00	330.00
	Variations: 1st issue - smaller, darker, snow on sides of steps; 2nd issue - larger, lighter, no snow on steps.						
CIC87-3	PALACE THEATRE	5963-3	Porcelain	NO	✓ RETIRED 1989	45.00	925.00
	Variations: in size, paint trim and snow.						
CIC87-4	CHRISTMAS IN THE CITY	6512-9	Porcelain	SET OF 3	✓ RETIRED 1990	112.00	375.00
	Variations: all three buildings vary from dark to light colors.						
CIC87-5	TOY SHOP AND PET STORE	6512-9	Porcelain	1 of a 3 pc set	✓ RETIRED 1990	37.50	150.00
CIC87-6	BAKERY	6512-9	Porcelain	1 of a 3 pc set	✓ RETIRED 1990	37.50	95.00
CIC87-7	TOWER RESTAURANT	6512-9	Porcelain	1 of a 3 pc set	✓ RETIRED 1990	37.50	175.00

CIC88-1

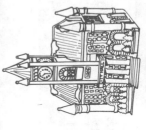

CHOCOLATE SHOPPE

Paneled roof between first and second story extends to shop signs. Building over Chocolate Shoppe rises three stories plus attic. Above Brown Brothers Bookstore is one short story plus attic. Stone facade has heart panels at base while bookstore has sign and canopy over window.

CIC88-2

CITY HALL

Imposing fortress with four towers at corners plus repeat design on clock tower. Broad steps plus large columns establish entry doors. Stone arches accent first floor windows plus tower window. Planters with evergreens on either side of steps.

CIC88-3

HANK'S MARKET

Grocery store as corner shop with boxes/barrels of produce on display. Rolled awnings over sign. Brick building with painted brick on upper sections of second story. Two upper windows are multi-paned with half-circle sunburst, other window has awning. Two chimneys on steeply pitched roof.

CIC88-4

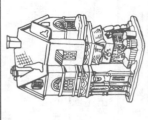

VARIETY STORE

Corner store in two story brick building. Garland decorated awnings extend out to shelter display windows and shoppers. Separate door for upper story. Second floor corner window projects out as rounded tower and support column underneath becomes part of entry. Next door shop is barbershop with striped pole outside. Small eyeglass shop completes trio.

ART CHART #	NAME	ITEM #	MATERIAL	SET?	❢	MARKET STATUS	ORIGINAL SRP	GREENBOOK TRUMKT PRICE
	VARIATIONS/MISC/COLLECTOR NOTES							
CIC88-1	CHOCOLATE SHOPPE	5968-4	Porcelain	NO	✓	RETIRED 1991	$ 40.00	$ 110.00
	Variations: varies from dark to light color.							
CIC88-2	CITY HALL	5969-2	Porcelain	NO	✓	RETIRED 1991	65.00	150.00
	Variation: smaller in size "Proof" version (none of the boxes had sleeves) @ $200.00. For color photo, see Second Edition, page 232.							
CIC88-3	HANK'S MARKET	5970-6	Porcelain	NO	✓	RETIRED 1992	40.00	78.00
CIC88-4	VARIETY STORE	5972-2	Porcelain	NO	✓	RETIRED 1990	45.00	135.00
	Same mold as the Drug Store from the Bachman's Hometown Series.							

THE HERITAGE VILLAGE COLLECTION – CHRISTMAS IN THE CITY

CIC89-1

RITZ HOTEL

Red doors complete columned entryway, red window canopy over each second story French window. Stone, block, and brick building. Cupola on attic window. Slate roof.

CIC89-2

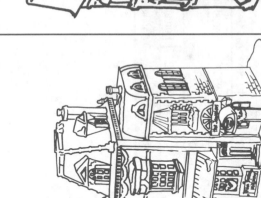

DOROTHY'S DRESS SHOP

Bright green door and awning, bay windows on first and second floor, mansard roof.

CIC89-3

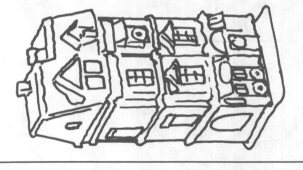

5607 PARK AVENUE TOWNHOUSE

Four stories with ground floor card and gift shop, curved corner turret, blue canopy over double French door entry.

CIC89-4

5609 PARK AVENUE TOWNHOUSE

Four stories with ground floor art gallery, double wood doors lead to apartments, blue canopy over entry.

ART CHART #	NAME	ITEM #	MATERIAL	SET?	🐤	MARKET STATUS	ORIGINAL SRP	GREENBOOK TRUMKT PRICE
	VARIATIONS/MISC/COLLECTOR NOTES							
CIC89-1	RITZ HOTEL	5973-0	Porcelain	NO	✓	CURRENT	$ 55.00	$ 55.00
CIC89-2	DOROTHY'S DRESS SHOP	5974-9	Porcelain	NO	✓	LTD. ED. 12,500	70.00	370.00
CIC89-3	5607 PARK AVENUE TOWNHOUSE	5977-3	Porcelain	NO	✓	RETIRED 1992	48.00	81.00
	Variation: earlier pieces have gilded trim at top of building, later production had dull gold colored paint.							
CIC89-4	5609 PARK AVENUE TOWNHOUSE	5978-1	Porcelain	NO	✓	RETIRED 1992	48.00	82.00
	Variation: earlier pieces have gilded trim at top of building, later production had dull gold colored paint.							

CIC90-2

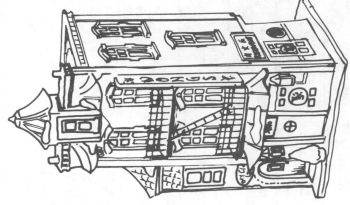

WONG'S IN CHINATOWN

Chinese restaurant and a laundry in brick building. Canopy over entry and at roof feature pagoda shape. Fire escape for second and third story tenants. Chinese characters highlight signs and entry.

CIC90-1

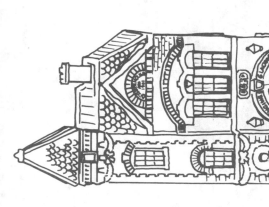

RED BRICK FIRE STATION

Brick Station House for Hook & Ladder Company. Large wood doors lead to equipment with separate door for upper level. Stone block detailing on turret and above upper floor windows. Formal pediment at front gable.

ART CHART #	NAME	ITEM #	MATERIAL	SET?	💰	MARKET STATUS	ORIGINAL SRP	GREENBOOK TRUMKT PRICE
			VARIATIONS/MISC/COLLECTOR NOTES					
CIC90-1	RED BRICK FIRE STATION	5536-0	Porcelain	NO	✓	CURRENT	$ 55.00	$ 55.00
CIC90-2	WONG'S IN CHINATOWN	5537-9	Porcelain	NO	✓	CURRENT	55.00	55.00

CIC91-1

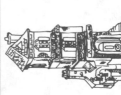

HOLLYDALE'S DEPARTMENT STORE

Corner curved front with awnings on windows, domed cupola, skylights on roof, and carved balustrade design on second story windows highlight store.

CIC91-2

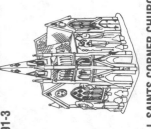

"LITTLE ITALY" RISTORANTE

Three story tall, narrow, stucco finish upper level above brick street level entry. Outdoor cafe serving pizza is behind side swinging doors. Balcony surrounds second and third story.

CIC91-3

ALL SAINTS CORNER CHURCH

Gothic style. Carved support ribs, denote Saints, arched windows, tall steeple with each corner capped by small steeples. Larger windows exhibit tracery design.

CIC91-4

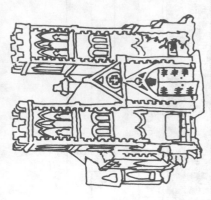

ARTS ACADEMY

Two story brick building has classrooms and practice halls. Corner columns and roof molding frame the front facade. Curved canopy over entrance repeats design of arched triple window with fan light, roof skylight & small tower window.

CIC91-5

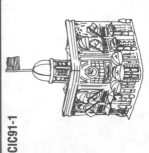

THE DOCTOR'S OFFICE

Four story brick building for Doctor, Dentist, and office space. Bow window is first level Doctor. Dentist windows have broad awning. Third floor window has balustrade design and pediment above, bricked archway entry to side of building.

CIC91-6

CATHEDRAL CHURCH OF ST. MARK'S

Front has look of fortification with two towers rising next to entry. Moldings are richly carved above double doors. Stone and brick with accented stone work framing walls and towers. Triple windows on each upper tower side.

ART CHART #	NAME	ITEM #	MATERIAL	SET?	✎ MARKET STATUS	ORIGINAL SRP	GREENBOOK TRU/MKT PRICE
	VARIATIONS/MISC/COLLECTOR NOTES						
CIC91-1	HOLLYDALE'S DEPARTMENT STORE	5534-4	Porcelain	NO	✓	CURRENT	$ 85.00
	Variation: holly on canopies - 3 main entrance only vs. 2nd floor canopies as well.					$ 75.00	
CIC91-2	"LITTLE ITALY" RISTORANTE	5538-7	Porcelain	NO	✓	CURRENT	52.00
						50.00	
CIC91-3	ALL SAINTS CORNER CHURCH	5542-5	Porcelain	NO	✓	CURRENT	105.00
						96.00	
CIC91-4	ARTS ACADEMY	5543-3	Porcelain	NO	✓	RETIRED 1993	80.00
						45.00	
CIC91-5	THE DOCTOR'S OFFICE	5544-1	Porcelain	NO	✓	CURRENT	60.00
						60.00	
CIC91-6	CATHEDRAL CHURCH OF ST. MARK'S	5549-2	Porcelain	NO	✓	LTD. ED. 17,500*	2850.00
	Early release to Gift Creations Concepts, Fall 1992. *Closed at an announced 3,024 pieces due to production problems.					120.00*	

1992

1992

CIC92-4

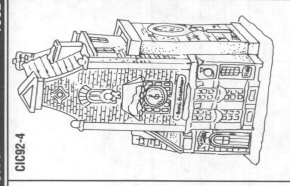

MUSIC EMPORIUM

Andrew Alberts music store highlights a musical score on one side wall with a store sign superimposed and decorated for the holidays. Signs on the facade advertise a specialty in violins, flutes, with a horn design above one entry door. Tallest of the three shops, building rises to three floors plus attic dormer. Street level windows tall and narrow topped by sign. Predominantly brick.

CIC92-3

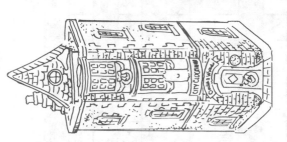

CITY CLOCKWORKS

Triangular shaped building with front angle blunted by semi-circular two story window treatment above entry to shop. Large clock hangs at right angles to store between sign and windows. Second clock next to entrance.

CIC92-2

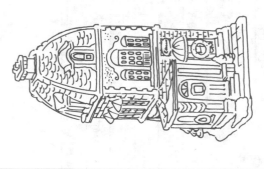

HABERDASHERY

Squared corner addition to three story building is entry for men's clothier. First floor front window topped by striped canopy and sign with store's name. Second floor triple windows topped by ornamental molding design and second floor side windows have triangular canopies. Brick, stone, and a roughcast pepple-dash facade construction.

CIC92-1

UPTOWN SHOPPES:

HABERDASHERY
CITY CLOCKWORKS
MUSIC EMPORIUM

ART CHART #	NAME	ITEM #	MATERIAL	SET?	⚫	MARKET STATUS	ORIGINAL SRP	GREENBOOK TRU/MKT PRICE
			VARIATIONS/MISC/COLLECTOR NOTES					
CIC92-1	UPTOWN SHOPPES	5531-0	Porcelain	SET OF 3	✓	CURRENT	$150.00	$150.00
CIC92-2	HABERDASHERY	5531-0	Porcelain	1 of a 3 pc set	✓	CURRENT	40.00	40.00
CIC92-3	CITY CLOCKWORKS	5531-0	Porcelain	1 of a 3 pc set	✓	CURRENT	56.00	56.00
CIC92-4	MUSIC EMPORIUM	5531-0	Porcelain	1 of a 3 pc set	✓	CURRENT	54.00	54.00

THE HERITAGE VILLAGE COLLECTION – CHRISTMAS IN THE CITY

1993 & 1994

CIC93-1

1993

WEST VILLAGE SHOPS:

POTTER'S TEA SELLER

SPRING ST. COFFEE HOUSE

CIC93-2

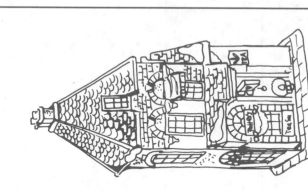

POTTER'S TEA SELLER

Stone 3 story shop sells tea or serves tea by the cup. Stone arches decorate windows. Green awning covers upper window above entry. Sign hangs in front of door to alert shoppers.

CIC93-3

SPRING ST. COFFEE HOUSE

Four story narrow building. Steps to main level lead to entry door covered by small pillared portico. Coffee ground to order & blended for taste plus an area for having a cup. Brick lower level topped by stucco upper story. Sign hangs from 3rd story to advertise shop.

1993 & 1994

CIC94-1

1994

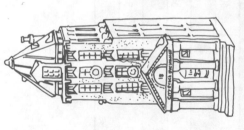

BROKERAGE HOUSE

Three story stone building gives impression of invincibility. Four pillars support large entry pediment which has name of Exchange carved into stone. Feeling of wealth is reinforced by gold embellishments.

ART CHART #	NAME	ITEM #	MATERIAL	SET?	⚫	MARKET STATUS	ORIGINAL SRP	GREENBOOK TRUMKT PRICE
	VARIATIONS/MISC/COLLECTOR NOTES							

1993

CIC93-1	WEST VILLAGE SHOPS	5880-7	Porcelain	SET OF 2	✓	CURRENT	$ 90.00	$ 90.00
CIC93-2	POTTER'S TEA SELLER	5880-7	Porcelain	1 of a 2 pc set	✓	CURRENT	45.00	45.00
CIC93-3	SPRING ST. COFFEE HOUSE	5880-7	Porcelain	1 of a 2 pc set	✓	CURRENT	45.00	45.00

1994

CIC94-1	BROKERAGE HOUSE	5881-5	Porcelain	NO	✓	CURRENT	48.00	48.00
	"18" is symbolic of initial D56 stock offering at $18.00.							

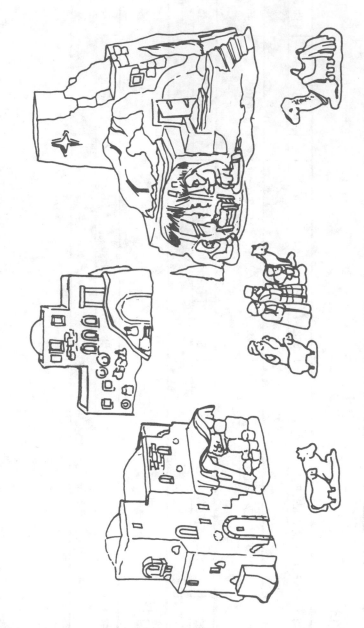

LITTLE TOWN OF BETHLEHEM

Replica of Holy Family Manger Scene with Three Wise Men and Shepherd.
Stone and sun-dried brick homes and shelters add Mid-East simplicity. Animals attentive to Holy Family.

ART CHART #	NAME	ITEM #	MATERIAL	SET?	⬤	MARKET STATUS	ORIGINAL SRP	GREENBOOK TRUMKT PRICE
			VARIATIONS/MISC/COLLECTOR NOTES					
LTB87-1	LITTLE TOWN OF BETHLEHEM	5975-7	Porcelain	SET OF 12	✓	CURRENT	$150.00	$150.00

THE HERITAGE VILLAGE COLLECTION – NORTH POLE

NP90-1

SANTA'S WORKSHOP

Multi-chimnied, many gabled home and workshop. Stone foundation with stucco and timber upper stories. Balconies extend off windows and hold garlands. Mailbox by front door.

NP90-2

NORTH POLE:

REINDEER BARN

ELF BUNKHOUSE

NP90-3

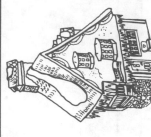

REINDEER BARN

Stone and stucco has stalls for all reindeer. Steeply pitched roof has cupola on ridge and step design on front of dormers. Roof vents and dutch stall doors provide ventilation.

NP90-4

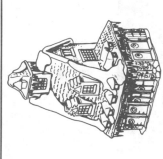

ELF BUNKHOUSE

Home for Santa's helpers, three stories with steeply pitched roof and protected chimney. Made of wood, stone, and stucco featuring bay windows, dormers, and a balcony.

ART CHART #	NAME	ITEM #	MATERIAL	SET?	↻	MARKET STATUS	ORIGINAL SRP	GREENBOOK TRUMKT PRICE
				VARIATIONS/MISC/COLLECTOR NOTES				
NP90-1	SANTA'S WORKSHOP	5600-6	Porcelain	NO	✓	RETIRED 1993	$ 72.00	$ 150.00
NP90-2	NORTH POLE	5601-4	Porcelain	SET OF 2	✓	CURRENT	70.00	80.00
NP90-3	REINDEER BARN	5601-4	Porcelain	1 of a 2 pc set	✓	CURRENT	35.00	40.00
	Common variation: a name duplicated, another omitted on reindeer stalls. For color photo, see Second Edition, page 232.							
NP90-4	ELF BUNKHOUSE	5601-4	Porcelain	1 of a 2 pc set	✓	CURRENT	35.00	40.00

NP91-4

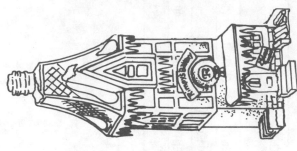

RIMPY'S BAKERY

Three storied, half wood timbered narrow building. Hipped - roof with gable on facade. Large eight paned front window with wood crib in front and on side.

NP91-3

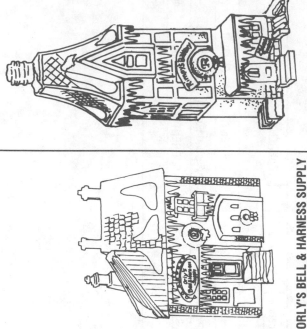

ORLY'S BELL & HARNESS SUPPLY

Stone steps lead to bell shop doorway with brick work design to frame it. Sleigh strap with bells above sign. Harness area has large wood doors that open to allow horse drawn carriage or wagon to enter. Window with balcony above, on 2nd story.

NP91-2

NORTH POLE SHOPS:

ORLY'S BELL & HARNESS SUPPLY

RIMPY'S BAKERY

NP91-1

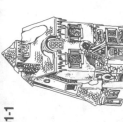

NEENEE'S DOLLS AND TOYS

Rough finish stucco and stone houses dolls, toys, and games.
Steeply pitched rear roof, red shuttered lattice-paned front second story windows, monogram within wreaths.

NP91-5

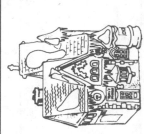

TASSY'S MITTENS & HASSEL'S WOOLIES

Two shops in connected buildings. Hassel's has corner turret window and oriel turret upper window. Tassy's has angled front window at ground and three arched windows on overhang second story. Gable has carved bough and berry design - roof angles steeply pitched.

175

ART CHART #	NAME	ITEM #	MATERIAL	SET?	🔔 MARKET STATUS	ORIGINAL SRP	GREENBOOK TRUMKT PRICE
	VARIATIONS/MISC/COLLECTOR NOTES						
NP91-1	NEENEE'S DOLLS AND TOYS	5620-0	Porcelain	NO	✓ CURRENT	$ 36.00	$ 37.50
	Early release to Showcase Dealers and Gift Creations Concepts.						
NP91-2	NORTH POLE SHOPS	5621-9	Porcelain	SET OF 2	✓ CURRENT	75.00	75.00
NP91-3	ORLY'S BELL & HARNESS SUPPLY	5621-9	Porcelain	1 of a 2 pc set	✓ CURRENT	37.50	37.50
NP91-4	RIMPY'S BAKERY	5621-9	Porcelain	1 of a 2 pc set	✓ CURRENT	37.50	37.50
NP91-5	TASSY'S MITTENS & HASSEL'S WOOLIES	5622-7	Porcelain	NO	✓ CURRENT	50.00	50.00

THE HERITAGE VILLAGE COLLECTION – NORTH POLE

NP92-3

ELFIE'S SLEDS & SKATES

Distinctive roof design with chimneys that are only visible outside from the second story. Roof hood projects out from walls to protect windows on house sides as well as sweeping down to help form large front window. Wreath with letter "E" in addition to shop signs.

NP92-2

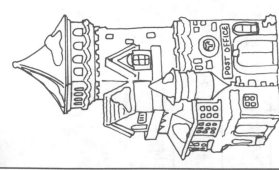

OBBIE'S BOOKS & LETRINKA'S CANDY

The tall narrow books and toys shop contrasts sharply with the shorter, wider, candy shop. Both shops have steep pitched roofs. A bay window on Obbie's side wall plus a number of dormer windows reinforce the angular look of the shop. Onion dome shaped chimney and cupola on roof ridge are unique to Letrinka's which also has a vertical timbered ground level design. Both shops have lettered wreaths by front entries.

NP92-1

POST OFFICE

Basis for building is turret with what appears to be a half-house on one side of main tower. Second floor features multi-paned windows, small curved turret between second and third floor could hold staircase and take up little wall space. Third floor has low balcony outside windows.

ART CHART #	NAME	ITEM #	MATERIAL	SET?	☝ MARKET STATUS	ORIGINAL SRP	GREENBOOK TRUMKT PRICE
		VARIATIONS/MISC/COLLECTOR NOTES					
NP92-1	POST OFFICE	5623-5	Porcelain	NO	✓ CURRENT	$ 45.00	$ 50.00
	Early release to Showcase Dealers.						
NP92-2	OBBIE'S BOOKS & LETRINKA'S CANDY	5624-3	Porcelain	NO	✓ CURRENT	70.00	70.00
NP92-3	ELFIE'S SLEDS & SKATES	5625-1	Porcelain	NO	✓ CURRENT	48.00	48.00

THE HERITAGE VILLAGE COLLECTION – NORTH POLE

NP93-1

NORTH POLE CHAPEL

Spire, containing brass bell rises at rear of Chapel. Fieldstone topped by timbered upper story. Double door front entry flanked by evergreens. Side chimney rises through roof with flue pipe capped by onion cap. Large wreath circled clock above entry.

NP93-2

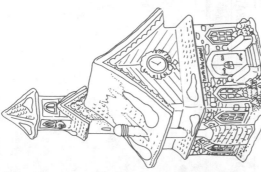

NORTH POLE EXPRESS DEPOT

Receiving area for all people and deliveries into and out of North Pole not going by Santa's sled. Roof line at lowest point is pagoda-like with an A-frame gable transversing a ridge. Stone chimney rises from rear of roof. Passenger door as well as freight doors.

NP93-3

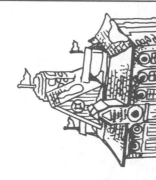

SANTA'S WOODWORKS

Lower level contains heavy equipment for sawing, debarking and trimming wood. Main woodworks level reached by wood stairs at side of open porch. Structure is a log house.

NP93-4

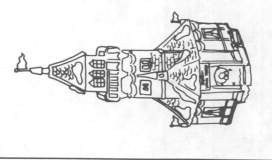

SANTA'S LOOKOUT TOWER

Pennants fly above door and top of tower which rises above trees to give Santa a clear picture of flight conditions. Balcony around highest story lets Santa check wind velocity.

ART CHART #	NAME	ITEM #	MATERIAL	SET?	🔔	MARKET STATUS	ORIGINAL SRP	GREENBOOK TRUMKT PRICE
	VARIATIONS/MISC/COLLECTOR NOTES							
NP93-1	NORTH POLE CHAPEL	5626-0	Porcelain	NO	✓	CURRENT	$ 45.00	$ 45.00
	Early release to Showcase Dealers and select buying groups.							
NP93-2	NORTH POLE EXPRESS DEPOT	5627-8	Porcelain	NO	✓	CURRENT	48.00	48.00
NP93-3	SANTA'S WOODWORKS	5628-6	Porcelain	NO	✓	CURRENT	42.00	42.00
NP93-4	SANTA'S LOOKOUT TOWER	5629-4	Porcelain	NO	✓	CURRENT	45.00	45.00

ACCESSORIES . . .   THE HERITAGE VILLAGE COLLECTION   ACCESSORIES . . .

HVA84-1

CAROLERS
Group of village people sing
or listen to carols.

HVA85-2

VILLAGE TRAIN
Three car porcelain train.

HVA86-3

CHRISTMAS CAROL FIGURES
Ebenezer Scrooge, Bob Cratchit carrying
Tiny Tim, boy with poulterer/goose.

HVA86-4

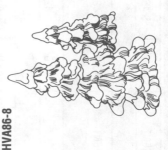

**LIGHTED TREE W/
CHILDREN AND LADDER**
Children climb ladder to decorate tree.

HVA86-5

SLEIGHRIDE
Two horses draw old fashioned
sleigh with a couple to enjoy ride.

HVA86-6

COVERED WOODEN BRIDGE
Simple wooden bridge with shingle
roof to protect travelers from weather.

HVA86-7

NEW ENGLAND WINTER SET
Stone well, man pushes woman
in swan sleigh, snow covered trees,
man pulling tree.

HVA86-8

PORCELAIN TREES
Two different size
snow covered evergreens.

ART CHART #	NAME	ITEM #	MATERIAL	SET?	🔔 MARKET STATUS	ORIGINAL SRP	GREENBOOK TRUMKT PRICE
	VARIATIONS/MISC/COLLECTOR NOTES						
HVA84-1	CAROLERS (1984) (DV)	6526-9	Porcelain	SET OF 3	RETIRED 1990	$ 10.00	$ 36.00
	There are three versions (sculpting/painting) of this set. Original "white post" @ $120.00. See footnote[1], page 211.						
HVA85-2	VILLAGE TRAIN (1985) (DV)	6527-7	Porcelain	SET OF 3	RETIRED 1986	12.00	455.00
	a/k/a "Brighton Village Train."						
HVA86-3	CHRISTMAS CAROL FIGURES (1986) (DV)	6501-3	Porcelain	SET OF 3	RETIRED 1990	12.50	65.00
HVA86-4	LIGHTED TREE W/CHILDREN AND LADDER (1986) (CIC)	6510-2	Porcelain	NO	✓ RETIRED 1989	35.00	350.00
	Original sleeve reads, "Christmas In The City."						
HVA86-5	SLEIGHRIDE (1986) (DV, NE)	6511-0	Porcelain	NO	RETIRED 1990	19.50	58.00
	See footnote[2], page 211.						
HVA86-6	COVERED WOODEN BRIDGE (1986) (NE)	6531-5	Porcelain	NO	RETIRED 1990	10.00	32.00
	See footnote[3], page 211.						
HVA86-7	NEW ENGLAND WINTER SET (1986) (NE)	6532-3	Porcelain	SET OF 5	RETIRED 1990	18.00	46.00
HVA86-8	PORCELAIN TREES (1986) (HV)	6537-4	Porcelain	SET OF 2	RETIRED 1992	14.00	36.00

HVA86-9

ALPINE VILLAGERS
Seated man, walking woman carrying book, dog pulling wagon with milk cans.

HVA87-10

FARM PEOPLE & ANIMALS
Man hauling logs. Woman and girl feeding geese. Goat pulls wagon and deer eat winter hay.

HVA87-11

BLACKSMITH
One man tends fire while smithy shoes horse and boy holds pail of nails.

HVA87-12

SILO & HAY SHED
Stone and stucco grain storage silo and elevated wood hay building.

HVA87-13

OX SLED
Heavy wood wagon on sled runners pulled by team of oxen. Driver plus small boy holding Christmas tree.

HVA87-14

CHRISTMAS IN THE CITY SIGN
Vertical emphasis on sign for Christmas In The City Collection.

HVA87-15

AUTOMOBILES
City delivery truck, checkered taxi, and roadster.

HVA87-16

CITY PEOPLE
Police officer, man walking dog, pretzel man with pushcart, mother and daughter with shopping bag, and woman collecting for the needy.

ART CHART #	NAME	ITEM #	MATERIAL	SET?	🔔 MARKET STATUS	ORIGINAL SRP	GREENBOOK TRUMKT PRICE
	VARIATIONS/MISC/COLLECTOR NOTES						
HVA86-9	ALPINE VILLAGERS (1986) (ALP)	6542-0	Porcelain	SET OF 3	RETIRED 1992	$ 13.00	$ 36.00
	Man and woman are thinner in later years of production.						
HVA87-10	FARM PEOPLE & ANIMALS (1987) (DV)	5901-3	Porcelain	SET OF 5	RETIRED 1989	24.00	80.00
HVA87-11	BLACKSMITH (1987) (DV)	5934-0	Porcelain	SET OF 3	RETIRED 1990	20.00	55.00
HVA87-12	SILO & HAY SHED (1987) (DV)	5950-1	Porcelain	SET OF 2	RETIRED 1989	18.00	140.00
	1st issue: the roof of silo has stripes of rust, gold and brown; 2nd issue: silo has close to solid brown roof.						
HVA87-13	OX SLED (1987) (DV)	5951-0	Porcelain	NO	RETIRED 1989	20.00	135.00
	Variation: tan pants and dark green seat cushion @ $225 (vs. blue pants on black seat cushion.)						
HVA87-14	CHRISTMAS IN THE CITY SIGN (1987)	5960-9	Porcelain	NO	RETIRED 1993	6.00	12.00
HVA87-15	AUTOMOBILES (1987) (CIC)	5964-1	Porcelain	SET OF 3	CURRENT	15.00	22.00
HVA87-16	CITY PEOPLE (1987) (CIC)	5965-0	Porcelain	SET OF 5	RETIRED 1990	27.50	50.00

HVA87-20

STONE BRIDGE
Varigated fieldstone arches over river.
Corner post has lamp.

HVA87-24

ALPINE VILLAGE SIGN

HVA87-19

SKATING POND
Low stone wall circles pond.
One child watches other child skating.
Two snow covered trees.

HVA87-23

NEW ENGLAND VILLAGE SIGN

HVA87-18

CITY WORKERS
Police constable, nurse, driver,
tradesman with packages.

HVA87-22

DICKENS' VILLAGE SIGN

HVA87-17

SHOPKEEPERS
Vendors of fruits, vegetables,
breads, cakes.

HVA87-21

VILLAGE WELL & HOLY CROSS
Old fashioned hand pump for water
housed in small gazebo...&...
Cross upon pedestal on stone step base.

185

ART CHART #	NAME	ITEM #	MATERIAL	SET?	MARKET STATUS	ORIGINAL SRP	GREENBOOK TRU/MKT PRICE
	VARIATIONS/MISC/COLLECTOR NOTES						
HVA87-17	SHOPKEEPERS (1987) (DV)	5966-8	Porcelain	SET OF 4	RETIRED 1988	$ 15.00	$ 35.00
	Along with the City Workers, the only figures to have "snow" sprinkled on them.						
HVA87-18	CITY WORKERS (1987) (DV)	5967-6	Porcelain	SET OF 4	RETIRED 1988	15.00	38.00
	Along with the Shopkeepers, the only figures to have "snow" sprinkled on them. Box reads "City People."						
HVA87-19	SKATING POND (1987) (DV, NE, CIC)	6545-5	Porcelain	NO	RETIRED 1990	24.00	75.00
	1st issue - made in Taiwan, ice is generally very light blue streaks; 2nd issue - made in Philippines, blue covers most of ice surface.						
HVA87-20	STONE BRIDGE (1987) (HV)	6546-3	Porcelain	NO	RETIRED 1990	12.00	80.00
	Variation in color from light to dark.						
HVA87-21	VILLAGE WELL & HOLY CROSS (1987) (DV)	6547-1	Porcelain	SET OF 2	RETIRED 1989	13.00	130.00
	1st issue - water is blue, birds are dark; 2nd issue - water has no color, birds are light.						
HVA87-22	DICKENS' VILLAGE SIGN (1987)	6569-2	Porcelain	NO	RETIRED 1993	6.00	18.00
HVA87-23	NEW ENGLAND VILLAGE SIGN (1987)	6570-6	Porcelain	NO	RETIRED 1993	6.00	14.00
HVA87-24	ALPINE VILLAGE SIGN (1987)	6571-4	Porcelain	NO	RETIRED 1993	6.00	28.00

HVA87-25

MAPLE SUGARING SHED
Two tapped trees, sled with bucket of syrup, & open walled shed w/cooking vat.

HVA88-29

NICHOLAS NICKLEBY CHARACTERS
Nicholas and sister Kate, Wackford Squeers with schoolbook, three children playing, and four-wheeled wagon.

HVA87-26

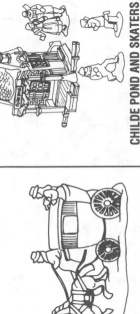

DOVER COACH
Passenger coach with one horse, driver, and coachman.

HVA88-30

SNOW CHILDREN
Girl finishes snowman while dog watches. Two boys push off on sled, another bellyflops on his sled.

HVA88-27

CHILDE POND AND SKATERS
Warming house, shutters latch against wind, wooden benches for skaters, brick building with birdhouse above door.

HVA88-31

VILLAGE HARVEST PEOPLE
Woman with butter churn, man loads pumpkins on cart, corn shocks, and pumpkins.

HVA88-28

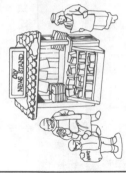

FEZZIWIG AND FRIENDS
Husband and wife bringing food to elderly neighbors.

HVA88-32

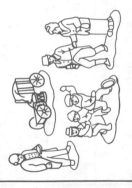

CITY NEWSSTAND
News vendor, magazine and newspaper wooden stand, woman reading paper, newsboy showing headlines.

ART CHART #	NAME		ITEM #	MATERIAL	SET?	💡	MARKET STATUS	ORIGINAL SRP	GREENBOOK TRUMKT PRICE
				VARIATIONS/MISC/COLLECTOR NOTES					
HVA87-25	MAPLE SUGARING SHED (1987)	(NE)	6589-7	Porcelain	SET OF 3		RETIRED 1989	$ 19.00	$ 210.00
HVA87-26	DOVER COACH (1987)	(DV)	6590-0	Porcelain	NO		RETIRED 1990	18.00	See Below*
	*Variations affect TRUMARKET Price, see footnote[4], page 211.								
HVA88-27	CHILDE POND AND SKATERS (1988)	(DV)	5903-0	Porcelain	SET OF 4		RETIRED 1991	30.00	85.00
HVA88-28	FEZZIWIG AND FRIENDS (1988)	(DV)	5928-5	Porcelain	SET OF 3		RETIRED 1990	12.50	48.00
	Addition to "Christmas Carol" grouping.								
HVA88-29	NICHOLAS NICKLEBY CHARACTERS (1988)	(DV)	5929-3	Porcelain	SET OF 4		RETIRED 1991	20.00	35.00
	Misspelled as Nicholas Nick'el"by on sleeve.								
HVA88-30	SNOW CHILDREN (1988)	(HV)	5938-2	Porcelain	SET OF 3		CURRENT	15.00	17.00
HVA88-31	VILLAGE HARVEST PEOPLE (1988)	(NE)	5941-2	Porcelain	SET OF 4		RETIRED 1991	27.50	45.00
	Sleeve reads "Harvest Time."								
HVA88-32	CITY NEWSSTAND (1988)	(CIC)	5971-4	Porcelain	SET OF 4		RETIRED 1991	25.00	42.00

. . . ACCESSORIES . . . THE HERITAGE VILLAGE COLLECTION . . . ACCESSORIES . . .

HVA88-33

VILLAGE TRAIN TRESTLE
Double arch trestle spans river.
One track on stone train bridge.

HVA88-34

ONE HORSE OPEN SLEIGH
Couple out for a ride in sleigh with canopy.
Lap robes protect against cold.

HVA88-35

CITY BUS & MILK TRUCK
Open back milk truck carries large
milk cans. Old fashioned city bus.

HVA88-36

SALVATION ARMY BAND
Five instrumentalists and conductor
in uniform of charitable organization.

HVA88-37

WOODCUTTER AND SON
Father splits logs and
son carries cordwood.

HVA88-38

RED COVERED BRIDGE
Wooden bridge spans Maple Creek
supported by stone bases.

HVA89-39

DAVID COPPERFIELD CHARACTERS
David Copperfield, Agnes, Mr. Wickfield,
Peggotty with young David and Emily,
Betsy Trotwood with Mr. Dick.

HVA89-40

VILLAGE SIGN WITH SNOWMAN
Snowman with top hat and scarf next to
brick pillars and Heritage Village Sign.

ART CHART #	NAME	ITEM #	MATERIAL	SET?	☎	MARKET STATUS	ORIGINAL SRP	GREENBOOK TRU MKT PRICE
	VARIATIONS/MISC/COLLECTOR NOTES							
HVA88-33	VILLAGE TRAIN TRESTLE (1988) (HV)	5981-1	Porcelain	NO		RETIRED 1990	$ 17.00	$ 60.00
	Sleeve reads "Stone Train Trestle."							
HVA88-34	ONE HORSE OPEN SLEIGH (1988) (HV)	5982-0	Porcelain	NO		RETIRED 1993	20.00	30.00
HVA88-35	CITY BUS & MILK TRUCK (1988) (CIC)	5983-8	Porcelain	SET OF 2		RETIRED 1991	15.00	36.00
	Box reads "Transport."							
HVA88-36	SALVATION ARMY BAND (1988) (CIC)	5985-4	Porcelain	SET OF 6		RETIRED 1991	24.00	50.00
HVA88-37	WOODCUTTER AND SON (1988) (NE)	5986-2	Porcelain	SET OF 2		RETIRED 1990	10.00	35.00
HVA88-38	RED COVERED BRIDGE (1988) (NE)	5987-0	Porcelain	NO		CURRENT	15.00	17.00
HVA89-39	DAVID COPPERFIELD CHARACTERS (1989) (DV)	5551-4	Porcelain	SET OF 5		RETIRED 1992	32.50	44.00
HVA89-40	VILLAGE SIGN WITH SNOWMAN (1989) (HV)	5572-7	Porcelain	NO		CURRENT	10.00	10.00
	Size is 3".							

HVA89-41

LAMPLIGHTER W/LAMP

Man carries lit torch to light street lamps for evening. Old fashioned lampost, small tree by post.

HVA89-42

ROYAL COACH

Royal Coat Of Arms on door of gold filigree decorated red coach, wheel base and undercarriage of cast metal, four gray horses with red and gold trim.

HVA89-43

CONSTABLES

One holds club, one with seated dog, one tips hat and stands by lampost.

HVA89-44

VIOLET VENDOR/CAROLERS/ CHESTNUT VENDOR

Elderly woman sells violet bunches from basket, man sells fresh roasted nuts, and two women singing carols.

HVA89-45

KINGS ROAD CAB

Two wheeled horse drawn carriage. Driver sits high and behind cab. Passengers protected from weather.

HVA89-46

CHRISTMAS MORNING FIGURES

Scrooge transformed - smiling, small boy by fence and lampost - waving, couple carrying presents.

HVA89-47

CHRISTMAS SPIRITS FIGURES

Scrooge with Ghost Of ...
1) Christmas Past, 2) Christmas Present, and 3) Future....&....Marley.

HVA89-48

FARM ANIMALS

Chickens, geese, sheep, ewe and lamb.

ART CHART #	NAME	ITEM #	MATERIAL	SET?	🔔 MARKET STATUS	ORIGINAL SRP	GREENBOOK TRU MKT PRICE
	VARIATIONS/MISC/COLLECTOR NOTES						
HVA89-41	LAMPLIGHTER W/LAMP (1989) (DV)	5577-8	Porcelain	SET OF 2	CURRENT	$ 9.00	$ 10.00
HVA89-42	ROYAL COACH (1989) (DV)	5578-6	Prcln/Metal	NO	RETIRED 1992	55.00	75.00
	Early release to National Association Of Limited Edition Dealers, 1990.						
HVA89-43	CONSTABLES (1989) (DV)	5579-4	Porcelain	SET OF 3	RETIRED 1991	17.50	55.00
HVA89-44	VIOLET VENDOR/CAROLERS/CHESTNUT VENDOR (1989) (DV)	5580-8	Porcelain	SET OF 3	RETIRED 1992	23.00	45.00
HVA89-45	KINGS ROAD CAB (1989) (DV)	5581-6	Porcelain	NO	CURRENT	30.00	30.00
HVA89-46	CHRISTMAS MORNING FIGURES (1989) (DV)	5588-3	Porcelain	SET OF 3	CURRENT	18.00	18.00
	Early release to National Association Of Limited Edition Dealers, 1989. Addition to "Christmas Carol" grouping.						
HVA89-47	CHRISTMAS SPIRITS FIGURES (1989) (DV)	5589-1	Porcelain	SET OF 4	CURRENT	27.50	27.50
	Addition to "Christmas Carol" grouping.						
HVA89-48	FARM ANIMALS (1989) (NE)	5945-5	Porcelain	SET OF 4	RETIRED 1991	15.00	36.00

HVA89-49

ORGAN GRINDER

Man turns handle to produce music for little monkey to dance. Woman and girl watch monkey.

HVA89-50

POPCORN VENDOR

Truck with red and white striped top. Vendor fills red and white bag. Little girl has a full popcorn bag.

HVA89-51

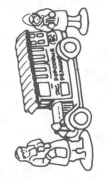

RIVER STREET ICE HOUSE CART

Horse pulls a blue and gray ice wagon for iceman

HVA89-52

CENTRAL PARK CARRIAGE

Gray horse pulls red and black carriage. Driver has mother and child as passengers.

HVA90-53

BUSY SIDEWALKS

Delivery boy, doorman, two elderly ladies, mother with toddler and baby in carriage.

HVA90-54

'TIS THE SEASON

Santa with bell and iron kettle for Season donations. Little girl gives to the needy.

HVA90-55

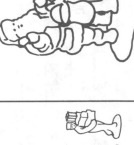

REST YE MERRY GENTLEMAN

Man sits on bench reading newspaper with purchases all around him.

HVA90-56

TOWN CRIER & CHIMNEY SWEEP

Crier rings bell and reads out announcements. A Sweep in top hat and tails carries chimney brush.

ART CHART #	NAME		ITEM #	MATERIAL	SET?	🏷	MARKET STATUS	ORIGINAL SRP	GREENBOOK TRU/MKT PRICE
	VARIATIONS/MISC/COLLECTOR NOTES								
HVA89-49	ORGAN GRINDER (1989)	(CIC)	5957-9	Porcelain	SET OF 3		RETIRED 1991	$ 21.00	$ 40.00
HVA89-50	POPCORN VENDOR (1989)	(CIC)	5958-7	Porcelain	SET OF 3		RETIRED 1992	22.00	35.00
HVA89-51	RIVER STREET ICE HOUSE CART (1989)	(CIC)	5959-5	Porcelain	NO		RETIRED 1991	20.00	45.00
HVA89-52	CENTRAL PARK CARRIAGE (1989)	(CIC)	5979-0	Porcelain	NO		CURRENT	30.00	30.00
HVA90-53	BUSY SIDEWALKS (1990)	(CIC)	5535-2	Porcelain	SET OF 4		RETIRED 1992	28.00	42.00
HVA90-54	'TIS THE SEASON (1990)	(CIC)	5539-5	Porcelain	NO		CURRENT	12.50	12.95
HVA90-55	REST YE MERRY GENTLEMAN (1990)	(CIC)	5540-9	Prcln/Metal	NO		CURRENT	12.50	12.95
HVA90-56	TOWN CRIER & CHIMNEY SWEEP (1990)	(DV)	5569-7	Porcelain	SET OF 2		CURRENT	15.00	16.00

194

HVA90-57

CAROLERS ON THE DOORSTEP
Four children sing carols to elderly man and woman - boys carry lanterns, girls have songbooks.

HVA90-61

TRIMMING THE NORTH POLE
One elf holds another to put greenery on North Pole sign while blue bird watches.

HVA90-58

HOLIDAY TRAVELERS
Train conductor, baggage handler, and man and woman passengers.

HVA90-62

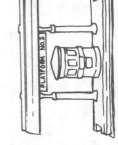

SANTA & MRS. CLAUS
Mrs. Claus with elf waves good-bye. Santa checks book before leaving N. Pole.

HVA90-59

THE FLYING SCOT TRAIN
Engine and wood supply car and two passenger cars with luggage carriers atop cars.

HVA90-63

SANTA'S LITTLE HELPERS
Elf stands on presents to hang wreath. Two elves move toy sack. One elf brings two reindeer to sleigh.

HVA90-60

VICTORIA STATION TRAIN PLATFORM
Ticket booth with windows all around, long metal roof to protect passengers.

HVA90-64

SLEIGH & EIGHT TINY REINDEER
Toys fill sleigh harnessed to Santa's eight reindeer.

ART CHART #	NAME		ITEM #	MATERIAL	SET?	♻	MARKET STATUS	ORIGINAL SRP	GREENBOOK TRU/MKT PRICE
	VARIATIONS/MISC/COLLECTOR NOTES								
HVA90-57	CAROLERS ON THE DOORSTEP (1990)	(DV)	5570-0	Porcelain	SET OF 4		RETIRED 1993	$ 25.00	$ 36.00
HVA90-58	HOLIDAY TRAVELERS (1990)	(DV)	5571-9	Porcelain	SET OF 3		CURRENT	22.50	25.00
HVA90-59	THE FLYING SCOT TRAIN (1990)	(DV)	5573-5	Porcelain	SET OF 4		CURRENT	48.00	50.00
HVA90-60	VICTORIA STATION TRAIN PLATFORM (1990)	(DV)	5575-1	Porcelain	NO		CURRENT	20.00	22.00
HVA90-61	TRIMMING THE NORTH POLE (1990)	(NP)	5608-1	Porcelain	NO		RETIRED 1993	10.00	22.00
HVA90-62	SANTA & MRS. CLAUS (1990)	(NP)	5609-0	Porcelain	SET OF 2		CURRENT	15.00	15.00
	Variation exists in title on book: "Good Boys" instead of "Good Kids."								
HVA90-63	SANTA'S LITTLE HELPERS (1990)	(NP)	5610-3	Porcelain	SET OF 3		RETIRED 1993	28.00	40.00
HVA90-64	SLEIGH & EIGHT TINY REINDEER (1990)	(NP)	5611-1	Porcelain	SET OF 5		CURRENT	40.00	42.00

HVA90-65

THE TOY PEDDLER

Toyman carries tray with toys.
Mother and son look at toy horse.
Little girl holds top.

HVA90-66

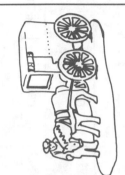

AMISH FAMILY

Mother carries apples in apron, father
stacks apple boxes, children sort apples.

HVA90-67

AMISH BUGGY

Amish man feeds brown horse harnessed
to family privacy curtained carriage.

HVA90-68

SLEEPY HOLLOW CHARACTERS

Man carving pumpkin,
Squire and Mrs. VanTassel,
Ichabod Crane with children.

HVA91-69

SKATING PARTY

Skating couple, boy, and girl.

HVA91-70

ALL AROUND THE TOWN

Man with "sandwich boards" as a
walking ad for "White Christmas."
Man with packages stops to get his
shoes shined from young boy.

HVA91-71

THE FIRE BRIGADE

Two firemen carry ladder and ax.
Fireman with pail takes moment
to pet mascot dalmatian.

HVA91-72

"CITY FIRE DEPT" FIRE TRUCK

Ladder attached to side, hose and nozzle
assembly on top and rear of red fire truck.

ART CHART #	NAME		ITEM #	MATERIAL	SET?	⚠	MARKET STATUS	ORIGINAL SRP	GREENBOOK TRU/MKT PRICE
	VARIATIONS/MISC/COLLECTOR NOTES								
HVA90-65	THE TOY PEDDLER (1990)	(ALP)	5616-2	Porcelain	SET OF 3		CURRENT	$ 22.00	$ 22.00
HVA90-66	AMISH FAMILY (1990)	(NE)	5948-0	Porcelain	SET OF 3		RETIRED 1992	20.00	28.00
	Early release to Showcase Dealers and the National Association Of Limited Edition Dealers. Variation: with mustache @ $40. For color photo, see Second Edition, page 231.								
HVA90-67	AMISH BUGGY (1990)	(NE)	5949-8	Porcelain	NO		RETIRED 1992	22.00	50.00
HVA90-68	SLEEPY HOLLOW CHARACTERS (1990)	(NE)	5956-0	Porcelain	SET OF 3		RETIRED 1992	27.50	45.00
HVA91-69	SKATING PARTY (1991)	(NE)	5523-9	Porcelain	SET OF 3		CURRENT	27.50	27.50
HVA91-70	ALL AROUND THE TOWN (1991)	(CIC)	5545-0	Porcelain	SET OF 2		RETIRED 1993	18.00	30.00
HVA91-71	THE FIRE BRIGADE (1991)	(CIC)	5546-8	Porcelain	SET OF 2		CURRENT	20.00	20.00
HVA91-72	"CITY FIRE DEPT." FIRE TRUCK (1991)	(CIC)	5547-6	Porcelain	NO		CURRENT	18.00	18.00

THE HERITAGE VILLAGE COLLECTION

HVA91-73

CAROLING THRU THE CITY
Singing man pulls sled with two boys, two women with young girl, man (alone) all with song books.

HVA91-74

OLIVER TWIST CHARACTERS
Mr. Brownlow in long coat, stovepipe hat, walks with cane. Oliver in rags next to food cart as another boy reaches to steal food, third boy holds sack.

HVA91-75

BRINGING HOME THE YULE LOG
Two boys pull on ropes to haul log. One girl holds lantern to light way and another walks alongside.

HVA91-76

POULTRY MARKET
Aproned poulterer holds game bird. Covered stand with display of turkeys and geese. Woman holds purchase as child watches.

HVA91-77

COME INTO THE INN
Innkeeper's wife reads note between sweeping snow from entry. Young boy with lantern lights way for coach driver. Gentleman with luggage waits to board coach.

HVA91-78

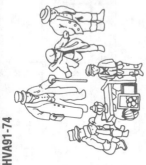

HOLIDAY COACH
Four horses pull coach full of travelers who ride inside and on topside seats. Coachman blows horn on arrival as driver guides horses.

HVA91-79

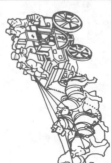

TOYMAKER ELVES
Two elves carry trunk of toys. One elf balances stack of toys. One elf has apron filled with toys.

HVA91-80

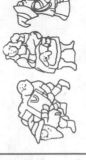

BAKER ELVES
One elf holds piece of belled harness from sleigh. One elf holds tray of baked goods. One elf takes a cookie from Sweets Cart.

ART CHART #	NAME		ITEM #	MATERIAL	SET?	🔔	MARKET STATUS	ORIGINAL SRP	GREENBOOK TRUMKT PRICE
	VARIATIONS/MISC/COLLECTOR NOTES								
HVA91-73	CAROLING THRU THE CITY (1991)	(CIC)	5548-4	Porcelain	SET OF 3		CURRENT	$ 27.50	$ 27.50
HVA91-74	OLIVER TWIST CHARACTERS (1991)	(DV)	5554-9	Porcelain	SET OF 3		RETIRED 1993	35.00	58.00
HVA91-75	BRINGING HOME THE YULE LOG (1991)	(DV)	5558-1	Porcelain	SET OF 3		CURRENT	27.50	28.00
HVA91-76	POULTRY MARKET (1991)	(DV)	5559-0	Porcelain	SET OF 3		CURRENT	30.00	32.00
	Variation: original "proof" version with patches on drape.								
HVA91-77	COME INTO THE INN (1991)	(DV)	5560-3	Porcelain	SET OF 3		CURRENT	22.00	22.00
HVA91-78	HOLIDAY COACH (1991)	(DV)	5561-1	Porcelain	NO		CURRENT	68.00	70.00
	Variation: gold chains vs. silver chains.								
HVA91-79	TOYMAKER ELVES (1991)	(NP)	5602-2	Porcelain	SET OF 3		CURRENT	27.50	27.50
HVA91-80	BAKER ELVES (1991)	(NP)	5603-0	Porcelain	SET OF 3		CURRENT	27.50	27.50

200

HVA92-84

VILLAGE PORCELAIN PINE, LARGE
Snow laden evergreen with a massive trunk. Some surface roots visible atop a bed of snow.

HVA92-88

LETTERS FOR SANTA
One elf carries bundles of letters, as another elf tries to lift sack of letters. Two additional elves arrive with reindeer cart filled with mail bags of letters for Santa.

HVA92-83

CHURCHYARD FENCE & GATE
Stone base with wrought iron atop, acted as barrier to protect land around church which usually included graveyard. One curved section, one straight section, one section with iron gate set in stone arch.

HVA92-87

WELCOME HOME
Boy reaches to hug Grandmother visiting for holiday as girl and Grandfather reach out to hug each other. Family pet joins the greeting.

HVA92-82

GATE HOUSE
Originated as tower over fortified entrance of a castle's perimeter wall. Brick base with arched entry made for passage of carriages/wagons. Windows generally narrow and shuttered to close against weather and for attack.

HVA92-86

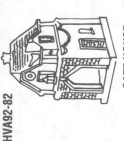

DON'T DROP THE PRESENTS!
Mother cautions father to take care as dog jumps up to sniff presents in father's arms. Daughter peeks out from mother's skirt as full shopping bag rests on snow. Son slips and tumbles in snow.

HVA91-81

MARKET DAY
Mother carrying baby and basket and daughter with basket of bread. Aproned merchant tips hat as he pushes sledge with bagged food. Man and boy rest on goat pulled cart while standing boy holds bag.

HVA92-85

VILLAGE PORCELAIN PINE, SMALL
Snow laden evergreen with a massive trunk. Some surface roots visible atop a bed of snow. Slightly shorter than Large Pine.

ART CHART #	NAME	ITEM #	MATERIAL	SET?	♻ MARKET STATUS	ORIGINAL SRP	GREENBOOK TRU MKT PRICE
	VARIATIONS/MISC/COLLECTOR NOTES						
HVA91-81	MARKET DAY (1991) (NE)	5641-3	Porcelain	SET OF 3	RETIRED 1993	$ 35.00	$ 48.00
HVA92-82	GATE HOUSE (1992) (HV, CIC)	5530-1	Porcelain	NO	SEE BELOW*	22.50	65.00
	*Available at 1992 Village Gatherings and select Showcase Dealer Open Houses. Variations in color of stone brick between shades of gray or blue.						
HVA92-83	CHURCHYARD FENCE & GATE (1992) (DV, NE, CIC)	5563-8	Porcelain	SET OF 3	DISCONTINUED*	15.00	40.00
	Early release to Gift Creations Concepts. *See footnote[5], page 211.						
HVA92-84	VILLAGE PORCELAIN PINE, LARGE (1992) (HV)	5218-3	Porcelain	NO	CURRENT	12.50	12.50
	Both large and small are illustrated.						
HVA92-85	VILLAGE PORCELAIN, SMALL (1992) (HV)	5219-1	Porcelain	NO	CURRENT	10.00	10.00
	Both large and small are illustrated.						
HVA92-86	DON'T DROP THE PRESENTS! (1992) (CIC)	5532-8	Porcelain	SET OF 2	CURRENT	25.00	25.00
HVA92-87	WELCOME HOME (1992) (CIC)	5533-6	Porcelain	SET OF 3	CURRENT	27.50	27.50
HVA92-88	LETTERS FOR SANTA (1992) (NP)	5604-9	Porcelain	SET OF 3	CURRENT	30.00	30.00

202

HVA92-89

TESTING THE TOYS

One elf rides downhill on a sled as two others try out a toboggan.

HVA92-90

BUYING BAKER'S BREAD

Man and woman lift basket together to carry loaves, plus she carries basket on arm. Man carries basket tray of bread while rest of loaves are carried in his basket backpack.

HVA92-91

HARVEST SEED CART

Boy lifts sack of corn to place on barrow. Man lifts barrow filled with corn sacks as one chicken pecks at sack and one chicken walks next to him. Girl holds white rooster and has basket resting on ground by her feet.

HVA92-92

TOWN TINKER

Traveling salesman with wheeled covered cart which he lifts and push/pulls. Tinker sold pots, pans, trinkets, silverware, and all manner of odds and ends, and made repairs as well, going from house to house, village to village.

HVA92-93

THE OLD PUPPETEER

Children watch puppet show. Stage on wheels with man moving the stringed marionettes to tell stories to audiences of all ages.

HVA92-94

THE BIRD SELLER

Woman holds up two bird cages. Delighted child and mother with woman who has made her purchase.

HVA92-95

VILLAGE STREET PEDDLERS

One man carries pole of fresh dressed rabbits. Second peddler wears wooden tray of spices to be sold in small pinches and ounces.

HVA92-96

CHURCHYARD GATE AND FENCE

Arched gate of stone and wrought iron connects to low stone fence topped by low wrought iron posts and connectors.

ART CHART #	NAME		ITEM #	MATERIAL	SET?	♻ ■	MARKET STATUS	ORIGINAL SRP	GREENBOOK TRUMKT PRICE
	VARIATIONS/MISC/COLLECTOR NOTES								
HVA92-89	TESTING THE TOYS (1992)	(NP)	5605-7	Porcelain	SET OF 2		CURRENT	$ 16.50	$ 16.50
HVA92-90	BUYING BAKERS BREAD (1992)	(ALP)	5619-7	Porcelain	SET OF 2		CURRENT	20.00	20.00
HVA92-91	HARVEST SEED CART (1992)	(DV, NE)	5645-6	Porcelain	SET OF 3		CURRENT	27.50	27.50
HVA92-92	TOWN TINKER (1992)	(DV, NE)	5646-4	Porcelain	SET OF 2		CURRENT	24.00	24.00
HVA92-93	THE OLD PUPPETEER (1992)	(DV)	5802-5	Porcelain	SET OF 3		CURRENT	32.00	32.00
HVA92-94	THE BIRD SELLER (1992)	(DV)	5803-3	Porcelain	SET OF 3		CURRENT	25.00	25.00
HVA92-95	VILLAGE STREET PEDDLERS (1992)	(DV)	5804-1	Porcelain	SET OF 2		CURRENT	16.00	16.00
HVA92-96	CHURCHYARD GATE AND FENCE (1992)	(DV, NE, CIC)	5806-8	Porcelain	SET OF 3		CURRENT	15.00	15.00

See footnote[5], page 211.

HVA93-100

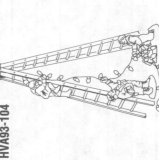

VILLAGE ANIMATED SKATING POND

Skaters move alone or as pair in set patterns on ice pond surface.

HVA92-99

VILLAGE EXPRESS VAN

Green delivery van advertises on time service. Rack on van roof holds wrapped packages.

HVA92-98

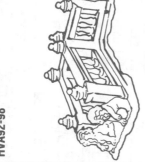

LIONHEAD BRIDGE

Massive bridge with two stone lions, each with one raised paw resting on a sphere.

HVA92-97

CHURCHYARD FENCE EXTENTIONS

Stone base with wrought iron posts and connectors to extend fence around church and graveyard.

HVA93-104

TOWN TREE TRIMMERS

Ladder and 3 helpers to decorate town tree.

HVA93-103

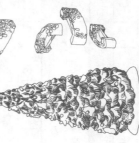
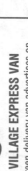

TOWN TREE

Decorated town tree and stone sections to encircle tree.

HVA93-102

STREET MUSICIANS

Girl gives coin to the street musicians.

HVA93-101

PLAYING IN THE SNOW

Children build and dress a snowman.

205

ART CHART #	NAME	ITEM #	MATERIAL	SET?	♥	MARKET STATUS	ORIGINAL SRP	GREENBOOK TRU/MKT PRICE
	VARIATIONS/MISC/COLLECTOR NOTES							
HVA92-97	CHURCHYARD FENCE EXTENTIONS (1992) (DV, NE, CIC)	5807-6	Porcelain	SET OF 4		CURRENT	$ 16.00	$ 16.00
	See footnote[5], page 211.							
HVA92-98	LIONHEAD BRIDGE (1992) (DV)	5864-5	Porcelain	NO		CURRENT	22.00	22.00
HVA92-99	VILLAGE EXPRESS VAN (1992) (DV, CIC)	5865-3	Porcelain	NO		CURRENT	25.00	25.00
	Color is green. Size is 4.5" x 3". See footnote[6], page 211.							
HVA93-100	VILLAGE ANIMATED SKATING POND (1993) (CIC)	5229-9	------	SET OF 15		CURRENT	60.00	60.00
HVA93-101	PLAYING IN THE SNOW (1993) (CIC)	5556-5	Porcelain	SET OF 3		CURRENT	25.00	25.00
HVA93-102	STREET MUSICIANS (1993) (CIC)	5564-6	Porcelain	SET OF 3		CURRENT	25.00	25.00
HVA93-103	TOWN TREE (1993) (CIC)	5565-4	Porcelain	SET OF 5		CURRENT	45.00	45.00
HVA93-104	TOWN TREE TRIMMERS (1993) (CIC)	5566-2	Porcelain	SET OF 4		CURRENT	32.50	32.50

THE HERITAGE VILLAGE COLLECTION

HVA93-105

CLIMB EVERY MOUNTAIN
3 climbers and companion
St. Bernard dog roped together for safety.

HVA93-106

WOODSMEN ELVES
Elves cut tree and wood to
warm North Pole buildings.

HVA93-107

SING A SONG FOR SANTA
Caroling North Pole elves.

HVA93-108

NORTH POLE GATE
Entry gate to North Pole Village.

HVA93-109

KNIFE GRINDER
Man powered grinding wheel keeps
sharp edge for knives and tools.

HVA93-110

BLUE STAR ICE HARVESTERS
Men cut up pond, lake,
and river ice for use in icehouse
for food storage and cooling.

HVA93-111

**CHELSEA MARKET
FRUIT MONGER & CART**
Pushcart vendor of
fresh fruits and vegetables.

HVA93-112

**CHELSEA MARKET
FISH MONGER & CART**
Pushcart vendor of fresh fish.

ART CHART #	NAME		ITEM #	MATERIAL	SET?	🖐	MARKET STATUS	ORIGINAL SRP	GREENBOOK TRUMKT PRICE
					VARIATIONS/MISC/COLLECTOR NOTES				
HVA93-105	CLIMB EVERY MOUNTAIN (1993)	(ALP)	5613-8	Porcelain	SET OF 4		CURRENT	$ 27.50	$ 27.50
HVA93-106	WOODSMEN ELVES (1993)	(NP)	5630-8	Porcelain	SET OF 3		CURRENT	30.00	30.00
HVA93-107	SING A SONG FOR SANTA (1993)	(NP)	5631-6	Porcelain	SET OF 3		CURRENT	28.00	28.00
HVA93-108	NORTH POLE GATE (1993)	(NP)	5632-4	Porcelain	NO		CURRENT	32.50	32.50
HVA93-109	KNIFE GRINDER (1993)	(NE)	5649-9	Porcelain	SET OF 2		CURRENT	22.50	22.50
HVA93-110	BLUE STAR ICE HARVESTERS (1993)	(NE)	5650-2	Porcelain	SET OF 2		CURRENT	27.50	27.50
HVA93-111	CHELSEA MARKET FRUIT MONGER & CART (1993)	(DV)	5813-0	Porcelain	SET OF 2		CURRENT	25.00	25.00
HVA93-112	CHELSEA MARKET FISH MONGER & CART (1993)	(DV)	5814-9	Porcelain	SET OF 2		CURRENT	25.00	25.00

. . . ACCESSORIES . . .   THE HERITAGE VILLAGE COLLECTION   . . . ACCESSORIES . . .

HVA93-113

CHELSEA MARKET FLOWER MONGER & CART
Pushcart vendor of fresh cut flowers and nosegays.

HVA93-114

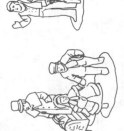

CHELSEA LANE SHOPPERS
Woman and girl, each with flowers. Couple walking with package and basket. Gentleman with walking stick.

HVA93-115

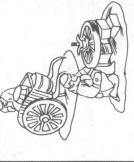

VISION OF A CHRISTMAS PAST
Innkeeper with coach dogs, traveling merchant, 2 young travelers.

HVA93-116

C. BRADFORD, WHEELWRIGHT & SON
Father and son wagon wheel makers and repairers.

HVA93-117

BRINGING FLEECES TO THE MILL
Shepherd takes wagonload of fleeces to market. Child stands with sheep.

HVA93-118

DASHING THROUGH THE SNOW
Horse drawn sleigh takes couple for ride across snowy roads.

HVA93-119

CHRISTMAS AT THE PARK
Seated father, mother and child. Seated boy and girl with dog.

HVA93-120

VILLAGE STREETCAR
Track setup for inner city traveling. Car lights up. Passengers visible thru windows.

ART CHART #	NAME		ITEM #	MATERIAL	SET?	☺	MARKET STATUS	ORIGINAL SRP	GREENBOOK TRUMKT PRICE
	VARIATIONS/MISC/COLLECTOR NOTES								
HVA93-113	CHELSEA MARKET FLOWER MONGER & CART (1993)	(DV)	5815-7	Porcelain	SET OF 2		CURRENT	$ 27.50	$ 27.50
HVA93-114	CHELSEA LANE SHOPPERS (1993)	(DV)	5816-5	Porcelain	SET OF 4		CURRENT	30.00	30.00
HVA93-115	VISION OF A CHRISTMAS PAST (1993)	(DV)	5817-3	Porcelain	SET OF 3		CURRENT	27.50	27.50
HVA93-116	C. BRADFORD, WHEELWRIGHT & SON (1993)	(DV)	5818-1	Porcelain	SET OF 2		CURRENT	24.00	24.00
HVA93-117	BRINGING FLEECES TO THE MILL (1993)	(DV)	5819-0	Porcelain	SET OF 2		CURRENT	35.00	35.00
HVA93-118	DASHING THROUGH THE SNOW (1993)	(DV)	5820-3	Porcelain	NO		CURRENT	32.50	32.50
HVA93-119	CHRISTMAS AT THE PARK (1993)	(CIC)	5866-1	Porcelain	SET OF 3		CURRENT	27.50	27.50
HVA94-120	VILLAGE STREETCAR (1994)	(CIC)	5240-0	------	SET OF 10		CURRENT	65.00	65.00
	Passengers' Silhouettes on windows.								

HVA94-121

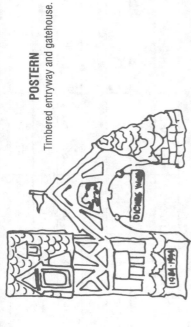

POSTERN

Timbered entryway and gatehouse.

ART CHART #	NAME		ITEM #	MATERIAL	SET?	♻	MARKET STATUS	ORIGINAL SRP	GREENBOOK TRUMKT PRICE
				VARIATIONS/MISC/COLLECTOR NOTES					
HVA94-121	POSTERN (1994)	(DV)	9871-0	Porcelain	NO		1994 ANNUAL	$ 17.50	$ 17.50
	Dickens' Village Ten Year Anniversary Piece. Cornerstone with dates. Special commemorative imprint on the bottom.								

HVA FOOTNOTES:

[1] There are 3 versions of the **Carolers**:
- *1st issue* - white post, viola is very light with dark brown trim, very little detail in figures, made in Taiwan.
- *2nd issue* - black post, viola is one color, slightly more detail in figures, made in Taiwan.
- *3rd issue* - black post, viola has darker trim, largest of 3 sets, made in Philippines.

[2] There are 2 versions of the **Sleighride**:
- *1st issue* - original sleeve reads, "Dickens Sleighride" - man has a narrow white scarf with red polka dots.
- *2nd issue* - man's scarf and lapels are white with red polka dots. Gray horse is more spotted.

[3] There are 2 versions of the **Covered Wooden Bridge**:
- *1st issue* - dark roof, made in Taiwan.
- *2nd issue* - light roof, made in Philippines.

[4] There are 3 versions of the **Dover Coach**:
- *1st issue* - Coachman has no mustache, wheels are crude, made in Taiwan, GREENBOOK TRUMARKET PRICE @ $125.
- *2nd issue* - Coachman has mustache, wheels are more round, made in Taiwan, two long recesses on underside of base, GNBK TRUMKT PRICE @ $65.
- *3rd issue* - Coachman has mustache, wheels are round, made in Sri Lanka @ $75.

[5] There were two different sets of **Churchyard Gate & Fences** introduced in 1992:
- The first one, "Churchyard Fence Gate" (1992 - 1992), Set of 3, was Item # 5563-8. It was a mid-year introduction and a GCC Exclusive. The set of 3 included one gate, one wall, and one corner. This version was pictured in the Quarterly in gray but was shipped in brown.
- The second one, "Churchyard Gate And Fence" (1992 - Current), Set of 3, is Item # 5806-8 and includes one gate and two corners.
- There is also "Churchyard Fence Extensions" (1992 - Current), Set of 4, Item #5807-6, which is four straight wall pieces.

[6] The **Village Express Van** was manufactured in black on a limited basis. The black version is a replica of the actual life-size van which has been on display at the Collectible Expositions and trade shows. Special Edition black Village Express Vans were given to D56 sales reps and GCC dealers. In addition, collectors who attended Bachman's September 1993 Gathering had the opportunity to purchase one for $20.00. The 1994 Gatherings will have a black van with the dealer's logo on one side ($22.50 SRP).

There is also an extremely limited gold "Road Show Limited Edition" version of the Village Express Van.

ADDITIONAL VILLAGE ACCESSORIES . . .

TREES . . .

	5111-0	Christmas Wreaths	Set of 8 1" & .75"	Discontinued
	5112-8	SV Garland Trim	3 pcs/pkg Each pc 24" long	Discontinued
	5115-2	Frosted Topiary Village Garden	Set of 8 4 cones, 4 ovals	Discontinued
	5175-6	Frosted Norway Pines	Set of 3 7", 9", & 11"	$12.95/set
	5181-0	Bare Branch Winter Oak, Small	Each 4.25"	4.50/ea
	5182-9	Bare Branch Winter Oak, Large	Each 7.75"	8.00/ea
	5183-7	Sisal Tree Set	Set of 7 4 cones & 3 ovals	Discontinued
	5184-5	Winter Oak Tree with 2 Red Birds	Each	Discontinued

Item #	Description		Discontinued
5185-3	Topiary Garden Sisal	36 pc asst 2.5", 4", 6", 8", & 12"	
5200-0	Frosted Topiary Cone Trees, Large	2/pkg 11.5"	$12.50/pkg
5201-9	Frosted Topiary Cone Trees, Medium	Set of 4 2 @ 7.5" & 2 @ 6"	10.00/set
5202-7	Frosted Topiary Trees, Large	Set of 8 4" ea - 4 cones, 4 oblong	12.50/set
5203-5	Frosted Topiary Trees, Small	Set of 8 4 @ 2" round, 4 @ 3" high	7.50/set
5205-1	Village Evergreen Trees	Set of 3 3.25", 4.25", & 6.5"	12.95/set
5216-7	Village Winter Birch Tree	Each 11.5"	12.50/ea
5221-3	Pine Cone Trees	Set of 2 8.75" & 7.25"	15.00/set
5231-0	Frosted Spruce Tree	Each 15"	12.50/ea

Item # = New for 1994

... ADDITIONAL VILLAGE ACCESSORIES ...

... TREES continued

	Item #	Description	Details	Price
	5232-9	Frosted Spruce Tree	Each 22"	$27.50/ea
	5419-4	Sisal Wreaths	6/pkg 1" diameter	4.00/pkg
	5527-1	Pole Pine Forest	Set of 5 4 trees in a snow base, 10" x 5" x 12"	48.00/set
	5528-0	Pole Pine Tree, Small	Each 8"	10.00/ea
	5529-8	Pole Pine Tree, Large	Each 10.5"	12.50/ea
	6582-0	Papier-Mache Frosted Evergreen Trees	Set of 3 4.5", 6.5", & 8.5"	16.00/set
	6595-1	Spruce Tree with Wooden Base, Small	Each 6"	3.50/ea
	6597-8	Spruce Tree with Wooden Base, Medium	Each 9"	5.00/ea

	Item #	Description		
	6598-6	Spruce Tree with Wooden Base, Large	Each 12"	7.00/ea
ELECTRICAL				
	5213-2	"Lights Out" Remote Control — Turns lights on/off in up to 60 houses at once	4" x 2.75"	$25.00/ea
	5502-6	AC/DC Adapter for Battery Operated Accessories		14.00/ea
	9902-8	Single Cord Set with Light Bulb		3.50/set
	9924-4	Replacement Light Bulb	3/pkg	2.00/pkg
	9926-0	Battery Operated Light	Each 6 watts, 12 volts	Discontinued
	9927-9	6 Socket Lite Set with Bulbs	Each	12.50/set
	9933-3	Multi-Outlet Plug Strip, 6 Outlets	Each 12" x 2" x 1.5"	10.00/ea

 = New for 1994

... ADDITIONAL VILLAGE ACCESSORIES ...

LAMPS/LIGHTS

Item No.	Description	Specs	Price
3636-6	Heritage Village Street Lamp Set (2 "AA" Batteries)	6/pkg Cord 60" long, lamps 2.25" tall	$10.00/pkg
5206-0	Candles by the Doorstep (2 "AA" Batteries)	4/pkg 2.25"	6.95/pkg
5215-9	Village Mini Lights	14 bulbs 27" long cord	12.50/set
5416-0	Yard Lights (2 Santas, 2 Snowmen)	Set of 4 1.75"	12.95/set
5500-0	Traffic Light (2 "C" Batteries)	2/pkg 4.25"	11.00/pkg
5501-8	Railroad Crossing Sign (2 "C" Batteries)	2/pkg 4.25"	12.50/pkg
5503-4	Old World Streetlamp (2 "C" Batteries)	4/pkg 4"	Discontinued
5504-2	Turn Of The Century Lamppost (2 "C" Batteries)	4/pkg 4"	16.00/pkg

Item	Description	Size/Qty	Price
5505-0	Turn of the Century Lamppost (2 "C" Batteries)	6/pkg 4"	Discontinued
5512-3	Heritage Village Utility Accessories 2 stop signs, 4 parking meters, 2 traffic lights	Set of 8 1.75" - 3"	12.50/set
5993-5	Streetlamp Wrapped in Garland	2/pkg 4"	Discontinued
5996-0	Double Street Lamps (2 "C" Batteries)	4/pkg 3.5"	13.00/pkg

SNOW

Item	Description	Size/Qty	Price
4995-6	Blanket of New Fallen Snow	2' x 5' x 1"	$ 7.50/ea
4996-4	"Let It Snow" Crystals, Plastic Snow	8 oz box	Discontinued
4998-1	Real Plastic Snow	7 oz bag	3.00/bag
4999-9	Real Plastic Snow	2 lb box	10.00/box

. . . ADDITIONAL VILLAGE ACCESSORIES . . .

FENCES

	5204-3	Snow Fence, Flexible Wood & Wire	Each 2" high x 36" long	$ 7.00/ea
	5207-8	Frosty Tree-Lined Picket Fence	Each 5.75" x 2.5", 3 posts & 3 attached trees	6.50/ea
	5212-4	Tree-Lined Courtyard Fence	Each 1.5" high x 4" long	4.00/ea
	5220-5	Courtyard Fence with Steps	Each 1.25" high x 4.25" long	4.00/ea
	5234-5	Chain Link Fence with Gate	Set of 3 2", 4.5"	12.00/set
	5235-3	Chain Link Fence Extensions	Set of 4 4.5"	15.00/set
	5506-9	Lamp Post/Fence (2 "AA" Batteries)	Set of 10 2 lamps, 4 posts, 4 fence pcs	Discontinued
	5508-5	Lamp Post/Fence Extension	Set of 12 6 posts & 6 fence pcs	Discontinued

Item #	Description		Price
5514-0	Wrought Iron Village Gate with Fence, Green	Set of 9 gate & 4 fence pcs w/4 posts, 9.25" x 3"	15.00/set
5515-8	Village Wrought Iron Fence Extension	Set of 9 4 fence pieces & 5 posts, 9.25" x 3"	12.50/set
5541-7	Subway Entrance	Each 4.5" x 2.75" x 4.5"	15.00/ea
5998-6	Wrought Iron Fence (White & Black or White & Green)	Each 4" long	2.50/ea
5999-4	Wrought Iron Fence (White & Black)	4/pkg 4" long	10.00/pkg

MOUNTAINS

Item #	Description		Price
5226-4	Village Mountains with Frosted Sisal Trees, Small	Set of 5 12" x 10.5" x 8", 4 trees	$ 32.50/set
5227-2	Village Mountains with Frosted Sisal Trees, Medium	Set of 8 22" x 12" x 10.5", 7 trees, 1 niche to display Village piece	65.00/set
5228-0	Village Mountains with Frosted Sisal Trees, Large	Set of 14 35" x 13" x 15.5", 13 trees, can accomodate 3 lighted pieces	150.00/set

Item # = New for 1994

. . . ADDITIONAL VILLAGE ACCESSORIES . . .

TRIMS . . .

5208-6	Mylar Skating Pond	2 sheets/pkg 25.25" x 18" each	$ 6.00/pkg
5210-8	Brick Road	2 strips/pkg 4.75" x 36" each	10.00/pkg
5984-6	Cobblestone Road	2 strips/pkg 4.75" x 36" each	10.00/set
5211-6	Acrylic Icicles	4/pkg 18" long each	4.50/pkg
5511-5	"Christmas Eave" Trim (bulb garland, non-electric)	Each 24" long	3.50/ea
5513-1	Town Square Gazebo	Each 6"	19.00/ea
5516-6	Christmas In The City Boulevard 4 pieces sidewalk, 4 removable 5" trees, 2 benches, 4 hitching posts	Set of 14	Discontinued
5217-5	Tacky Wax	Each 1" diameter x 1" deep tub	2.00/tub

Item #	Description	Specification	Price
5214-0	Heritage Village Mailbox & Fire Hydrant HV Mail Service - Green & Red, 1.5" & 1"	Set of 2	5.00/set
5230-2	Wrought Iron Park Bench	Each 2.25"	5.00/ea
5233-7	Sled & Skis	Set of 2 2" & 2.25"	6.00/set
5456-9	Windmill	Each 11.5"	20.00/ea
5517-4	Heritage Mailbox & Fire Hydrant USPO - Red, White, & Blue	Set of 2	Discontinued
5805-0	English Post Box	Each 2.25"	4.50/ea
5524-7	"Village Sounds" Tape with Speakers	23 minute tape, 12' cord	25.00/set
5525-5	"Village Sounds" Tape	23 minutes, continuous play	8.00/ea
5417-8	It's A Grand Old Flag	2/pkg 2.25"	4.00/pkg

Item # = New for 1994

... ADDITIONAL VILLAGE ACCESSORIES

... *TRIMS continued*

	Item #	Description	Detail	Price
	5526-3	Heritage Banners	Set of 4, 2 each of 2 1.25"	$ 6.00/set
	9953-8	Heritage Village Collection Promotional Sign	GREENBOOK TRUMARKET Price is $18.00.	Discontinued
	9948-1	Snow Village Promotional Sign	GREENBOOK TRUMARKET Price is $12.00.	Discontinued
	948-2	Heritage Village Collection Promotional Logo Banner	Each Giveaway at 1992 events.	Discontinued

VILLAGE BRITE LITES

	Item #	Description	Detail	Price
	5222-1	"I Love My Village"	6.5"	$ 15.00/ea
	5223-0	"Merry Christmas"	7.5"	15.00/ea
	5224-8	Flashing Reindeer	3.25"	13.50/ea

	Item #	Description	Size	Price
	5225-6	Village Brite Lites Adapter		10.00/ea
	5236-1	Fence, Animated	Set of 4 / 11"	25.00/set
	5237-0	Snowman, Animated	3.75"	20.00/ea
	5238-8	Tree, Animated	3.5"	13.50/ea
	5239-6	Santa, Animated	3.5"	20.00/ea
	9846-9	Department 56, Animated	5"	10.00 ea

TRAINS

	Item #	Description	Detail	Price
	5997-8	Village Express HO Scale Train / Black engine. GREENBOOK TRUMARKET Price is $300.00	Set of 5	Discontinued
	5980-3	Village Express HO Scale Train / Red and silver engine	Set of 5	$100.00/set

Item # = New for 1994

New Snowbunnies:

2600-0	I've Got A Surprise!	$15.00
2601-8	Oops! I Dropped One!	16.00
2602-6	A Tisket, A Tasket	15.00
2603-4	I'll Paint The Top ...	30.00
2604-2	Surprise! It's Me!	25.00
2606-9	Tra-La-La	37.50
2607-7	Help Me Hide The Eggs	25.00
2608-5	Easter Delivery	27.50
2609-3	Let's Do The Bunny-Hop!	32.50
2610-7	A Tisket, A Tasket	32.50

Snowbabies

1986 • D56 introduces the first 16 Snowbabies

1987 • first Snowbabies retirement

1988 • the first Snowbabies limited edition, Frosty Frolic - limited to 4,800
pieces, is introduced

1989 • Miniature Snowbabies made of painted pewter are introduced

1993 • D56's second event piece, Can I Open It Now?, is made available at
selected dealers' Open House Events

1994 • first Snowbabies piece featuring an adult person - Jack Frost -
is introduced

SNOWBABIES

SB86-1

CATCH A FALLING STAR
Seated Snowbaby with outstretched arms.

SB86-2

SNOWBABY SITTING
Snowbaby sitting with open arms.

SB86-3

SNOWBABY CRAWLING

SB86-4

SNOWBABY WINGED
Winged Snowbaby sitting with open arms.

SB86-5

GIVE ME A PUSH!
Snowbaby with open arms seated on sled.

SB86-6

HOLD ON TIGHT!
Snowbaby lying on a sled.

SB86-7

BEST FRIENDS
Snowbabies put arms around each other.

SB86-8

SNOWBABY NITE LITE
Snowbaby sitting with open arms.

ART CHART #	NAME / TYPE OF PRODUCT	ITEM #	MATERIAL	SET?	♥ NOTES	MARKET STATUS	ORIGINAL SRP	GREENBOOK TRUMKT PRICE
SB86-1	**CATCH A FALLING STAR** MUSIC BOX (7")	7950-2	Porcelain	NO		RETIRED 1987	$ 27.50	$ 545.00
SB86-2	**SNOWBABY SITTING** LITE-UP, CLIP-ON ORNAMENT (2.75")	7952-9	Porcelain	NO	✓	RETIRED 1990	7.00	36.00
SB86-3	**SNOWBABY CRAWLING** LITE-UP, CLIP-ON ORNAMENT (3.75")	7953-7	Porcelain	NO	✓	RETIRED 1992	7.00	20.00
SB86-4	**SNOWBABY WINGED** LITE-UP, CLIP-ON ORNAMENT (2.75")	7954-5	Porcelain	NO	✓	RETIRED 1990	7.00	38.00
	For smaller version, also in porcelain, see: 1987 #7976-6.							
SB86-5	**GIVE ME A PUSH!** FIGURINE (3.25")	7955-3	Porcelain	NO		RETIRED 1990	12.00	54.00
	For same subject, miniature, in handpainted pewter, see: 1989 #7601-5.							
SB86-6	**HOLD ON TIGHT!** FIGURINE (3.25")	7956-1	Porcelain	NO		CURRENT	12.00	13.50
	For same subject, miniature, in handpainted pewter, see: 1989 #7600-7.							
SB86-7	**BEST FRIENDS** FIGURINE (3.75")	7958-8	Porcelain	NO		RETIRED 1989	12.00	118.00
	For same subject, miniature, in handpainted pewter, see: 1989 #7604-0.							
SB86-8	**SNOWBABY NITE LITE** NITE LITE (5.75")	7959-6	Porcelain	NO	✓	RETIRED 1989	15.00	230.00

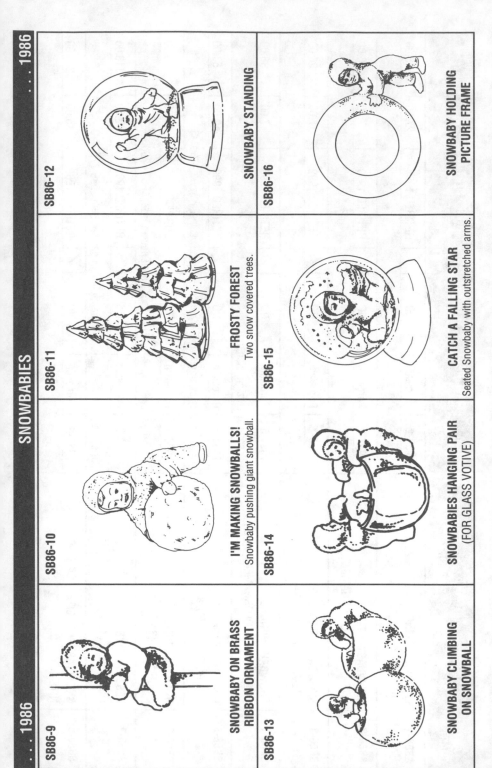

SB86-9

SNOWBABY ON BRASS RIBBON ORNAMENT

SB86-10

I'M MAKING SNOWBALLS!
Snowbaby pushing giant snowball.

SB86-11

FROSTY FOREST
Two snow covered trees.

SB86-12

SNOWBABY STANDING

SB86-13

SNOWBABY CLIMBING ON SNOWBALL

SB86-14

SNOWBABIES HANGING PAIR
(FOR GLASS VOTIVE)

SB86-15

CATCH A FALLING STAR
Seated Snowbaby with outstretched arms.

SB86-16

SNOWBABY HOLDING PICTURE FRAME

ART CHART #	NAME TYPE OF PRODUCT	ITEM #	MATERIAL	SET?	MARKET STATUS NOTES	ORIGINAL SRP	GREENBOOK TRUMKT PRICE
SB86-9	**SNOWBABY ON BRASS RIBBON ORNAMENT** ORNAMENT (7.5")	7961-8	Porcelain	NO	RETIRED 1989	$ 8.00	$ 112.00
SB86-10	**I'M MAKING SNOWBALLS!** FIGURINE (3.25")	7962-6	Porcelain	NO	RETIRED 1992	12.00	30.00
	For same subject, miniature, in handpainted pewter, see: 1989 #7602-3.						
SB86-11	**FROSTY FOREST** ACCESSORY (5" & 6")	7963-4	Porcelain	SET OF 2	CURRENT	15.00	20.00
	For same subject, miniature, in handpainted pewter, see: 1989 #7612-0.						
SB86-12	**SNOWBABY STANDING** WATERGLOBE (4.5")	7964-2	Glass/Resin	NO	RETIRED 1987	7.50	400.00
SB86-13	**SNOWBABY CLIMBING ON SNOWBALL** BISQUE VOTIVE W/CANDLE (3.75")	7965-0	Porcelain	SET OF 2	RETIRED 1989	15.00	65.00
SB86-14	**SNOWBABIES HANGING PAIR** FOR GLASS VOTIVE W/CANDLE (not included) (3.5")	7966-9	Porcelain	PAIR	RETIRED 1989	15.00	140.00
SB86-15	**CATCH A FALLING STAR** WATERGLOBE (4.5")	7967-7	Glass/Resin	NO	RETIRED 1987	18.00	550.00
SB86-16	**SNOWBABY HOLDING PICTURE FRAME** PICTURE FRAME (4.75")	7970-7	Porcelain	SET OF 2	RETIRED 1987	15.00	550.00

NE = Not Established

SNOWBABIES

SB87-1

MOON BEAMS
Snowbaby sits on crescent moon.

SB87-5

SNOWBABY ADRIFT
Snowbaby on a snowflake.

SB87-2

TUMBLING IN THE SNOW!
Snowbabies tumbling.

SB87-6

SNOWBABIES CLIMBING ON TREE
One Snowbaby watches
another climbing tree.

SB87-3

DOWN THE HILL WE GO!
Two Snowbabies on a toboggan.

SB87-7

WHEN YOU WISH UPON A STAR
Snowbaby sitting on snowball.

SB87-4

DON'T FALL OFF!
Snowbaby sitting on a snowball.

SB87-8

SNOWBABY WITH WINGS
Snowbaby sits with outstretched arms.

231

ART CHART #	NAME / TYPE OF PRODUCT	ITEM #	MATERIAL	SET?	🔔	MARKET STATUS	ORIGINAL SRP	GREENBOOK TRUMKT PRICE
SB87-1	**MOON BEAMS** HANGING ORNAMENT (3.75")	7951-0	Porcelain	NO		CURRENT	$7.50	$8.50
SB87-2	**TUMBLING IN THE SNOW!** FIGURINES (2" - 3.25")	7957-0	Porcelain	SET OF 5		RETIRED 1993	35.00	70.00
	For same subject, miniature, in handpainted pewter, see: 1989 #7614-7.							
SB87-3	**DOWN THE HILL WE GO!** FIGURINE (2.75")	7960-0	Porcelain	NO		CURRENT	20.00	22.50
	For same subject, miniature, in handpainted pewter, see: 1989 #7606-6.							
SB87-4	**DON'T FALL OFF!** FIGURINE (5.5")	7968-5	Porcelain	NO		RETIRED 1990	12.50	62.00
	For same subject, miniature, in handpainted pewter, see: 1989 #7603-1.							
SB87-5	**SNOWBABY ADRIFT** LITE-UP, CLIP-ON ORNAMENT	7969-3	Porcelain	NO	✓	RETIRED 1990	8.50	92.00
SB87-6	**SNOWBABIES CLIMBING ON TREE** FIGURINES (8")	7971-5	Porcelain	SET OF 2		RETIRED 1989	25.00	535.00
	Baby on top of trees is separate.							
SB87-7	**WHEN YOU WISH UPON A STAR** MUSIC BOX (6.5")	7972-3	Porcelain	NO		RETIRED 1993	30.00	45.00
	Tune: "When You Wish Upon A Star."							
SB87-8	**SNOWBABY WITH WINGS** LIGHTED WATERGLOBE (5.5")	7973-1	Glass/Resin	NO	✓	RETIRED 1988	20.00	385.00
	Light works on batteries.							

SNOWBABIES

SB87-9

WINTER SURPRISE!
Two Snowbabies peek out of gift box.

SB87-10

SNOWBABIES RIDING SLEDS
Snowbabies sled down
hill between evergreen trees.

SB87-11

SNOWBABY-MINI, WINGED PAIR
Seated Snowbaby with open arms.

ART CHART #	NAME / TYPE OF PRODUCT	ITEM #	MATERIAL	SET?	🔔 MARKET STATUS	ORIGINAL SRP	GREENBOOK TRUMKT PRICE
					NOTES		
SB87-9	**WINTER SURPRISE!** FIGURINE (3")	**7974-0**	Porcelain	NO		RETIRED 1992	$ 15.00	$ 35.00
	For same subject, miniature, in handpainted pewter, see: 1989 #7607-4.						
SB87-10	**SNOWBABIES RIDING SLEDS** JUMBO WATERGLOBE/MUSIC BOX (7.25")	**7975-8**	Glass/Resin	NO		RETIRED 1988	40.00	650.00
	Tune: "Winter Wonderland."						
SB87-11	**SNOWBABY-MINI, WINGED PAIR** LITE-UP, CLIP-ON ORNAMENT (2.25")	**7976-6**	Porcelain	2/PKG	✓	CURRENT	9.00	12.00
	For same subject, full size, in porcelain, see: 1986 #7954-5.						

NE = Not Established

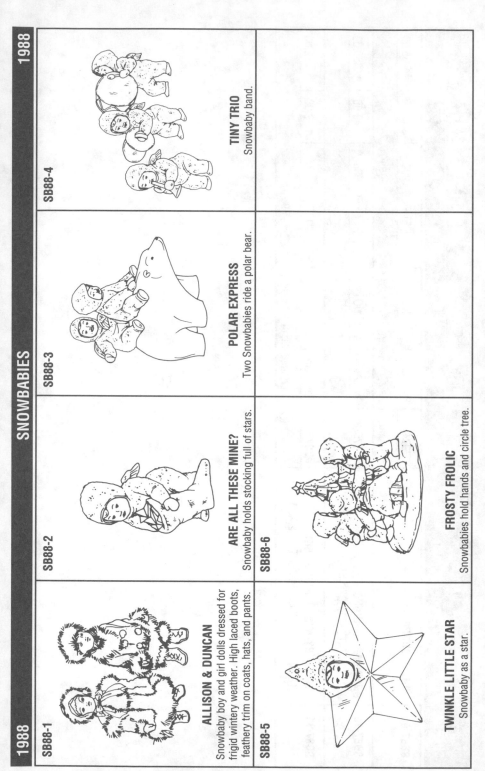

SB88-1

ALLISON & DUNCAN
Snowbaby boy and girl dolls dressed for frigid wintery weather. High laced boots, feathery trim on coats, hats, and pants.

SB88-2

ARE ALL THESE MINE?
Snowbaby holds stocking full of stars.

SB88-3

POLAR EXPRESS
Two Snowbabies ride a polar bear.

SB88-4

TINY TRIO
Snowbaby band.

SB88-5

TWINKLE LITTLE STAR
Snowbaby as a star.

SB88-6

FROSTY FROLIC
Snowbabies hold hands and circle tree.

ART CHART #	NAME / TYPE OF PRODUCT	ITEM #	MATERIAL	SET?	⚫ MARKET STATUS	ORIGINAL SRP	GREENBOOK TRUMKT PRICE
					NOTES		
SB88-1	ALLISON & DUNCAN DOLLS	7730-5	Papier Mache	SET OF 2	RETIRED 1989	$200.00	$700.00
SB88-2	ARE ALL THESE MINE? FIGURINE (3.5")	7977-4	Porcelain	NO	CURRENT	10.00	12.50
	For same subject, miniature, in handpainted pewter, see: 1989 #7605-8.						
SB88-3	POLAR EXPRESS FIGURINE (5.75")	7978-2	Porcelain	NO	RETIRED 1992	22.00	55.00
	For same subject, miniature, in handpainted pewter, see: 1989 #7609-0.						
SB88-4	TINY TRIO FIGURINES (3.5")	7979-0	Porcelain	SET OF 3	RETIRED 1990	20.00	102.00
	For same subject, miniature, in handpainted pewter, see: 1989 #7615-5.						
SB88-5	TWINKLE LITTLE STAR ORNAMENT (5")	7980-4	Porcelain	NO	RETIRED 1990	7.00	82.00
SB88-6	FROSTY FROLIC FIGURINE (5")	7981-2	Porcelain	NO	LTD. ED. 4,800	35.00	785.00
	For same subject, miniature, in handpainted pewter, see: 1989 #7613-9.						

SNOWBABIES

SB89-1

HELPFUL FRIENDS
Snowbaby and penguins with box of stars.

SB89-2

FROSTY FUN
Snowbabies building a snowman.

SB89-3

ALL FALL DOWN
Ice-skating Snowbabies fall down.

SB89-4

FINDING FALLEN STARS
Snowbabies collect fallen stars in basket.

SB89-5

PENGUIN PARADE
Penguins follow Snowbaby playing flute.

SB89-6

**ICY IGLOO
W/SWITCH, CORD, & BULB**
Snow house.

SB89-7

NOEL
Flying Snowbaby plays horn.

SB89-8

SURPRISE!
Snowbaby peeks out of gift box.

ART CHART #	NAME / TYPE OF PRODUCT	ITEM #	MATERIAL	SET?	💡	MARKET STATUS	ORIGINAL SRP	GREENBOOK TRUMKT PRICE
						NOTES		
SB89-1	HELPFUL FRIENDS FIGURINE (6")	7982-0	Porcelain	NO		RETIRED 1993	$ 30.00	$ 55.00
		For same subject, miniature, in handpainted pewter, see: 1989 #7608-2.						
SB89-2	FROSTY FUN FIGURINE (4")	7983-9	Porcelain	NO		RETIRED 1991	27.50	55.00
		For same subject, miniature, in handpainted pewter, see: 1989 #7611-2.						
SB89-3	ALL FALL DOWN FIGURINES (4.25")	7984-7	Porcelain	SET OF 4		RETIRED 1991	36.00	60.00
		For same subject, miniature, in handpainted pewter, see: 1989 #7617-1.						
SB89-4	FINDING FALLEN STARS FIGURINE (6")	7985-5	Porcelain	NO		LTD. ED. 6,000	32.50	165.00
		For same subject, miniature, in handpainted pewter, see: 1989 #7618-0.						
SB89-5	PENGUIN PARADE FIGURINE (5")	7986-3	Porcelain	NO		RETIRED 1992	25.00	52.00
		For same subject, miniature, in handpainted pewter, see: 1989 #7616-3.						
SB89-6	ICY IGLOO W/SWITCH, CORD, & BULB ACCESSORY (7.5")	7987-1	Porcelain	NO	✓	CURRENT	37.50	37.50
		For same subject, miniature, in handpainted pewter, see: 1989 #7610-4.						
SB89-7	NOEL HANGING ORNAMENT (4.5")	7988-0	Porcelain	NO		CURRENT	7.50	7.50
SB89-8	SURPRISE! HANGING ORNAMENT (3")	7989-8	Porcelain	NO		CURRENT	12.00	12.00

SNOWBABIES

SB89-9

STAR BRIGHT
Snowbaby climbs on a star.

SB89-10

LET IT SNOW
Snowbabies ride on polar bear.

ART CHART #	NAME TYPE OF PRODUCT	ITEM #	MATERIAL	SET?	♪	MARKET STATUS	ORIGINAL SRP	GREENBOOK TRUMKT PRICE
					NOTES			
SB89-9	**STAR BRIGHT** HANGING ORNAMENT (4")	**7990-1**	Porcelain	NO		CURRENT	$ 7.50	$ 7.50
SB89-10	**LET IT SNOW** WATERGLOBE/MUSIC BOX (4")	**7992-8**	Glass/Resin	NO		RETIRED 1993	25.00	35.00
		Tune: "Winter Wonderland."						

SNOWBABIES

SB90-1

NEVER RELEASED.

WHAT ARE YOU DOING?

SB90-2

ALL TIRED OUT
Snowbaby takes a nap.

SB90-3

ROCK-A-BYE BABY
Snowbaby naps on crescent moon
with garland of stars.

SB90-4

PENGUIN

SB90-6

POLAR BEAR

SB90-6

TWINKLE LITTLE STARS
Three Snowbabies sing carols.

SB90-7

WISHING ON A STAR
Penguin watches Snowbaby
holding up star to wish upon.

SB90-8

READ ME A STORY
Snowbaby reads story to penguin.

ART CHART #	NAME TYPE OF PRODUCT	ITEM #	MATERIAL	SET?	🔔	MARKET STATUS	ORIGINAL SRP	GREENBOOK TRUMKT PRICE
					NOTES			
SB90-1	**WHAT ARE YOU DOING?** WATERGLOBE/MUSIC BOX	7935-9	Never released. Production problems. Penguins on outside of waterglobe too fragile.					
			Tune: "Twinkle, Twinkle, Little Star."					
SB90-2	**ALL TIRED OUT** WATERGLOBE/MUSIC BOX (7")	7937-5	Glass/Resin	NO		RETIRED 1992	$ 55.00	$ 68.00
			Tune: "Brahms Lullaby."					
SB90-3	**ROCK-A-BYE BABY** HANGING ORNAMENT (3.5")	7939-1	Porcelain	NO		CURRENT	7.00	7.50
SB90-4	**PENGUIN** LITE-UP, CLIP-ON ORNAMENT (3")	7940-5	Porcelain	NO	✓	RETIRED 1992	5.00	15.00
SB90-5	**POLAR BEAR** LITE-UP, CLIP-ON ORNAMENT (3.5")	7941-3	Porcelain	NO	✓	RETIRED 1992	5.00	18.00
SB90-6	**TWINKLE LITTLE STARS** FIGURINES (4")	7942-1	Porcelain	SET OF 2		RETIRED 1993	37.50	55.00
			For same subject, miniature, in handpainted pewter, see: 1990 #7621-0.					
SB90-7	**WISHING ON A STAR** FIGURINE (3.5")	7943-0	Porcelain	NO		CURRENT	20.00	22.00
			For same subject, miniature, in handpainted pewter, see: 1991 #7626-0.					
SB90-8	**READ ME A STORY!** FIGURINE (3.5")	7945-6	Porcelain	NO		CURRENT	25.00	25.00
			For same subject, miniature, in handpainted pewter, see: 1990 #7622-8.					

SNOWBABIES

SB90-9

WE WILL MAKE IT SHINE!
Snowbabies hang stars on tree.

SB90-10

PLAYING GAMES IS FUN!
Snowbabies play London Bridge
with penguins.

SB90-11

A SPECIAL DELIVERY
Snowbaby on snowshoes delivers star.

SB90-12

WHO ARE YOU?
Snowbaby and penguin with walrus.

ART CHART #	NAME / TYPE OF PRODUCT	ITEM #	MATERIAL	SET?	MARKET STATUS	ORIGINAL SRP	GREENBOOK TRU MKT PRICE
SB90-9	**WE WILL MAKE IT SHINE!** FIGURINE (7.5")	7946-4	Porcelain	NO	RETIRED 1992	$ 45.00	$ 80.00
SB90-10	**PLAYING GAMES IS FUN!** FIGURINE (5")	7947-2	Porcelain	NO	RETIRED 1993-	30.00	55.00
	NOTES: For same subject, miniature, in handpainted pewter, see: 1990 #7623-6.						
SB90-11	**A SPECIAL DELIVERY** FIGURINE (4")	7948-0	Porcelain	NO	CURRENT	13.50	15.00
	NOTES: For same subject, miniature, in handpainted pewter, see: 1990 #7624-4.						
SB90-12	**WHO ARE YOU?** FIGURINE (2.5")	7949-9	Porcelain	NO	LTD. ED. 12,500	32.50	125.00
	NOTES: Early release to Gift Creations Concepts.						

SNOWBABIES

SB91-1

I'LL PUT UP THE TREE!
Snowbaby holds small tree with star.

SB91-2

WHY DON'T YOU TALK TO ME?
Snowbaby asks snowman a question.

SB91-3

I MADE THIS JUST FOR YOU!
Snowbaby carrying a star wreath.

SB91-4

IS THAT FOR ME?
One Snowbaby holds present
for another.

SB91-5

POLAR SIGN
Penguin looks at Collector's Sign.

SB91-6

THIS IS WHERE WE LIVE!
Snowbaby shows walrus
and polar bear The Pole.

SB91-7

WAITING FOR CHRISTMAS
Two Snowbabies sitting on opposite sides
of present - one watches, one naps.

SB91-8

DANCING TO A TUNE
Snowbaby plays concertina as
two Snowbabies dance.

ART CHART #	NAME / TYPE OF PRODUCT	ITEM #	MATERIAL	SET?	❓ MARKET STATUS	ORIGINAL SRP	GREENBOOK TRUMKT PRICE
					NOTES		
SB91-1	I'LL PUT UP THE TREE! / FIGURINE (4")	6800-4	Porcelain	NO	CURRENT	$24.00	$25.00
	Early release to Gift Creations Concepts. For same subject, miniature, in handpainted pewter, see: 1991 #7627-9.						
SB91-2	WHY DON'T YOU TALK TO ME? / FIGURINE (4")	6801-2	Porcelain	NO	CURRENT	24.00	24.00
	For same subject, miniature, in handpainted pewter, see: 1991 #7625-2.						
SB91-3	I MADE THIS JUST FOR YOU! / FIGURINE (4.25")	6802-0	Porcelain	NO	CURRENT	15.00	15.00
	For same subject, miniature, in handpainted pewter, see: 1991 #7628-7.						
SB91-4	IS THAT FOR ME? / FIGURINES (4.25")	6803-9	Porcelain	SET OF 2	RETIRED 1993	32.50	50.00
	For same subject, miniature, in handpainted pewter, see: 1991 #7631-7.						
SB91-5	POLAR SIGN / ACCESSORY (3.5")	6804-7	Porcelain	NO	CURRENT	20.00	20.00
SB91-6	THIS IS WHERE WE LIVE! / FIGURINE (5")	6805-5	Porcelain	NO	CURRENT	60.00	60.00
SB91-7	WAITING FOR CHRISTMAS / FIGURINE (2.75")	6807-1	Porcelain	NO	RETIRED 1993	27.50	45.00
	For same subject, miniature, in handpainted pewter, see: 1991 #7629-5.						
SB91-8	DANCING TO A TUNE / FIGURINES (4")	6808-0	Porcelain	SET OF 3	CURRENT	30.00	30.00
	For same subject, miniature, in handpainted pewter, see: 1991 #7630-9.						

SNOWBABIES

SB91-9

FISHING FOR DREAMS
Snowbaby ice fishing for a star watched by two Puffins.

SB91-10

SWINGING ON A STAR
Snowbaby seated on swing holds large star.

SB91-11

MY FIRST STAR
Snowbaby icicle with star ornament.

SB91-12

PLAYING GAMES IS FUN
Snowbabies play London Bridge with two penguins.

SB91-13

PENGUIN PARADE
One Snowbaby plays flute, one Snowbaby watches as penguins parade to tune.

SB91-14

FROSTY FROLIC
Top Tier: Snowbabies circle tree.
Bottom Tier: Snowbabies play instruments for penguins.

SB91-15

PLAY ME A TUNE
Snowbaby plays a horn as penguin listens.

SB91-16

PEEK-A-BOO
Snowbaby covers eyes with hands playing with penguins.

ART CHART #	NAME / TYPE OF PRODUCT	ITEM #	MATERIAL	SET?	🔔 NOTES	MARKET STATUS	ORIGINAL SRP	GREENBOOK TRU/MKT PRICE
SB91-9	**FISHING FOR DREAMS** FIGURINE (4")	6809-8	Porcelain	NO		CURRENT	$ 28.00	$ 28.00
SB91-10	**SWINGING ON A STAR** ORNAMENT (3.5")	6810-1	Porcelain	NO		CURRENT	9.50	10.00
SB91-11	**MY FIRST STAR** ORNAMENT (6.75")	6811-0	Porcelain	NO		CURRENT	7.00	7.50
SB91-12	**PLAYING GAMES IS FUN!** REVOLVING MUSIC BOX (6")	7632-5	Wood/Resin	NO	Tune: "Twinkle, Twinkle Little Star."	RETIRED 1993	72.00	NE
SB91-13	**PENGUIN PARADE** REVOLVING MUSIC BOX (7")	7633-3	Wood/Resin	NO	Tune: "Brahms Lullaby."	CURRENT	72.00	72.00
SB91-14	**FROSTY FROLIC** 2-TIER MUSIC BOX (10.25")	7634-1	Wood/Resin	NO	Tune: "Let It Snow."	RETIRED 1993	110.00	NE
SB91-15	**PLAY ME A TUNE** WATERGLOBE/MUSIC BOX (5")	7936-7	Bisque	NO	Tune: "We Wish You A Merry Christmas."	RETIRED 1993	50.00	75.00
SB91-16	**PEEK-A-BOO** WATERGLOBE/MUSIC BOX (6.5")	7938-3	Bisque	NO	Tune: "Jingle Bells."	RETIRED 1993	50.00	75.00

SNOWBABIES

SB91-17

SNOWBABIES ADVENT TREE
WITH 24 ORNS

ART CHART #	NAME / TYPE OF PRODUCT	ITEM #	MATERIAL	SET?	🔔 NOTES	MARKET STATUS	ORIGINAL SRP	GREENBOOK TRU MKT PRICE
SB91-17	**SNOWBABIES ADVENT TREE W/24 ORNS** MUSIC BOX	7635-0	Tune: "We Wish You A Merry Christmas."			CURRENT	$135.00	$135.00

250

SNOWBABIES

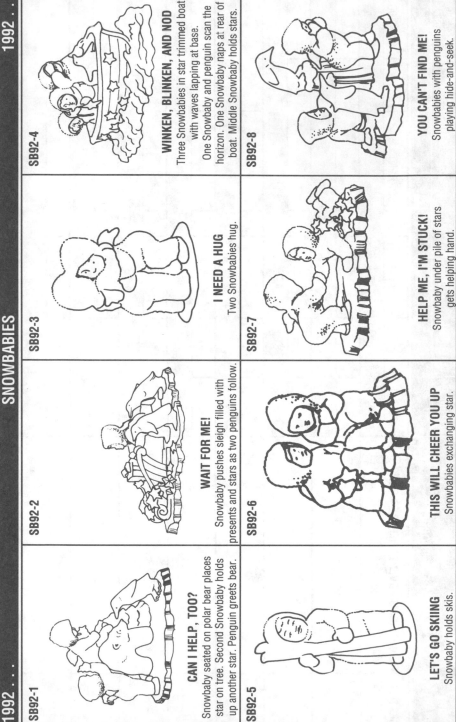

SB92-4

WINKEN, BLINKEN, AND NOD
Three Snowbabies in star trimmed boat with waves lapping at base. One Snowbaby and penguin scan the horizon. One Snowbaby naps at rear of boat. Middle Snowbaby holds stars.

SB92-8

YOU CAN'T FIND ME!
Snowbabies with penguins playing hide-and-seek.

SB92-3

I NEED A HUG
Two Snowbabies hug.

SB92-7

HELP ME, I'M STUCK!
Snowbaby under pile of stars gets helping hand.

SB92-2

WAIT FOR ME!
Snowbaby pushes sleigh filled with presents and stars as two penguins follow.

SB92-6

THIS WILL CHEER YOU UP
Snowbabies exchanging star.

SB92-1

CAN I HELP, TOO?
Snowbaby seated on polar bear places star on tree. Second Snowbaby holds up another star. Penguin greets bear.

SB92-5

LET'S GO SKIING
Snowbaby holds skis.

ART CHART #	NAME / TYPE OF PRODUCT	ITEM #	MATERIAL	SET?	MARKET STATUS / NOTES	ORIGINAL SRP	GREENBOOK TRUMKT PRICE
SB92-1	CAN I HELP, TOO? / FIGURINE (5")	6806-3	Porcelain	NO	LTD. ED. 18,500	$48.00	$90.00
SB92-2	WAIT FOR ME! / FIGURINE (4.5")	6812-8	Porcelain	NO	CURRENT	48.00	48.00
			For same subject, miniature, in handpainted pewter, see: 1992 #7641-4.				
SB92-3	I NEED A HUG / FIGURINE (4.25")	6813-6	Porcelain	NO	CURRENT	20.00	20.00
			For same subject, miniature, in handpainted pewter, see: 1992 #7640-6.				
SB92-4	WINKEN, BLINKEN, AND NOD / FIGURINE (5")	6814-4	Porcelain	NO	CURRENT	60.00	65.00
			Early release to Gift Creation Concepts. For same subject, miniature, in handpainted pewter, see: 1993 #7658-9.				
SB92-5	LET'S GO SKIING / FIGURINE (4.5")	6815-2	Porcelain	NO	CURRENT	15.00	15.00
			For same subject, miniature, in handpainted pewter, see: 1992 #7636-8.				
SB92-6	THIS WILL CHEER YOU UP / FIGURINE (4.25")	6816-0	Porcelain	NO	CURRENT	30.00	30.00
			Early release to Ideation. For same subject, miniature, in handpainted pewter, see: 1992 #7639-2.				
SB92-7	HELP ME, I'M STUCK! / FIGURINE (3.75")	6817-9	Porcelain	NO	CURRENT	32.50	32.50
			For same subject, miniature, in handpainted pewter, see: 1992 #7638-4.				
SB92-8	YOU CAN'T FIND ME! / FIGURINE (5")	6818-7	Porcelain	NO	CURRENT	45.00	45.00
			For same subject, miniature, in handpainted pewter, see: 1992 #7637-6.				

SNOWBABIES

SB92-9

LOOK WHAT I CAN DO!
Snowbaby juggling stars.

SB92-10

SHALL I PLAY FOR YOU?
Snowbaby playing drum.

SB92-11

YOU DIDN'T FORGET ME!
Snowbaby getting mail.

SB92-12

STARS-IN-A-ROW, TIC-TAC-TOE
Snowbabies playing tic-tac-toe.

SB92-13

JUST ONE LITTLE CANDLE
Snowbaby holding candle.

SB92-14

JOIN THE PARADE
Snowbaby marching with friends.

SB92-15

SNOWBABIES ICICLE WITH STAR ORNAMENT

SB92-16

WHAT WILL I CATCH?
Snowbaby fishing.

ART CHART #	NAME / TYPE OF PRODUCT	ITEM #	MATERIAL	SET?	☝ MARKET STATUS	ORIGINAL SRP	GREENBOOK TRUMKT PRICE
					NOTES		
SB92-9	**LOOK WHAT I CAN DO!** FIGURINE (5")	6819-5	Porcelain	NO	CURRENT	$ 16.50	$ 16.50
SB92-10	**SHALL I PLAY FOR YOU?** FIGURINE (4")	6820-9	Porcelain	NO	CURRENT	16.50	16.50
	For same subject, miniature, in handpainted pewter, see: 1992 #7642-2.						
SB92-11	**YOU DIDN'T FORGET ME!** FIGURINE (4.5")	6821-7	Porcelain	NO	CURRENT	32.50	32.50
	For same subject, miniature, in handpainted pewter, see: 1992 #7643-0.						
SB92-12	**STARS-IN-A-ROW, TIC-TAC-TOE** FIGURINE (4.5")	6822-5	Porcelain	NO	CURRENT	32.50	32.50
SB92-13	**JUST ONE LITTLE CANDLE** FIGURINE (4")	6823-3	Porcelain	NO	CURRENT	15.00	15.00
	For same subject, miniature, in handpainted pewter, see: 1992 #7644-9.						
SB92-14	**JOIN THE PARADE** FIGURINE (4.5")	6824-1	Porcelain	NO	CURRENT	37.50	37.50
	For same subject, miniature, in handpainted pewter, see: 1992 #7645-7.						
SB92-15	**SNOWBABIES ICICLE WITH STAR** ORNAMENTS (7.25")	6825-0	Porcelain	SET OF 4	CURRENT	16.00	16.00
SB92-16	**WHAT WILL I CATCH?** MUSIC BOX (5.5")	6826-8	Porcelain	NO	CURRENT	48.00	48.00
	Tune: "Catch A Falling Star."						

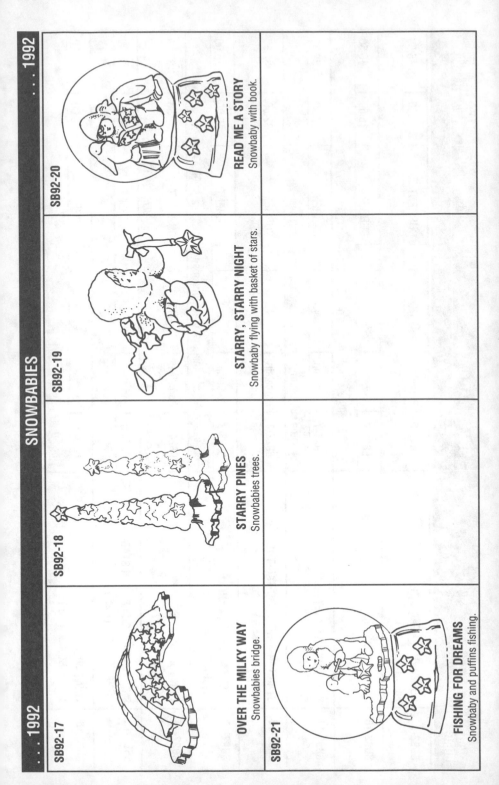

SNOWBABIES

SB92-17

OVER THE MILKY WAY
Snowbabies bridge.

SB92-18

STARRY PINES
Snowbabies trees.

SB92-19

STARRY, STARRY NIGHT
Snowbaby flying with basket of stars.

SB92-20

READ ME A STORY
Snowbaby with book.

SB92-21

FISHING FOR DREAMS
Snowbaby and puffins fishing.

ART CHART #	NAME / TYPE OF PRODUCT	ITEM #	MATERIAL	SET?	MARKET STATUS	ORIGINAL SRP	GREENBOOK TRUMKT PRICE
SB92-17	**OVER THE MILKY WAY** FIGURINE (3")	6828-4	Porcelain	NO	CURRENT	$ 32.00	$ 32.00
SB92-18	**STARRY PINES** FIGURINES (8.5" & 6.5")	6829-2	Porcelain	SET OF 2	CURRENT	17.50	17.50
SB92-19	**STARRY, STARRY NIGHT** ORNAMENT (4.5")	6830-6	Porcelain	NO	CURRENT	12.50	12.50
SB92-20	**READ ME A STORY** WATERGLOBE/MUSIC BOX (4")	6831-4	Bisque	NO	CURRENT	32.50	32.50
	Tune: "Twinkle, Twinkle, Little Star."						
SB92-21	**FISHING FOR DREAMS** WATERGLOBE/MUSIC BOX (4")	6832-2	Bisque	NO	CURRENT	32.50	32.50
	Tune: "Catch A Falling Star."						

NOTES

SNOWBABIES

SB93-1

LOOK WHAT I FOUND
Two polar bear cubs discovered by Snowbaby in snow house shelter.

SB93-2

CROSSING STARRY SKIES
Snowbaby paddles in kayak across star strewn ice.

SB93-3

I'LL TEACH YOU A TRICK
Snowbaby teaches penguin to jump through hoop.

SB93-4

I FOUND YOUR MITTENS!
Snowbaby holds mittens as second Snowbaby hugs cold hands to keep warm.

SB93-5

SO MUCH WORK TO DO!
Snowbaby gathers stars with a shovel.

SB93-6

CAN I OPEN IT NOW?
Seated Snowbaby holds gift wrapped present.

SB93-7

NOW I LAY ME DOWN TO SLEEP
Snowbaby says bedtime prayers.

SB93-8

Annual Production Mark on piece - brass plate with one snowflake.

SOMEWHERE IN DREAMLAND
Snowbabies nap on moon watched by bear, puffen and penguin.

ART CHART #	NAME / TYPE OF PRODUCT	ITEM #	MATERIAL	SET?	🔔 MARKET STATUS	ORIGINAL SRP	GREENBOOK TRUMKT PRICE
					NOTES		
SB93-1	LOOK WHAT I FOUND FIGURINE (3.75")	6833-0	Porcelain	NO	CURRENT	$ 45.00	$ 45.00
		Early release to Showcase Dealers and select buying groups.					
SB93-2	CROSSING STARRY SKIES FIGURINE (5")	6834-9	Porcelain	NO	CURRENT	35.00	35.00
		Early release to Showcase Dealers and select buying groups.					
SB93-3	I'LL TEACH YOU A TRICK FIGURINE (3.75")	6835-7	Porcelain	NO	CURRENT	24.00	24.00
		Early release to Showcase Dealers and select buying groups.					
SB93-4	I FOUND YOUR MITTENS! FIGURINES (4.25")	6836-5	Porcelain	SET OF 2	CURRENT	30.00	30.00
		Early release to Showcase Dealers and select buying groups.					
SB93-5	SO MUCH WORK TO DO! FIGURINE (3.75")	6837-3	Porcelain	NO	CURRENT	18.00	18.00
		Early release to Showcase Dealers and select buying groups.					
SB93-6	CAN I OPEN IT NOW? FIGURINE (2.75")	6838-1	Porcelain	NO	1993 ANNUAL	15.00	35.00
		1993 Event Piece.					
SB93-7	NOW I LAY ME DOWN TO SLEEP FIGURINE (3.5")	6839-0	Porcelain	NO	CURRENT	13.50	13.50
		For same subject, miniature, in handpainted pewter, see: 1993 #7657-0.					
SB93-8	SOMEWHERE IN DREAMLAND FIGURINE (7.25")	6840-3	Porcelain	NO	CURRENT	85.00	85.00
		For same subject, miniature, in handpainted pewter, see: 1993 #7656-2.					

. . . . . 1993 . . . . 1993 . . .

SNOWBABIES

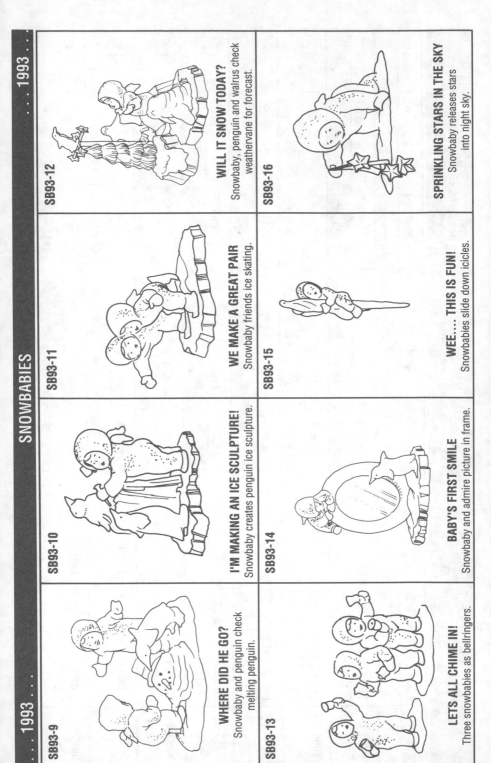

SB93-9

WHERE DID HE GO?
Snowbaby and penguin check melting penguin.

SB93-10

I'M MAKING AN ICE SCULPTURE!
Snowbaby creates penguin ice sculpture.

SB93-11

WE MAKE A GREAT PAIR
Snowbaby friends ice skating.

SB93-12

WILL IT SNOW TODAY?
Snowbaby, penguin and walrus check weathervane for forecast.

SB93-13

LET'S ALL CHIME IN!
Three snowbabies as bellringers.

SB93-14

BABY'S FIRST SMILE
Snowbaby and admire picture in frame.

SB93-15

WEE.... THIS IS FUN!
Snowbabies slide down icicles.

SB93-16

SPRINKLING STARS IN THE SKY
Snowbaby releases stars into night sky.

ART CHART #	NAME TYPE OF PRODUCT	ITEM #	MATERIAL	SET?	⬇ MARKET STATUS	ORIGINAL SRP	GREENBOOK TRUMKT PRICE
					NOTES		
SB93-9	WHERE DID HE GO? FIGURINE (4.25")	6841-1	Porcelain	NO	CURRENT	$ 35.00	$ 35.00
		For same subject, miniature, in handpainted pewter, see: 1993 #7654-6.					
SB93-10	I'M MAKING AN ICE SCULPTURE! FIGURINE (4.50")	6842-0	Porcelain	NO	CURRENT	30.00	30.00
		Originally shipped in boxes that read, "I'm An Artist."					
SB93-11	WE MAKE A GREAT PAIR FIGURINE (4")	6843-8	Porcelain	NO	CURRENT	30.00	30.00
		For same subject, miniature, in handpainted pewter, see: 1993 #7652-0.					
SB93-12	WILL IT SNOW TODAY? FIGURINES (6.25")	6844-6	Porcelain	NO	CURRENT	45.00	45.00
		For same subject, miniature, in handpainted pewter, see: 1993 #7653-8.					
SB93-13	LET'S ALL CHIME IN! FIGURINE (4")	6845-4	Porcelain	SET OF 2	CURRENT	37.50	37.50
		For same subject, miniature, in handpainted pewter, see: 1993 #7655-4.					
SB93-14	BABY'S FIRST SMILE PICTURE FRAME (6.50")	6846-2	Porcelain	NO	CURRENT	30.00	30.00
SB93-15	WEE... THIS IS FUN! ORNAMENT (6.50")	6847-9	Porcelain	NO	CURRENT	13.50	13.50
SB93-16	SPRINKLING STARS IN THE SKY ORNAMENT (6.75")	6848-9	Porcelain	NO	CURRENT	12.50	12.50

260

SNOWBABIES

SB93-17

SO MUCH WORK TO DO!
Snowbaby gathers stars with a shovel.

SB93-18

YOU DIDN'T FORGET ME!
Snowbaby getting mail.

SB93-19

I'M SO SLEEPY
Snowbaby naps on crescent moon.

SB93-20

LET IT SNOW
Snowbabies gathering and placing stars.

SB93-21

PENGUIN PARADE
Snowbaby with flute & penguins.

SB93-22

WISHING ON A STAR
Penguin watches Snowbaby holding up star to wish upon.

SB93-23

CAN I OPEN IT NOW?
Seated Snowbaby holds gift wrapped present.

SB93-24

READING A STORY
Snowbaby reading.

ART CHART #	NAME / TYPE OF PRODUCT	ITEM #	MATERIAL	SET?	MARKET STATUS	ORIGINAL SRP	GREENBOOK TRUMKT PRICE
					NOTES		
SB93-17	**SO MUCH WORK TO DO!** WATERGLOBE, MUSIC BOX (6")	6849-7	Porcelain	NO	CURRENT	$ 32.50	$ 32.50
	Tune: "Whistle While You Work."						
SB93-18	**YOU DIDN'T FORGET ME!** WATERGLOBE, MUSIC BOX (6")	6850-0	Porcelain	NO	CURRENT	32.50	32.50
	Tune: "Have Yourself A Merry Little Christmas."						
SB93-19	**I'M SO SLEEPY** REVOLVING MUSIC BOX (7")	6851-9	Porcelain	NO	CURRENT	37.50	37.50
	Tune: "Brahms' Lullaby."						
SB93-20	**LET IT SNOW** ANIMATED BOOK MUSIC BOX	6857-8	Porcelain	NO	CURRENT	100.00	100.00
SB93-21	**PENGUIN PARADE** ACRYLIC MUSIC BOX (2.75")	7646-5	Porcelain	NO	CURRENT	20.00	20.00
	Tune: "Winter Wonderland."						
SB93-22	**WISHING ON A STAR** ACRYLIC MUSIC BOX (2.75")	7647-3	Porcelain	NO	CURRENT	20.00	20.00
	Tune: "When You Wish Upon a Star."						
SB93-23	**CAN I OPEN IT NOW?** ACRYLIC MUSIC BOX (2.75")	7648-1	Porcelain	NO	CURRENT	20.00	20.00
	Tune: "Happy Birthday."						
SB93-24	**READING A STORY** ACRYLIC MUSIC BOX (2.75")	7649-0	Porcelain	NO	CURRENT	20.00	20.00
	Tune: "Brahms' Lullaby."						

SNOWBABIES

SB93-25

FROSTY FUN
Snowbabies build a snowman.

SB93-26

PLAY ME A TUNE
Snowbaby plays a flute as penguin listens.

263

ART CHART #	NAME TYPE OF PRODUCT	ITEM #	MATERIAL	SET?	MARKET STATUS	ORIGINAL SRP	GREENBOOK TRUMKT PRICE
SB93-25	FROSTY FUN ACRYLIC MUSIC BOX (2.75")	7650-3	Porcelain	NO	CURRENT	$ 20.00	$ 20.00
	Tune: "Frosty The Snowman."				NOTES		
SB93-26	PLAY ME A TUNE ACRYLIC MUSIC BOX (2.75")	7651-1	Porcelain	NO	CURRENT	20.00	20.00
	Tune: "Joy To The World."						

SNOWBABIES

SB94-1

I'M RIGHT BEHIND YOU!
Four Snowbabies take turns sledding down a hill.

SB94-2

THERE'S ANOTHER ONE!
Snowbaby pushing wheelbarrow collecting stars.

SB94-3

JACK FROST... A TOUCH OF WINTER'S MAGIC
Holding a star wand with stars, Jack Frost protects Snowbaby and friends from wind with his robe.

SB94-4

GATHERING STARS IN THE SKY
Snowbaby rests on floating star.

SB94-5

WHERE DID YOU COME FROM?
Snowbaby asks rabbit question while building ice block sign wall.

SB94-6

FIRST STAR JINGLEBABY
Snowbaby as a jinglebell carries first star of night.

SB94-7

LITTLE DRUMMER JINGLEBABY
Snowbaby as a drum playing jinglebell.

265

ART CHART #	NAME TYPE OF PRODUCT	ITEM #	MATERIAL	SET?	MARKET STATUS	ORIGINAL SRP	GREENBOOK TRUMKT PRICE
					NOTES		
SB94-1	I'M RIGHT BEHIND YOU! FIGURINE (2")	6852-7	Porcelain	NO	CURRENT	$ 60.00	$ 60.00
		Early release to NALED.					
SB94-2	THERE'S ANOTHER ONE! FIGURINE (4.25")	6853-5	Porcelain	NO	CURRENT	24.00	24.00
		Early release to Ideation.					
SB94-3	JACK FROST... A TOUCH OF WINTER'S MAGIC FIGURINE (10")	6854-3	Porcelain	NO	CURRENT	90.00	90.00
		Early release to GCC.					
SB94-4	GATHERING STARS IN THE SKY ORNAMENT	6855-1	Porcelain	NO	CURRENT	12.50	12.50
SB94-5	WHERE DID YOU COME FROM? FIGURINE	6856-0	Porcelain	NO	CURRENT	40.00	40.00
		Early release to Retail Resource.					
SB94-6	FIRST STAR JINGLEBABY ORNAMENT (3.5")	6858-6	Porcelain	NO	CURRENT	10.00	10.00
SB94-7	LITTLE DRUMMER JINGLEBABY ORNAMENT (3.5")	6859-4	Porcelain	NO	CURRENT	10.00	10.00

SNOWBABIES MINIATURES

SM89-1

HOLD ON TIGHT!
Snowbaby lying on a sled.

SM89-2

GIVE ME A PUSH!
Snowbaby with open arms seated on sled.

SM89-3

I'M MAKING SNOWBALLS!
Snowbaby pushing giant snowball.

SM89-4

DON'T FALL OFF!
Snowbaby sitting on a snowball.

SM89-5

BEST FRIENDS
Snowbabies put arms around each other.

SM89-6

ARE ALL THESE MINE?
Snowbaby holds stocking full of stars.

SM89-7

DOWN THE HILL WE GO!
Two Snowbabies on toboggan.

SM89-8

WINTER SURPRISE!
Two Snowbabies peek out of gift box.

267

ART CHART #	NAME / TYPE OF PRODUCT	ITEM #	MATERIAL	SET?	🔔 MARKET STATUS	ORIGINAL SRP	GREENBOOK TRUMKT PRICE
					NOTES		
SM89-1	HOLD ON TIGHT! MINIATURE (1.5")	7600-7	Pewter	NO	CURRENT	$ 7.00	$ 7.00
	For same subject, full size, in porcelain, see: 1986 #7956-1.						
SM89-2	GIVE ME A PUSH! MINIATURE (1.5")	7601-5	Pewter	NO	CURRENT	7.00	7.00
	For same subject, full size, in porcelain, see: 1986 #7955-3.						
SM89-3	I'M MAKING SNOWBALLS! MINIATURE (1.5")	7602-3	Pewter	NO	CURRENT	7.00	7.00
	For same subject, full size, in porcelain, see: 1986 #7962-6.						
SM89-4	DON'T FALL OFF! MINIATURE (1.5")	7603-1	Pewter	NO	CURRENT	7.00	7.00
	For same subject, full size, in porcelain, see: 1987 #7968-5.						
SM89-5	BEST FRIENDS MINIATURE (1.5")	7604-0	Pewter	NO	CURRENT	10.00	10.00
	For same subject, full size, in porcelain, see: 1986 #7958-8.						
SM89-6	ARE ALL THESE MINE? MINIATURE (1.5")	7605-8	Pewter	NO	RETIRED 1992	7.00	22.00
	For same subject, full size, in porcelain, see: 1988 #7977-4.						
SM89-7	DOWN THE HILL WE GO! MINIATURES (1")	7606-6	Pewter	SET OF 2	CURRENT	13.50	13.50
	For same subject, full size, in porcelain, see: 1987 #7960-0.						
SM89-8	WINTER SURPRISE! MINIATURE (1")	7607-4	Pewter	NO	CURRENT	13.50	13.50
	For same subject, full size, in porcelain, see: 1987 #7974-0.						

SM89-9

HELPFUL FRIENDS
Snowbaby and penguins
with box of stars.

SM89-10

POLAR EXPRESS
Two Snowbabies ride a polar bear.

SM89-11

ICY IGLOO W/TREE
Snow house.

SM89-12

FROSTY FUN
Snowbabies build a snowman.

SM89-13

FROSTY FOREST
Two evergreens.

SM89-14

FROSTY FROLIC
Snowbabies hold hands and circle tree.

SM89-15

TUMBLING IN THE SNOW!

SM89-16

TINY TRIO
Snowbaby band.

ART CHART #	NAME / TYPE OF PRODUCT	ITEM #	MATERIAL	SET?	NOTES	MARKET STATUS	ORIGINAL SRP	GREENBOOK TRUMKT PRICE
SM89-9	HELPFUL FRIENDS MINIATURES (1" - 1.5")	7608-2	Pewter	SET OF 4		RETIRED 1992	$ 13.50	$ 30.00
		For same subject, full size, in porcelain, see: 1989 #7982-0.						
SM89-10	POLAR EXPRESS MINIATURES (2.5")	7609-0	Pewter	2/PKG		RETIRED 1992	13.50	35.00
		For same subject, full size, in porcelain, see: 1988 #7978-2.						
SM89-11	ICY IGLOO W/TREE MINIATURE ACCESSORIES (2")	7610-4	Pewter	SET OF 2		RETIRED 1992	7.50	22.00
		For same subject, full size, in porcelain, see: 1989 #7987-1.						
SM89-12	FROSTY FUN MINIATURES (1.5")	7611-2	Pewter	SET OF 2		CURRENT	13.50	13.50
		For same subject, full size, in porcelain, see: 1989 #7983-9.						
SM89-13	FROSTY FOREST MINIATURE ACCESSORIES (2" & 1.5")	7612-0	Pewter	SET OF 2		CURRENT	12.00	12.00
		For same subject, full size, in porcelain, see: 1986 #7963-4.						
SM89-14	FROSTY FROLIC MINIATURES (1.5" - 2.5")	7613-9	Pewter	SET OF 4		RETIRED 1993	24.00	38.00
		For same subject, full size, in porcelain, see: 1988 #7981-2.						
SM89-15	TUMBLING IN THE SNOW! MINIATURES (1" - 1.5")	7614-7	Pewter	SET OF 5		RETIRED 1992	30.00	74.00
		For same subject, full size, in porcelain, see: 1987 #7957-0.						
SM89-16	TINY TRIO MINIATURES (1.25" - 1.5")	7615-5	Pewter	SET OF 3		RETIRED 1993	18.00	32.00
		For same subject, full size, in porcelain, see: 1986 #7979-0.						

SNOWBABIES MINIATURES

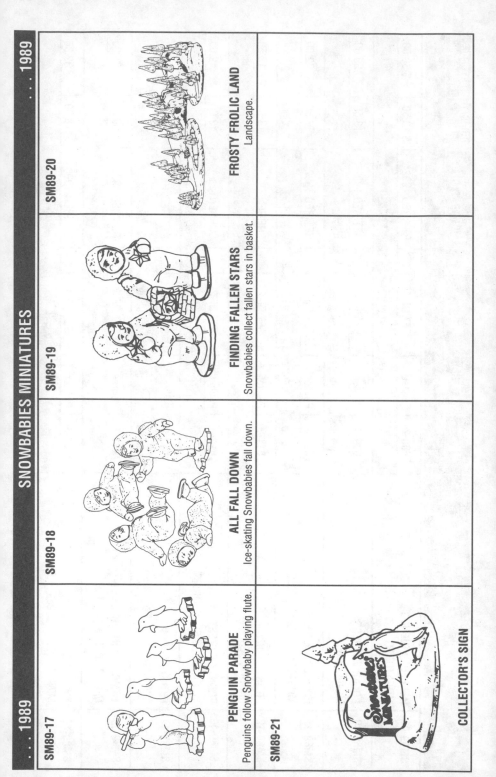

SM89-17

PENGUIN PARADE
Penguins follow Snowbaby playing flute.

SM89-18

ALL FALL DOWN
Ice-skating Snowbabies fall down.

SM89-19

FINDING FALLEN STARS
Snowbabies collect fallen stars in basket.

SM89-20

FROSTY FROLIC LAND
Landscape.

SM89-21

COLLECTOR'S SIGN

ART CHART #	NAME / TYPE OF PRODUCT	ITEM #	MATERIAL	SET?	MARKET STATUS	ORIGINAL SRP	GREENBOOK TRU/MKT PRICE
SM89-17	PENGUIN PARADE MINIATURES (.75" - 1.5")	7616-3	Pewter	SET OF 4	RETIRED 1993	$ 12.50	$ 28.00
	NOTES	For same subject, full size, in porcelain, see: 1989 #7986-3.					
SM89-18	ALL FALL DOWN MINIATURES (1.5")	7617-1	Pewter	SET OF 4	RETIRED 1993	25.00	35.00
		For same subject, full size, in porcelain, see: 1989 #7984-7.					
SM89-19	FINDING FALLEN STARS MINIATURES (1.5")	7618-0	Pewter	SET OF 2	RETIRED 1992	12.50	35.00
		For same subject, full size, in porcelain, see: 1989 #7985-5.					
SM89-20	FROSTY FROLIC LAND MINIATURE ACCESSORY (16" X 8")	7619-8	Resin	SET OF 4	CURRENT	96.00	96.00
SM89-21	COLLECTOR'S SIGN MINIATURE ACCESSORY (1.5")	7620-1	Pewter	NO	CURRENT	7.00	7.00

SNOWBABIES MINIATURES

SM90-1

TWINKLE LITTLE STARS
Three Snowbabies sing carols.

SM90-2

READ ME A STORY!
Snowbaby reads story to penguins

SM90-3

PLAYING GAMES IS FUN!
Snowbabies play London Bridge
with penguins.

SM90-4

A SPECIAL DELIVERY
Snowbaby on snowshoes delivers star.

ART CHART #	NAME TYPE OF PRODUCT	ITEM #	MATERIAL	SET?	● MARKET STATUS	ORIGINAL SRP	GREENBOOK TRUMKT PRICE
					NOTES		
SM90-1	TWINKLE LITTLE STARS MINIATURES (1.25")	7621-0	Pewter	SET OF 2	RETIRED 1993	$ 15.00	$ 28.00
	For same subject, full size, in porcelain, see: 1990 #7942-1.						
SM90-2	READ ME A STORY! MINIATURE (1.25")	7622-8	Pewter	NO	CURRENT	11.00	11.00
	For same subject, full size, in porcelain, see: 1990 #7945-6.						
SM90-3	PLAYING GAMES IS FUN! MINIATURES (1.25")	7623-6	Pewter	SET OF 2	RETIRED 1993	13.50	22.00
	For same subject, full size, in porcelain, see: 1990 #7947-2.						
SM90-4	A SPECIAL DELIVERY MINIATURE (1.25")	7624-4	Pewter	NO	RETIRED 1993	7.00	14.00
	For same subject, full size, in porcelain, see: 1990 #7948-0.						

SNOWBABIES MINIATURES

SM91-1

WHY DON'T YOU TALK TO ME?
Snowbaby asks snowman a question.

SM91-2

WISHING ON A STAR
Penguin watches Snowbaby holding up star to wish upon.

SM91-3

I'LL PUT UP THE TREE!
Snowbaby holds small tree with star.

SM91-4

I MADE THIS JUST FOR YOU!
Snowbaby carrying a star wreath.

SM91-5

WAITING FOR CHRISTMAS
Two Snowbabies sitting on opposite sides of present - one watches, one naps.

SM91-6

DANCING TO A TUNE
Snowbaby plays concertina as two Snowbabies dance.

SM91-7

IS THAT FOR ME?
One Snowbaby holds present for another.

ART CHART #	NAME / TYPE OF PRODUCT	ITEM #	MATERIAL	SET?	MARKET STATUS / NOTES	ORIGINAL SRP	GREENBOOK TRUMKT PRICE
SM91-1	WHY DON'T YOU TALK TO ME? / MINIATURES (1.5")	7625-2	Pewter	SET OF 2	CURRENT	$ 12.00	$ 12.00
		For same subject, full size, in porcelain, see: 1991 #6801-2.					
SM91-2	WISHING ON A STAR / MINIATURE (1.25")	7626-0	Pewter	NO	CURRENT	10.00	10.00
		For same subject, full size, in porcelain, see: 1990 #7943-0.					
SM91-3	I'LL PUT UP THE TREE! / MINIATURE (1.25")	7627-9	Pewter	NO	CURRENT	9.00	9.00
		For same subject, full size, in porcelain, see: 1991 #6800-4.					
SM91-4	I MADE THIS JUST FOR YOU! / MINIATURE (1.25")	7628-7	Pewter	NO	CURRENT	7.00	7.00
		For same subject, full size, in porcelain, see: 1991 #6802-0.					
SM91-5	WAITING FOR CHRISTMAS / MINIATURE (1.25")	7629-5	Pewter	NO	RETIRED 1993	12.50	22.00
		For same subject, full size, in porcelain, see: 1991 #6807-1.					
SM91-6	DANCING TO A TUNE / MINIATURES (1.5")	7630-9	Pewter	SET OF 3	RETIRED 1993	$ 18.00	32.00
		For same subject, full size, in porcelain, see: 1991 #6808-0.					
SM91-7	IS THAT FOR ME? / MINIATURES (1.5")	7631-7	Pewter	SET OF 2	RETIRED 1993	12.50	18.00
		For same subject, full size, in porcelain, see: 1991 #6803-9.					

SNOWBABIES MINIATURES

SM92-1

LET'S GO SKIING
Snowbaby holds skis.

SM92-2

YOU CAN'T FIND ME!
Snowbaby with penguins playing hide-and-seek.

SM92-3

HELP ME, I'M STUCK!
Snowbaby under pile of stars gets helping hand.

SM92-4

THIS WILL CHEER YOU UP
Snowbabies exchanging star.

SM92-5

I NEED A HUG
Two Snowbabies hug.

SM92-6

WAIT FOR ME!
Snowbaby pushes sled filled with presents and stars as two penguins follow.

SM92-7

SHALL I PLAY FOR YOU?
Snowbaby playing drum.

SM92-8

YOU DIDN'T FORGET ME
Snowbaby getting mail.

ART CHART #	NAME / TYPE OF PRODUCT	ITEM #	MATERIAL	SET?		MARKET STATUS	ORIGINAL SRP	GREENBOOK TRUMKT PRICE
					NOTES			
SM92-1	LET'S GO SKIING MINIATURE (1.5")	7636-8	Pewter	NO		CURRENT	$7.00	$7.00
		For same subject, full size, in porcelain, see: 1992 #6815-2.						
SM92-2	YOU CAN'T FIND ME! MINIATURES (1.5")	7637-6	Pewter	SET OF 4		CURRENT	22.50	22.50
		For same subject, full size, in porcelain, see: 1992 #6818-7.						
SM92-3	HELP ME, I'M STUCK! MINIATURES (1.5")	7638-4	Pewter	SET OF 2		CURRENT	15.00	15.00
		For same subject, full size, in porcelain, see: 1992 #6817-9.						
SM92-4	THIS WILL CHEER YOU UP MINIATURE (1.5")	7639-2	Pewter	NO		CURRENT	13.75	13.75
		For same subject, full size, in porcelain, see: 1992 #6816-0.						
SM92-5	I NEED A HUG MINIATURE (1.5")	7640-6	Pewter	NO		CURRENT	10.00	10.00
		For same subject, full size, in porcelain, see: 1992 #6813-6.						
SM92-6	WAIT FOR ME! MINIATURES (3")	7641-4	Pewter	SET OF 4		CURRENT	22.50	22.50
		For same subject, full size, in porcelain, see: 1992 #6812-8.						
SM92-7	SHALL I PLAY FOR YOU? MINIATURE (1.5")	7642-2	Pewter	NO		CURRENT	7.00	7.00
		For same subject, full size, in porcelain, see: 1992 #6820-9.						
SM92-8	YOU DIDN'T FORGET ME MINIATURES (1.5")	7643-0	Pewter	SET OF 3		CURRENT	17.50	17.50
		For same subject, full size, in porcelain, see: 1992 #6821-7.						

SM92-9

JUST ONE LITTLE CANDLE
Snowbaby holding candle.

SM92-10

JOIN THE PARADE
Snowbaby marching with friends.

ART CHART #	NAME / TYPE OF PRODUCT	ITEM #	MATERIAL	SET?	MARKET STATUS	ORIGINAL SRP	GREENBOOK TRUMKT PRICE
SM92-9	**JUST ONE LITTLE CANDLE** MINIATURE (1.5")	**7644-9**	Pewter	NO	CURRENT	$ 7.00	$ 7.00
	NOTES: For same subject, full size, in porcelain, see: 1992 #6823-3.						
SM92-10	**JOIN THE PARADE** MINIATURES (3")	**7645-7**	Pewter	SET OF 4	CURRENT	22.50	22.50
	NOTES: For same subject, full size, in porcelain, see: 1992 #6824-1.						

SNOWBABIES MINIATURES

SM93-4

LET'S ALL CHIME IN!
Three Snowbabies as bellringers.

SM93-3

WHERE DID HE GO?
Snowbaby and penguin check melting snowman.

SM93-7

WINKEN, BLINKEN, & NOD
Three Snowbabies in star trimmed boat with waves lapping at base. One Snowbaby and penguin scan the horizon. One Snowbaby naps at rear of boat. Middle Snowbaby holds stars.

SM93-2

WILL IT SNOW TODAY?
Snowbaby, penguin, and walrus check weathervane for forecast.

SM93-6

NOW I LAY ME DOWN TO SLEEP
Snowbaby says bedtime prayers.

SM93-1

WE MAKE A GREAT PAIR
Snowbaby friends ice skating.

SM93-5

SOMEWHERE IN DREAMLAND
Snowbabies nap on Moon watched by bear, puffen and penguin.

ART CHART #	NAME / TYPE OF PRODUCT	ITEM #	MATERIAL	SET?	🕯 MARKET STATUS	ORIGINAL SRP	GREENBOOK TRUMKT PRICE
SM93-1	WE MAKE A GREAT PAIR / MINIATURE (1.5")	7652-0	Pewter	NO	CURRENT	$ 13.50	$ 13.50
		For same subject, full size, in porcelain, see: 1993 # 6843-8.					
SM93-2	WILL IT SNOW TODAY? / MINIATURES (3.5")	7653-8	Pewter	SET OF 5	CURRENT	22.50	22.50
		For same subject, full size, in porcelain, see: 1993 # 6844-6.					
SM93-3	WHERE DID HE GO? / MINIATURES (1.75")	7654-6	Pewter	SET OF 4	CURRENT	20.00	20.00
		For same subject, full size, in porcelain, see: 1993 # 6841-1.					
SM93-4	LET'S ALL CHIME IN! / MINIATURES (1.75")	7655-4	Pewter	SET OF 2	CURRENT	20.00	20.00
		For same subject, full size, in porcelain, see: 1993 # 6845-4.					
SM93-5	SOMEWHERE IN DREAMLAND / MINIATURES (3.0")	7656-2	Pewter	SET OF 5	CURRENT	30.00	30.00
		For same subject, full size, in porcelain, see: 1993 # 6840-3.					
SM93-6	NOW I LAY ME DOWN TO SLEEP / MINIATURE (1.25")	7657-0	Pewter	NO	CURRENT	7.00	7.00
		For same subject, full size, in porcelain, see: 1993 # 6839-0.					
SM93-7	WINKEN, BLINKEN, & NOD / MINIATURES (2.0")	7658-9	Pewter	SET OF 2	CURRENT	27.50	27.50
		For same subject, full size, in porcelain, see: 1992 # 6814-4.					

SNOW VILLAGE RETIRED BUILDINGS

5000-8	1984	Town Hall	5034-2	1985	Congregational Church
5001-3	1979	Mountain Lodge	5035-0	1986	Trinity Church
5001-6	1985	Grocery	5036-9	1985	Summit House
5002-1	1979	Gabled Cottage	5037-7	1986	New School House
5002-4	1984	Victorian Cottage	5039-3	1986	Parish Church
5003-2	1985	Governor's Mansion	5041-5	1986	Waverly Place
5003-9	1979	The Inn	5042-3	1986	Twin Peaks
5004-0	1986	Turn Of The Century	5043-1	1986	2101 Maple
5004-7	1979	Country Church	5044-0	1991	Village Market
5005-4	1979	Steepled Church	5045-8	1986	Stucco Bungalow
5005-9	1986	Main Street House	5046-6	1988	Williamsburg House
5006-2	1979	Small Chalet	5047-4	1987	Plantation House
5006-7	1989	St. Anthony Hotel & Post Office	5048-2	1988	Church Of The Open Door
5007-0	1979	Victorian House	5049-0	1987	Spruce Place
5007-5	1986	Stratford House	5050-4	1987	Duplex
5008-3	1987	Haversham House	5051-2	1988	Depot And Train With 2 Train Cars
5008-8	1979	Mansion			
5009-1	1985	Galena House	5052-0	1987	Ridgewood
5009-6	1979	Stone Church	5054-2	1982	Victorian
5010-5	1987	River Road House	5054-7	1990	Kenwood House
5011-2	1984	Homestead	5055-9	1981	Knob Hill
5012-0	1980	General Store	5056-7	1981	Brownstone
5012-1	1986	Delta House	5057-5	1981	Log Cabin
5013-0	1989	Snow Village Factory	5058-3	1984	Countryside Church
5013-8	1980	Cape Cod	5059-1	1980	Stone Church
5014-6	1986	Nantucket	5060-1	1988	Lincoln Park Duplex
5015-3	1979	Skating Rink / Duck Pond Set	5060-9	1982	School House
			5061-7	1981	Tudor House
5015-6	1986	Bayport	5062-5	1980	Mission Church
5016-1	1989	Small Double Trees	5062-8	1988	Sonoma House
5017-2	1984	Skating Pond	5063-3	1980	Mobile Home
5019-9	1990	Cathedral Church	5063-6	1988	Highland Park House
5019-9	1984	Street Car	5065-2	1988	Beacon Hill House
5020-2	1984	Centennial House	5065-8	1982	Giant Trees
5021-0	1984	Carriage House	5066-0	1988	Pacific Heights House
5022-9	1984	Pioneer Church	5066-6	1980	Adobe House
5023-7	1984	Swiss Chalet	5067-4	1981	Cathedral Church
5024-5	1983	Bank	5067-9	1989	Ramsey Hill House
5025-3	1984	Gingerbread House	5068-2	1982	Stone Mill House
5026-1	1984	Village Church	5068-7	1988	Saint James Church
5027-0	1990	Springfield House	5070-9	1982	Colonial Farm House
5028-8	1986	Gothic Church	5071-7	1988	Carriage House
5029-6	1985	Parsonage	5071-7	1982	Town Church
5030-0	1988	Lighthouse	5072-5	1984	Wooden Clapboard
5031-8	1985	Wooden Church	5073-3	1982	English Cottage
5032-6	1984	Fire Station	5073-3	1990	Toy Shop
5033-4	1985	English Tudor	5074-1	1984	Barn

SNOW VILLAGE RETIRED BUILDINGS continued

5076-8	1990	Apothecary
5076-8	1983	Corner Store
5077-6	1983	Bakery
5077-6	1991	Bakery
5078-4	1987	Diner
5078-4	1982	English Church
5080-6	1989	Large Single Tree
5081-4	1983	Gabled House
5081-4	1992	Red Barn
5082-2	1983	Flower Shop
5082-2	1991	Jefferson School
5083-0	1984	New Stone Church
5084-9	1984	Chateau
5085-6	1985	Train Station With 3 Train Cars
5089-0	1992	Farm House
5091-1	1989	Fire Station No. 2
5092-0	1989	Snow Village Resort Lodge
5114-4	1991	Jingle Belle Houseboat
5119-5	1992	Colonial Church
5120-9	1992	North Creek Cottage
5121-7	1990	Maple Ridge Inn
5122-5	1992	Village Station And Train
5123-3	1992	Cobblestone Antique Shop
5124-1	1991	Corner Cafe
5125-0	1990	Single Car Garage
5126-8	1991	Home Sweet Home/ House & Windmill
5127-6	1992	Redeemer Church
5128-4	1991	Service Station
5141-1	1990	Palos Verdes
5142-0	1993	Paramount Theater
5143-8	1992	Doctor's House
5144-6	1993	Courthouse
5145-4	1992	Village Warming House
5149-7	1992	J. Young's Granary
5151-9	1992	56 Flavors Ice Cream Parlor
5152-7	1992	Morningside House
5153-5	1993	Mainstreet Hardware
5154-3	1993	Village Realty
5155-1	1992	Spanish Mission Church
5156-0	1993	Prairie House
5401-1	1993	The Honeymooner Motel
5405-4	1993	Finklea's Finery

SNOW VILLAGE RETIRED ACCESSORIES

5018-0	1990	Snowman With Broom		5133-0	1991	Water Tower
5038-5	1985	Scottie With Tree		5134-9	1993	Kids Decorating The
5040-7	1988	Monks-A-Caroling				Village Sign
5053-9	1987	Singing Nuns		5136-5	1990	Woody Station Wagon
5056-3	1987	Snow Kids Sled, Skis		5137-3	1991	School Bus,
5057-1	1988	Family Mom/Kids,				Snow Plow
		Goose/Girl		5147-0	1992	Choir Kids
5059-8	1988	Santa/Mailbox		5148-9	1990	Special Delivery
5064-1	1986	Carolers		5158-6	1993	Down The Chimney
5069-0	1986	Ceramic Car				He Goes
5079-2	1986	Ceramic Sleigh		5159-4	1993	Sno-jet Snowmobile
5094-6	1990	Kids Around The Tree		5160-8	1992	Sleighride
5095-4	1987	Girl/Snowman, Boy		5161-6	1992	Here We Come
5096-2	1988	Shopping Girls With				A Caroling
		Packages		5162-4	1992	Home Delivery
5102-0	1988	3 Nuns W/Songbooks		5163-2	1993	Fresh Frozen Fish
5103-9	1988	Praying Monks		5168-3	1991	Kids Tree House
5104-7	1989	Children In Band		5169-1	1992	Bringing Home
5105-5	1990	Caroling Family				The Tree
5107-1	1990	Christmas Children		5170-5	1991	Skate Faster Mom
5108-0	1989	For Sale Sign		5172-1	1991	Through The Woods
5109-8	1993	Village Park Bench		5173-0	1991	Statue Of Mark Twain
5113-6	1990	Snow Kids		5174-8	1991	Calling All Cars
5116-0	1992	Man On Ladder		5179-9	1990	Mailbox
		Hanging Garland		5197-7	1992	Special Delivery
5117-9	1990	Hayride		5409-7	1993	Winter Fountain
5118-7	1990	School Children		5411-9	1992	Come Join The Parade
5129-2	1990	Apple Girl/		5412-7	1992	Village Marching Band
		Newspaper Boy		5414-3	1993	Snowball Fort
5130-6	1991	Woodsman And Boy		5415-1	1993	Country Harvest
5131-4	1992	Doghouse/Cat In		6459-9	1984	Monks-A-Caroling
		Garbage Can		8183-3	1991	Sisal Tree Lot

MEADOWLAND RETIRED PIECES

5050-0	1980	Thatched Cottage
5051-8	1980	Countryside Church
5052-6	1980	Aspen Trees
5053-4	1980	Sheep

DICKENS' VILLAGE RETIRED BUILDINGS

5550-6	1992	David Copperfield		5926-9	1993	The Mermaid
5550-6	1992	Mr. Wickfield				Fish Shoppe
		Solicitor		5926-9	1993	White Horse Bakery
5550-6	1992	Betsy Trotwood's		5926-9	1993	Walpole Tailors
		Cottage		5927-7	1991	Ivy Glen Church
5550-6	1992	Peggotty's Seaside		6507-2	1989	Dickens' Lane Shops
		Cottage		6507-2	1989	Thomas Kersey
5553-0	1993	Oliver Twist				Coffee House
5553-0	1993	Brownlow House		6507-2	1989	Cottage Toy Shop
5553-0	1993	Maylie Cottage		6507-2	1989	Tuttles Pub
5567-0	1992	Bishops Oast House		6508-0	1990	Blythe Pond
5583-2	1991	Cobles Police Station				Mill House
5584-0	1992	Theatre Royal		6515-3	1988	The Original Shops Of
5900-5	1989	Barley Bree				Dickens' Village
5900-5	1989	Farmhouse		6515-3	1988	Crowntree Inn
5900-5	1989	Barn		6515-3	1988	Candle Shop
5902-1	1990	Counting House &		6515-3	1988	Green Grocer
		Silas Thimbleton		6515-3	1988	Golden Swan Baker
		Barrister		6515-3	1988	Bean And Son
5916-1	1988	Kenilworth Castle				Smithy Shop
5924-2	1990	Cobblestone Shops		6515-3	1988	Abel Beesley Butcher
5924-2	1990	The Wool Shop		6515-3	1988	Jones & Co. Brush &
5924-2	1990	Booter And Cobbler				Basket Shop
5924-2	1990	T. Wells Fruit &		6516-1	1989	Dickens' Village
		Spice Shop				Church
5925-0	1991	Nicholas Nickleby		6518-8	1988	Dickens' Cottages
5925-0	1991	Nicholas Nickleby		6518-8	1988	Thatched Cottage
		Cottage		6518-8	1988	Stone Cottage
5925-0	1991	Wackford Squeers		6518-8	1988	Tudor Cottage
		Boarding School		6528-5	1989	Chadbury Station
5926-9	1993	Merchant Shops				And Train
5926-9	1993	Poulterer		6549-8	1989	Brick Abbey
5926-9	1993	Geo. Weeton				
		Watchmaker				

ALPINE VILLAGE RETIRED BUILDINGS

5615-4	1993	Bahnhof
5952-8	1989	Josef Engel Farmhouse
6541-2	1991	Alpine Church

NEW ENGLAND VILLAGE RETIRED BUILDINGS

5931-5	1989	Weston Train Station	5954-4	1993	Ichabod Crane's Cottage
5939-0	1990	Cherry Lane Shops	5955-2	1993	Sleepy Hollow Church
5939-0	1990	Ben's Barbershop	6530-7	1989	New England Village
5939-0	1990	Otis Hayes	6530-7	1989	Apothecary Shop
		Butcher Shop	6530-7	1989	General Store
5939-0	1990	Anne Shaw Toys	6530-7	1989	Livery Stable &
5940-4	1991	Ada's Bed And			Boot Shop
		Boarding House	6530-7	1989	Steeple Church
5942-0	1991	Berkshire House	6530-7	1989	Brick Town Hall
5943-9	1992	Jannes Mullet Amish	6530-7	1989	Red Schoolhouse
		Farm House	6530-7	1989	Nathaniel Bingham
5944-7	1992	Jannes Mullet Amish			Fabrics
		Barn	6538-2	1989	Jacob Adams Farmhouse
5954-4	1993	Sleepy Hollow			& Barn
5954-4	1993	Sleepy Hollow School	6539-0	1990	Steeple Church
5954-4	1993	Van Tassel Manor	6544-7	1990	Timber Knoll Log Cabin

CHRISTMAS IN THE CITY RETIRED BUILDINGS

5543-3	1993	Arts Academy
5961-7	1989	Sutton Place Brownstones
5962-5	1990	The Cathedral
5963-3	1989	Palace Theatre
5968-4	1991	Chocolate Shoppe
5969-2	1991	City Hall
5970-6	1992	Hank's Market
5972-2	1990	Variety Store
5977-3	1992	5607 Park Ave Townhouse
5978-1	1992	5609 Park Ave Townhouse
6512-9	1990	Christmas In The City
6512-9	1990	Toy Shop & Pet Store
6512-9	1990	Bakery
6512-9	1990	Tower Restaurant

NORTH POLE RETIRED BUILDING

5600-6	1993	Santa's Workshop

HERITAGE VILLAGE RETIRED ACCESSORIES

5535-2	1992	Busy Sidewalks
5545-0	1993	All Around The Town
5551-4	1992	David Copperfield Characters
5554-9	1993	Oliver Twist Characters
5570-0	1993	Carolers On The Doorstep
5578-6	1992	Royal Coach
5579-4	1991	Constables
5580-8	1992	VioletVendor/Carolers/Chestnut Vendor
5608-1	1993	Trimming The North Pole
5610-3	1993	Santa's Little Helpers
5641-3	1993	Market Day
5901-3	1989	Farm People & Animals
5903-0	1991	Childe Pond And Skaters
5928-5	1990	Fezziwig And Friends
5929-3	1991	Nicholas Nickleby Characters
5934-0	1990	Blacksmith
5941-2	1991	Village Harvest People
5945-5	1991	Farm Animals
5948-0	1992	Amish Family
5949-8	1992	Amish Buggy
5950-1	1989	Silo & Hay Shed
5951-0	1989	Ox Sled
5956-0	1992	Sleepy Hollow Characters
5957-9	1991	Organ Grinder
5958-7	1992	Popcorn Vendor
5959-5	1991	River Street Ice House Cart
5960-9	1993	Christmas In The City Sign
5965-0	1990	City People
5966-8	1988	Shopkeepers
5967-6	1988	City Workers
5971-4	1991	City Newsstand
5981-1	1990	Village Train Trestle
5982-0	1993	One Horse Open Sleigh
5983-8	1991	City Bus & Milk Truck
5985-4	1991	Salvation Army Band
5986-2	1990	Woodcutter And Son
6501-3	1990	Christmas Carol Figures
6510-2	1989	Lighted Tree W/ Children & Ladder
6511-0	1990	Sleighride
6526-9	1990	Carolers
6527-7	1986	Village Train
6531-5	1990	Covered Wooded Bridge
6532-3	1990	New England Winter Set
6537-4	1992	Porcelain Trees
6542-0	1992	Alpine Villagers
6545-5	1990	Skating Pond
6546-3	1990	Stone Bridge
6547-1	1989	Village Well & Holy Cross
6569-2	1993	Dickens' Village Sign
6570-6	1993	New England Village Sign
6571-4	1993	Alpine Village Sign
6589-7	1989	Maple Sugaring Shed
6590-0	1990	Dover Coach

SNOWBABIES RETIRED PIECES

6803-9	1993	Is That For Me?	7964-2	1987	Snowbaby Standing
6807-1	1993	Waiting For Christmas	7965-0	1989	Snowbaby Climbing
7632-5	1993	Playing Games Is Fun			On Snowball
7634-1	1993	Frosty Frolic	7966-9	1989	Snowbabies Hanging
7730-5	1989	Allison & Duncan			Pair
7936-7	1993	Play Me A Tune	7967-7	1987	Catch A Falling Star
7937-5	1992	All Tired Out	7968-5	1990	Don't Fall Off!
		W'globe/Music Box	7969-3	1990	Snowbaby Adrift
7938-3	1993	Peek-A-Boo	7970-7	1987	Snowbaby Holding
7940-5	1992	Penguin Ornament			Picture Frame
7941-3	1992	Polar Bear Ornament	7971-5	1989	Snowbaby Climbing
7942-1	1993	Twinkle Little Stars			On Tree
7946-4	1992	We Will Make It Shine	7972-3	1994	Snowbaby On
7947-2	1993	Playing Games Is Fun!			A Snowball
7950-2	1987	Catch A Falling Star	7973-1	1988	Snowbaby With Wings
7952-9	1990	Snowbaby Sitting	7974-0	1992	Winter Surprise!
7953-7	1992	Snowbaby Crawling	7975-8	1988	Snowbabies Riding
		Ornament			Sleds
7954-5	1990	Snowbaby Winged	7978-2	1992	Polar Express
7955-3	1990	Give Me A Push!	7979-0	1990	Tiny Trio
7957-0	1993	Tumbling In The Snow!	7980-4	1990	Twinkle Little Star
7958-8	1989	Best Friends	7982-0	1993	Helpful Friends
7959-6	1989	Snowbaby Nite Lite	7983-9	1991	Frosty Fun
7961-8	1989	Snowbaby On Brass	7984-7	1991	All Fall Down
		Ribbon Ornament	7986-3	1992	Penguin Parade
7962-6	1992	I'm Making Snowballs!	7992-8	1993	Let It Snow

SNOWBABIES MINIATURES RETIRED PIECES

7605-8	1992	Are All These Mine?
7608-2	1992	Helpful Friends
7609-0	1992	Polar Express
7610-4	1992	Icy Igloo With Tree
7613-9	1993	Frosty Frolic
7614-7	1992	Tumbling In The Snow
7615-5	1993	Tiny Trio
7616-3	1993	Penguin Parade
7617-1	1993	All Fall Down
7618-0	1992	Finding Fallen Stars
7621-0	1993	Twinkle Little Stars
7623-6	1993	Playing Games Is Fun!
7624-4	1993	A Special Delivery
7629-5	1993	Waiting For Christmas
7630-9	1993	Dancing To A Tune
7631-7	1993	Is That For Me?

LIMITED EDITIONS

DICKENS' VILLAGE LIMITED EDITIONS:
5585-9 ...Ruth Marion Scotch Woolen 17,500
5586-7 ...Green Gate Cottage 22,500
5904-8 ...C. Fletcher Public House 12,500
6502-1 ...Norman Church 3,500
6519-6 ...Dickens' Village Mill 2,500
6568-4 ...Chesterton Manor House 7,500

NEW ENGLAND VILLAGE LIMITED EDITIONS:
6543-1 ...Smythe Woolen Mill 7,500

CHRISTMAS IN THE CITY LIMITED EDITIONS:
5549-2 ...Cathedral Church Of St. Mark 17,500   Announced, Actual Production 3,024
5974-9 ...Dorothy's Dress Shop 12,500

SNOWBABIES LIMITED EDITIONS:
6806-3 ...Can I Help, Too? 18,500
7949-9 ...Who Are You? 12,500
7981-2 ...Frosty Frolic 4,800
7985-2 ...Finding Fallen Stars 6,000

EVENT PIECES (all are also Annuals)
5530-1	Gate House	1992
6838-1	Can I Open It Now?	1993
9871-0	Postern	1994

ANNUALS
5441-0	Nantucket Renovation	1993
5809-2	Boarding & Lodging School	1993
9872-8	Dedlock Arms Ornament	1994

SERIES

AMERICAN ARCHITECTURE SERIES (SV)
5156-0	Prairie House
5157-8	Queen Anne Victorian
5403-8	Southern Colonial
5404-6	Gothic Farmhouse
5437-2	Craftsman Cottage

CHARLES DICKENS' SIGNATURE SERIES (HV) (all are also Annuals)
5750-9	Crown & Cricket Inn	1992
5751-7	The Pied Bull Inn	1993
5752-5	Dedlock Arms	1994

Peter George

Greetings, fellow collectors! Welcome to one of the new sections of GREENBOOK, the GREENBOOK Historian. In it you will find answers to some common and not so common questions. Some of these answers are based on fact and others, where necessary, are my opinion. Hopefully, they will answer some of the questions that you may have or assist you in forming your own opinions. Also, to keep things light, I've included a few anecdotes. I think you will find them amusing.

Before going on, let me tell you a little bit about myself and how I became a Department 56 collector. For years, my family and friends had listened to me say how I wanted to buy these Dickens houses that I had seen while traveling.

When my wife, Jeanne, and I became engaged, one of the presents we received from my mother was two of the three Cobblestone Shops. She had seen them in a store near her home in Maine and decided to buy them. When we realized that there was a third building, we started our search for the Wool Shop. While in Virginia, we went into a store to see if we could find it there, but no luck. We did notice, however, other pieces priced at 10 or 20 times their original value. When we questioned the store owner about this, she told us that the pieces retire and can appreciate. I was hooked though Jeanne wasn't really sure why.

Now, I needed to know more and wanted to find retired pieces that I liked. Running up a rather large phone bill over the course of several days, I managed to locate a few. When I located someone selling retired pieces, the routine was the same: "Do you have this piece? How much? I'll take it." "Do you have this piece? How much? I'll take it." "Do you have the Village Mill? How much? I'll think about it!"

Well, when I am very interested in something, I have a habit of immersing myself in it. I wanted to know more, much more. I was told that if I wanted to learn about collectibles, I should attend the International Collectible Exposition in South Bend. So I pointed the car west and headed to South Bend. There, I met people who were publishing information on the villages, but it was not what I was looking for. Come to find out, what I was looking for didn't exist. So, when I returned home, I informed Jeanne that I was going to create an informative publication about these wondrous little houses. She simply nodded her head and said, "O.K., Honey." I figured there had to be other collectors who were searching for the same thing that I was and, I am happy to say, I was right. The result: *the Village Chronicle.*

At the time of this printing, I have published *the Village Chronicle* for three years and have enjoyed every minute of it. I can't think of a better way to make a living. Not only do I work with something I love, but I also get to meet wonderful people throughout the country. There are two things that have made this journey even nicer. One is Jeanne coming to work for the Chronicle as the editor and the other is being asked to be the GREENBOOK Historian. As they say, life doesn't get any better than this.

As for our collection, we have expanded it a little. It now includes not only Dickens' Village, but also Christmas in the City, North Pole, Snowbabies, Snowbunnies, Merry Makers, Lite-ups, Winter Silhouette, D56 waterglobes, D56 ornaments (especially older ones) and much of the giftware. Oh yes, we added Snow Village during the past year, too. I was once told there is something in the paint used on Department 56 products that gets you hooked. If you don't want to collect it, don't touch it. I'm glad I didn't listen.

Now that you know a little about me, please read on and enjoy!

I was speaking to a collector recently who told me about an experience he had at a Swap & Sell. He was standing at his table where he had a number of pieces for sale when another collector, apparently fairly new to the hobby, approached, looked matter-of-factly at a Village Mill and asked what the price was. The seller proudly responded "47" knowing that this was a more than fair price for a piece that was commonly being sold for $5000. "I'll take it," the buyer replied while handing over a $100 bill. A bit perplexed, the seller then explained that "47" referred to $4700, not $47. There was no Village Mill sold that day.

Quite often we get calls in our office from collectors who are looking for assistance in determining which variation of a particular piece they own. It isn't too difficult to help them if it is a variation with a mold change or identifying marks. If the piece only has a color change, however, it isn't easy, if at all possible, to do over the phone. An example of this is the New England Village Berkshire House. One day we got a call from a collector who couldn't determine if they had the Williamsburg Blue or Teal variation. After speaking to them for a few minutes it was obvious that they had a good sense of humor so I decided to have a little fun instead of just explaining the difficulty of trying to do this by phone. I began by asking them if they had the piece in front of them. "Yes." Is there a window nearby? Again, "Yes." I instructed them to take the piece over to the window, hold the phone up to the piece and I would let them know which one they had. There was a moment of silence and then laughter. The moral of the story is, if at all possible, have someone who knows the pieces well take a look at them in person. By doing this, there is little room for error.

I like to use these two stories to illustrate my feelings regarding whether or not you should only purchase pieces with a box and sleeve.

At a Swap & Sell that I attended a collector walked up to a table that had a General Store on it. He began to look it over when he noticed that there was also a General Store on the next table. Now, he was looking at the two of them, alternating from one to the other. The major difference between the two was that one of them had no box or sleeve, though it was priced to reflect this. In fact, if there was any other difference, it was that the one with no box or sleeve was the nicer of the two buildings. Back to the story. This selection process went on for quite some time with the collector trying to decide which to buy. By now, this was attracting a little attention. Not only were the two sellers looking on with much interest, a few other collectors and I were also anxious to see which one he would buy. Then came the decision. All eyes and ears were focused on the two General Stores. And he chose...the one with the box for $100 more. As the collector went out the door we thought, there goes a $100 box.

I got a call one day from a collector who wanted to know my opinion on a matter. The question at hand was whether or not they should buy a Chesterton Manor for $600. My first question was, "How many pieces is it in?" They said that it was in fine condition but...it didn't have a box or sleeve. I couldn't believe it, the chance to buy a piece for at least $1000 less than what it usually sells for just because it didn't have a box and sleeve. What a country! My answer was, of course, yes, yes, yes. And if they decided not to buy it, let me know and I would. Do you know what kind of box you could have made for $1000?

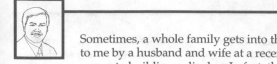

Sometimes, a whole family gets into the displays. This is the case as it was told to me by a husband and wife at a recent event. They are very creative when it comes to building a display. In fact, their display has actual running water in one of its waterways. A few days after setting up the display, the husband noticed that the water was evaporating much more quickly than he would have imagined. During the same time, his wife had realized that their cat had not been drinking his water. When they told each other of their observations, it was clear what was happening. Marvin, the tabby, had been lapping up the babbling brook.

As more collectors are including running water in their displays, they are encountering new and often unexpected situations. This little story is one about a waterway in a display that Marvin the cat, from the previous story, would have surely liked. Jeanne and I were invited to dinner at a collectors home in a neighboring state. When we arrived, the couple proudly showed us their wonderful displays which included Dickens' Village, Alpine Village, North Pole and New England Village. All were exceptionally nice, but the New England display really caught our attention because it had running water. We had seen displays with water in them before, but this was special. There is a small pond on one of the upper levels of the village. From this pond, the water flows through and over rocks making a waterfall as it descends to a lower level. From this point, it flows along a stream that travels under a bridge, along railroad tracks and into a larger pond. From here, the water drains into a bucket where a recirculating pump continuously sends it back up to the upper pond to keep the cycle flowing. Looking closer, we realized that, in the upper pond, there were a number of very small gold fish. What a great touch. But, as we said, there can be unexpected problems. The collectors brought to our attention a small screen in the rocks above the waterfall that prevents their particular problem from reoccurring. It seems that these goldfish are so small they can fit through the spaces in the rocks. You guessed it! These little guys went for a long swim. Through the rocks and over the waterfall they went. They continued down the stream, under the bridge, past the tracks, into the pond and through the drain hole. Plop...into the bucket. From here they were rescued by the collectors who, after installing the screen, placed them back into the upper pond.

As I travel throughout the country, I often have a slight problem with clashing of accents. Having been born and raised here, I have a Rhode Island accent which can be best described as a cross between Boston and Brooklyn accents. We have a habit of not pronouncing "R's" when we should, yet we do place them where they do not belong. Below are two situations where my accent has confused others and myself!

While giving a seminar on the secondary market, I began to talk about buying and selling pieces with flaws and how different types of *flaws* affect the value of a piece. One collector who was obviously confused by this topic raised their hand and asked if I was referring to the base of a building because they were not aware of any buildings with *floors* in them, let alone different types.

Jeanne and I were the guests of a Collectors' Club in the Midwest and had dinner with a few of the collectors before the meeting. During dinner, we were discussing different Department 56 collectibles and, wanting to mention the Upstairs Downstairs Bears, I asked if anyone collected bears. One of the collectors then turned to me and said no, but her husband collected steins. At that point I was confused and did not realize the confusion that my accent had caused. For Rhode Islanders, "bear" and "beer" are pronounced alike.

I was giving a Seminar at an Event and was asked by a collector if they should ever consider buying a piece that was chipped, had a flaw, or cracked. I answered that if the problem with the piece didn't bother them and it was priced where they thought it was a good buy, then certainly they should consider it and actually buy it if they wanted. After all, some pieces are priced out of the range of some collectors and, if they really want that piece, buying one with a flaw of some type may be the only way they could afford it. I went on to tell the group that, in the next room at the Swap & Sell, there was a Palace Theatre that had a small piece broken off of one of the back bottom corners, but it was selling for only $425 (at this time, they were averaging $900). Well, now I know how a teacher feels when the bell rings. About 10 collectors immediately stood up and left the room. The first one to find the right table left with a great buy.

With all of the Gatherings, Open Houses and other events taking place across the country, there are a few problems that often arise as collectors travel to attend them. One of the dilemmas that is usually overlooked (especially by first—time attendees to a distant event) is how to get the items that you bought safely back to your home.

One instance was at a large, weekend-long event. At the end, there were two couples who were leaving in the same car. Witnessing their predicament, it became rather obvious that they either had not planned on, or not realized, how much room the houses, accessories and other items that they purchased would take. The problem was magnified by the fact that they were driving a compact car. Their first move was to put packages in the hatchback. This was followed by having the two women sitting in the back seat load packages on their laps and up to the roof. Next, one of the men sat in the passenger's seat while the other man loaded him up with bundles. Finally, the driver got in and, as the car went down the street, it was difficult to tell that there was anyone other than the driver inside.

Don't get me wrong, not realizing how much room will be needed in the car is not an experience of the novice alone. Jeanne and I found ourselves in a similar situation. The problem occurred after an event that took place halfway across the country. I had driven to the event and Jeanne, having work to finish in the office, had taken a flight two days later and met me there. When the event concluded, we had taken our displays and other items from our booth outside to be loaded into the car. What we had not realized was that, though everything had fit in the car for the ride out, we had not considered Jeanne's luggage or Jeanne for that matter, for the ride back. (I had loaded so much into the car before leaving home that even the passenger's seat was full.) It took us about an hour of loading and unloading, but we finally managed to make enough room to leave the passenger's seat available for Jeanne. This was not the end, however. Since Jeanne had driven the car from its parking space to the loading area, the driver's seat was close to the steering wheel. So close, in fact, that I couldn't get in the car. And, with the car packed to the inch, the seat couldn't be pushed back. After another hour of loading and unloading, we were on our way.

But, traveling is not restricted to driving. What do you do with all your purchases when you fly? Two couples who live in the northeast had given this matter some thought before an event. They would be flying and knew that we would be driving. They asked if there would be enough room in the car to take the pieces that they would purchase home with us. I told them that we would take anything that they could fit in the back seat. Furthermore, for one retired piece and the price of one bus ticket, I would take anything they could fit in the passenger's seat as well.

Q: *Is it advisable to purchase any pieces that do not have a box or sleeve? How much does not having a box or sleeve effect the value of a piece on the secondary market?*

A: Anyone who has attended one of my seminars has certainly heard my views on this subject which is there is no right or wrong answer. How's that for a definite maybe?

Actually, the answer depends on the particular piece that you are purchasing and why. If you are buying a piece from a primary dealer, certainly you should always try to get a box and sleeve. There would be few reasons to buy a current piece without these. When you are buying a piece on the secondary market, however, things are not as simple. Before deciding if you should buy a piece without a box or sleeve, you should take a few things into consideration. First, are you buying the piece for your own enjoyment or for investment? If for investment, by all means, try to get a piece with a box and sleeve. It will be much easier to sell on the secondary market and will command a higher price. If buying for enjoyment, however, don't let the fact that it doesn't have a box or sleeve make you pass on it. If it is a piece that you really like and it is priced fairly, buy it. Always remember, you are buying a building or accessory and they are what really matters. The box and sleeve are just that - a box and sleeve.

There is no hard and fast rule to how much less a piece without a box and sleeve should sell for on the secondary market. A starting place would be approximately 10% less than a piece of the same quality with a box and sleeve. You have to keep in mind that this is only a reference point and that the percentage usually increases as the dollar value decreases. Let me explain. If you had a piece worth $500, then the same piece would be worth roughly $450 without the box and sleeve. The buyer and seller could use that as a starting point to negotiate the final selling price. If you took 10% off a piece averaging $100, however, a buyer would most likely opt to pass on the $90 price and spend the extra $10 to get one with a box and sleeve.

You may have noticed that in the above paragraph I specifically compared pieces "of the same quality." What I mean by this is that before being able to compare the actual cost of pieces, you should be certain that those pieces are of equal quality. A high quality building or accessory without a box and sleeve is worth every bit as much or more than a like piece of lower quality with a box and sleeve.

Q: *We have heard terms like factory flaw, firing crack and others. What are the differences in the types of flaws?*

A: I'll try to explain what the terms mean for the more common problems that you may see. *Factory Flaw* is a term that encompasses many imperfections that would have occurred at the factory during the manufacturing of the piece. One of these imperfections is a *chip*. A chip that is a factory flaw differs from an ordinary chip in that it, more than likely, would have occurred before the painting process. Because of this, it will have paint over the area where the piece has been broken off. A piece that was chipped later would show porcelain or ceramic at the break. Another factory flaw would be a *Firing Line*. This is a line that develops in the piece during the firing process. It resembles a thin pencil line on the piece though you cannot feel or remove it.

A close relative to the firing line is the *Firing Crack*. This also occurs during the firing process yet can actually be felt when running your fingernail over it. Other flaws that would be referred to as factory flaws include paint that may have been inadvertently rubbed off leaving the porcelain or ceramic to show through. This happens occasionally on the corners of roofs. Also, any mark or impression in the porcelain or ceramic that would have been made while the piece was still wet would fit under this heading. Flaws that occur after a piece is manufactured can be just about anything imaginable. This would include, but not be limited to, cracks and chips, missing attachments (you should be able to tell if a missing attachment was never put on at the factory or broken off later by looking to see if the piece is painted or not where the attachment should have been), and attachments that have been broken off and glued back into position.

Q: *Does a piece that has been signed by the artist who designed it have a higher value than one that has not been signed?*

A: Generally, a piece that has been signed by the artist will sell for more than its normal secondary value. There does not appear to be a high demand for these pieces relative to the piece without a signature. One signature that has demanded a $50 higher price is that of Jeanne-Marie Dickens. Crown & Cricket Inns that are accompanied by a certificate of authenticity that bears her signature have sold well on the secondary market.

One problem that does present itself when you have the opportunity to purchase a signed piece is how can you be certain that the signature is truly that of the person to whom it is said to belong. This doesn't seem to have been a problem, though, with Department 56 pieces.

Q: *I am familiar with the term "variation," but have also heard the term "mistake." How do they differ?*

A: A variation, as you may know, is a piece that is different in some fashion than other forms of the same piece. The most notable variations are mold changes. This term is applied when a piece has been made from one mold design and then subsequent pieces are made from another mold design. An example of this is the New England Village Ada's Bed & Boarding where the rear steps, among other features, changed. They were part of the main building in the first mold and became a separate piece that was joined to the main building in the second mold.

Another type of variation is a color change. Though usually not as dramatic a change as that of a mold change, many collectors seek these variations as well. Some color variations are very dramatic, however. Examples include Peggotty's Cottage which was first issued with the unpainted hull (commonly referred to as the white or tan Peggotty's) and later produced with the green hull. Also, the Dickens' Village Church has been produced in five or possibly more known colors. In both of these examples the different colors command different prices on the secondary market. This is not the case with every piece, though. For instance, take the Norman Church. The lower numbered pieces are painted light gray that shows a lot of detail in the bricks. As the numbers get higher, they are painted with a darker gray. There is no difference in the secondary market price for either.

Yet another type of variation is changes in the embossment on the bottom of a piece. This has happened on a few occasions and collectors have differentiated between the embossments. The Nicholas Nickleby Cottage is a prime example of this. The first shipment of these had Nic"k"olas Nickleby stamped on the bottom. This was soon corrected to the proper Nicholas Nickleby. Collectors are apt to pay $25 to $50 more for the one with the "k." (By the way, have you ever noticed that Dept. 56 spelled the name on the box for the characters, Nicholas Nick"el"by?) It was an odd turn of events when a similar thing happened with the Blythe Pond. This had a twist, however. The first release of the piece was fine, but future releases had the name embossed on the bottom as By The Pond. Somewhere, they lost the "L." You would think that the incorrect version would be worth more, right? Wrong. Because there are many more incorrect pieces available, the correct version commands the higher price on the secondary market. This is a perfect example of how you never know what will be until it is.

Now for mistakes. Say, for instance, you have a Chocolate Shoppe with a sign turned upside down. This is a mistake. A building that never had one of the chimneys attached is also one. Pieces like these, where they may be literally one-of-a-kind, actually would sell for no more than a "normal" piece on the secondary market and possibly would sell for less. This may seem odd, but there is rarely demand for a piece such as this since no one would know to be looking for it. If you tried to sell it, a collector would most likely rather buy one that was correct. Should you find yourself with one of these, think of it as having a piece that no one else , or at least very few people, have.

Q: *Who sets the prices of the pieces on the secondary market?*

A: Actually, you do. What I mean is the collector who buys on the secondary market does. All the prices are set by supply and demand. If supply is short and demand is high, the asking price of a piece goes higher. At some point, when the price reaches a level where collectors are no longer willing to pay that price, supply will increase and, coupled with the low demand, the price will recede. Again, at a certain point determined only by the market, demand will increase and likewise the price.

The Cathedral Church of Saint Mark is a perfect example. When collectors were buying them as quickly as they could locate them on the secondary market, prices skyrocketed to $4000 and more in a matter of months. As the demand decreased, prices receded to half that. Recently, prices have begun to rise again.

Q: *Why are some items listed as "retired" and others as "discontinued?"*

A: Department 56 applies the word "retired" to buildings, accessories, Snowbabies and other collectibles when they are no longer being manufactured. "Discontinued" is applied to trees, trim and other non-collectible items once they are no longer being produced.

Q: *Would you suggest buying the villages as an investment?*

A: I have always suggested to collectors that they purchase the villages because they like them. To me this has always been the best investment because no matter what happens to their value, you will always have the pleasure they bring. If you do purchase village pieces for investment, however, be certain to learn as much as you can about the pieces you intend to buy - as you would with any investment. This includes the issue price, the current value, the 6-month and 1-year value history, which variation it is (if applicable), etc. With this information, you should be able to make a decision. Of course, one of the major factors in the decision is how much you will be paying for the piece. Keep in mind that, as with many investments, your capital is at risk.

Q: *Is there a way to be certain that I will be able to buy a limited edition when they become available?*

A: There is no way to guarantee that you will have the opportunity to purchase a limited edition, but you can improve your chances. The best way, in my opinion, is to support one dealer. In turn, that dealer will try to support you. Notice two things in these last two sentences. First, I said support "one" dealer. By doing this, you become more important to that dealer. It is then in their best interest to support you so that you will continue to make your purchases at their store. Second, is that the dealer will "try" to support you. Unfortunately, there are occasions when a dealer gets fewer pieces than they have valued customers. When this is the case, some collectors will unfortunately be disappointed. Many collectors who collect more than one village purchase pieces for one village at one store and pieces for another village at another store. This, they feel, will make them a valued customer at both stores.

Visit your dealer often, even when you are not making a purchase. Talk to them, ask for their advice, let them know who you are. By doing this, you will be in the dealer's mind when they are making a list of their best customers.

Q: *Should I be wary of buying retired pieces through brokers or classified ads?*

A: I believe that in any transaction you should be cautious. Before making any purchase, be it through a secondary market dealer or broker or through classified ads, there are a few things that you will want to know. First is the reputation of the person or company with whom you will be dealing. Ask fellow collectors if they know of them and what they have heard. You will find that most dealers and brokers enjoy an excellent reputation. Second, know what you are buying. If there are variations of the piece, for example, be certain that you and the seller are speaking of the same one. Next, you need to know the price. This sounds obvious, but it is important to know what the final cost to you will be including shipping and any additional fees. Equally important, you will want to know the condition of the piece, i.e. if it has flaws, chips, crack, etc. and if it has the box and sleeve. Knowing this, you will be able to determine if the price is fair. When dealing with a secondary market dealer or broker, be sure to ask them about their return policy in case you find a problem with the piece. Many dealers and brokers have very reasonable policies that allow you to inspect the piece before considering the deal final. Some, though this is usually the exception, do not. In any case, find out all the details.

When buying through classified ads, you will want to know the same information as dealing with dealers and brokers. Though most people selling through classifieds are individual collectors and do not have a return "policy," you will still want to discuss with them what happens if there is a problem with the piece. Many collectors are very wary of buying through classified ads, but I have purchased many pieces in this manner and have never encountered a problem. If this idea still makes you nervous, purchase your pieces through an established and reputable dealer or broker and you should be very pleased.

Q: *I have heard two terms, secondary dealer and secondary broker. What are the differences, if any?*

A: Both of these terms are used for people or companies who sell retired pieces. When a collector is making a purchase on the secondary market, there is little difference between the two and there is no advantage to buy from one or the other. The major difference between them is the method in which they obtain pieces that they sell. A dealer usually buys the pieces outright. They may have purchased the pieces from a retailer before the items retired and held them until they appreciated in value. Likewise, they may have purchased them from a collector and are reselling them. A broker, on the other hand, generally does not own the pieces he/she is selling. They list the pieces for collectors and act as the intermediary when a sale is made. The seller ships the piece to the broker and the buyer pays the broker. The broker then ships the piece to the buyer and sends the funds, less the broker's commission, to the seller.

Q: *I would like to know more about restored pieces. Should you buy a piece that has been restored? How can you tell if a piece has been restored?*

A: The subject of restoring pieces can be a delicate one. There are certain topics for which collectors have developed a strong opinion and this is one of them. Many collectors believe that if a piece is broken in any manner, it should not be restored. The fear of a restored piece being resold as if it was in its original condition is the basis for their reasoning. At least, they feel, the piece should be marked "restored" in order to declare its condition to a prospective buyer.

On the other hand, just as many collectors see no reason not to have a piece restored should it become damaged. Why should you have to look at a piece that is broken? After all, if your car is damaged, you have it restored. And, the auto repair shop does not mark the car as such. It is left to the owner's honesty to let the buyer know that it's not in its original condition.

One might argue that when buying a car there are methods that can be used to discover any body work that has been done. This is also true with collectibles. A black light, when directed towards a collectible, will cause foreign matter, such as glue, to glow. Many of us have suggested to producers of swap & sells to make available an area where collectors can inspect under a black light a piece they intend to buy. Remember, the percentage of collectibles that have been restored is extremely low. The chances of you purchasing a piece that has been restored and you not knowing it are just as low.

If you have a piece that is damaged and want to have it restored, be sure to have it done by a competent restoration expert. You can locate them in several ways. These include recommendations from other collectors or dealers, referring to the Yellow Pages under the heading of "Dolls - Repair" and consulting a local museum. Before having any work done, ask to view pieces on which they have worked. Also, ask for references and check them. An unqualified person may do more harm to a piece than the original damage.

Q: *Do you think that it is worth having my collection insured?*

A: Insuring your collection is a personal decision and one truly worth considering. Since most of us have many of our valuables insured against loss or damage, I think that we would be inclined to do the same with collectibles, especially those that are worth a significant amount of money. Insuring collectibles, however, is not as simple as insuring other property. Collectibles that have not appreciated in value can often be insured on a homeowner's or renter's policy. Those that have appreciated though, usually have to be insured on a separate policy, called a rider or scheduled policy.

Before insuring your collectibles, consult your agent and ask them as many questions as you can think of that pertain to the collectible. Tell them about the history of the collectible and how they retire and appreciate. You should have documentation for the pieces including, but not limited to, sales receipts, photos and / or anything else that the agent suggests. For retired pieces, you will also need documentation of the current value of the pieces. The most current edition of *GREENBOOK* will usually suffice. Above all, read the policy to be certain that it does what you need it to do.

Q: *Is there a difference in a piece that is made in Taiwan, the Philippines and China?*

A: A piece that is manufactured in factories located in all three countries will vary depending on the country of origin. Pieces made in Taiwan generally seem to be more subdued in color. Collectors who have been collecting the villages for years are often attracted to this style since it is what they have become accustomed to. The pieces produced in the Philippines usually have brilliant whites while those manufactured in China have vibrant reds, greens and blues. Once you see an example of a piece that has been made in each country, it becomes fairly easy to recognize the origin of other pieces.

You may also find size differences in a piece that is produced in different countries. Along with the color differences, this will cause multiple variations of a piece, making variations much more common than in the past. The question that arises is will you buy one of each variation? This brings us to another point. Many collectors ask which of the variations they should purchase. Taking into consideration that you will not be buying all three (if there are three, of course), there are usually two schools of thought. One is to purchase the piece when first issued no matter where it was manufactured. The other is to purchase the style that most appeals to you. I, for instance, like the Dickens' Village pieces that are made in Taiwan, but prefer pieces from China for Christmas in the City. Keep in mind that certain pieces may not be produced in the country that you like.

Q: How does Department 56 decide to retire pieces?

A: Department 56 usually does not explain why a piece is retired, but there are various reasons why they would decide to do so. The first reason that comes to mind is that D56 was not able to meet the profit margins that they require. This, in itself, could happen for a number of reasons. One would be that the piece was too difficult to manufacture. As a result, too much time and too many attempts would be necessary to produce a piece that meets their quality requirements. Another reason is a result of the piece's popularity, or lack of it. If collectors do not find a particular piece attractive, then that piece does not sell well. In turn, dealers do not reorder from D56 in as large a quantity as expected. Consequently, D56 produces fewer of these pieces making it less profitable. At this point, D56 would cease production and, at the proper time, retire the piece. When you think about it, it is ironic that a company can stop manufacturing an unpopular item which, in turn, makes it more popular and sell quickly at stores. Wouldn't a company like GM love to be able to say that they were no longer going to produce a car that was not popular and have it sell well as a result? This not being the case, they have to cut prices and offer incentives to both their dealers and the consumer.

Lack of profit is not the only reason that Department 56 decides to retire a piece, nor is it necessarily the primary one. A piece may be retired because it is the right time. By this, I mean that the piece may have been on the market for a few years, run its course and have been selected to retire to make room for a new introduction. Also, a piece could be retired to cause a little excitement. D56 could decide to retire a popular piece in its prime, or just after, and catch collectors off guard. Has this ever been done? Who's to say, but don't doubt it. Sacrificing some short term profits sometimes leads to larger dividends in the long run. And besides, it's trying to outguess D56, as well as understand some of their thinking, that makes retirements so much fun.

Q: Does Department 56 break the molds once a figurine has been retired?

A: Yes, Department 56 does break the mold after retiring a piece. Most companies do this, though it is not a requirement. When a company does break a mold, it is usually done for one of two reasons. It is done either as a ceremonious act showing that they will no longer produce the piece, or simply because they see no reason to warehouse a none productive piece of material.

A company that does not break its molds would not "reissue" a piece that has been retired because it would negatively effect the company's reputation. If a company had any intentions of reissuing a piece, it would "suspend" production as opposed to retiring the piece. In this situation, the company would decide at a later date whether to continue production or actually retire it.

Q: *How would you suggest staying informed about the latest news about Department 56 and the villages? It seems that I learn about things after everyone else.*

A: There are a number of ways to keep up with all the information, events, news and views about Department 56. One great way that is becoming very popular is collectors' clubs. Collectors have started clubs throughout the country and more are formed each day. If there is one in your area, I really suggest joining it for a few reasons. One is that you will meet many friendly people who have the same hobby as you. Also, it is an excellent forum for ideas and information. It is a great way to learn anything from creating displays to when events take place to buying and selling at a swap & sell. If you would like to know if there is a local your club in your area, call our office at *the Village Chronicle* and we will tell you where it is and who to contact.

A way of being informed that is often overlooked is your Department 56 dealer. Get to know your dealer well and ask them when you are in their store if they have heard any news. Very often they have recently learned something from their representative or a collector that they are willing to share.

Another way to keep informed is subscribing to publications that pertain to Department 56. One of these is, of course, *the Village Chronicle*, my publication. *the Village Chronicle* is a bimonthly magazine published to increase the enjoyment of collecting Department 56 Villages, Snowbabies, giftware and related items. Written exclusively about Department 56 collectibles, each issue is packed with news, ideas, display tips, questions & answers, club news, a calendar of Dept. 56 events, classified ads and always much more. In it, you will read articles written by nationally recognized collectors offering their knowledge and experience to others. *the Village Chronicle* keeps you informed about what's new, surprises you with new information on past releases and educates you on how to display them all. It is the magazine that keeps you where you want to be...informed and excited about the best little porcelain houses ever made. It's more than a newsletter and includes information that even D56's publication does not. *the Village Chronicle*, All The News That's Lit To Print.

The greatest part of publishing *the Village Chronicle* is talking to other collectors. If you have any questions that you would like answered or ideas that you would like to share, please call or write.

If you would like to add to your enjoyment of collecting Dept. 56 by subscribing to *the Village Chronicle*, you may do so by either mail or phone. Subscribe today - you won't want to miss an issue!

$21 for one year - 6 issues; $36 for 2 years - 12 issues
Canada residents: $25 for 1 year, $42 for 2 years
Visa & MasterCard accepted

the Village Chronicle
200 Post Road Box 311
Warwick RI 02888-1535
phone: 401-467-9343
fax: 401-467-9359

I look forward to hearing from you and...
May your home be merry and your houses be many!

WINTER SILHOUETTE

	Item #	Name	Status	Last or Current SRP
1987				**1987**
	*7774—7	Carolers Set of 4	Retired 1993 GREENBOOK TRUMARKET Price Not Established	$120.00
	8215—5	Snow Doves Set of 2	Retired 1992 GREENBOOK TRUMARKET Price Not Established	60.00
1988				**1988**
	*5595—6	Joy To The World Music Box	Retired 1990 GREENBOOK TRUMARKET Price Not Established	$ 42.00
	*7771—2	Sleighride	Current	60.00
	*7772—0	Skating Couple	Current	33.00
	*7773—9	Skating Children Set of 2	Current	32.00

302

	*8271—6	Silver Bells Music Box GREENBOOK TRUMARKET Price Not Established	Retired 1990	75.00
1989				**1989**
	6765—2	Three Kings Candle Holder Set of 3 GREENBOOK TRUMARKET Price Not Established	Retired 1992	$ 85.00
	6766—0	Camel W/Glass Votive GREENBOOK TRUMARKET Price Not Established	Retired 1993	25.00
	*7788—7	Father Christmas GREENBOOK TRUMARKET Price Not Established	Retired 1993	50.00
	*7789—5	Putting Up The Tree Set of 3	Current	88.00
	*7790—9	Bringing Home The Tree Set of 4 GREENBOOK TRUMARKET Price Not Established	Retired 1993	75.00
1990 …				**1990 …**
Art Not Available	6767—9	Angel Candle Holder W/Candle GREENBOOK TRUMARKET Price Not Established	Retired 1992	$ 32.50

* Originally part of the Lamplighter Series

WINTER SILHOUETTE

	Item #	Name	Status	Last or Current SRP
... 1990				**... 1990**
	6769—5	Lighted Nativity W/Switch, Cord & Bulb	Current	$ 37.50
	6770—9	Caroling Angel W/Brass Halo & Songbook	Current	15.00
	6771—7	Nativity Scene Set of 4, Antique Reproduction	Current	175.00
	6772—5	Old World Santa	Current	50.00
	*7791—7	Decorating The Mantel Set of 3	Current	60.00
1991				**1991**
	*7792—5	Bedtime Stories	Current	$ 40.00

	*7793—3	Hanging The Ornaments Set of 3	Current	30.00
	7794—1	Angel Candle Holder	Current	95.00
	7795—0	Santa's Sleigh & 4 Reindeer Set of 5	Current	125.00
	7796—8	Santa's Reindeer Set of 2	Current	27.00
	7797—6	Grandfather Clock	Current	27.50
	7798—4	Caroling Bells Set of 3	Current	60.00
	7799—2	Chimney Sweep	Retired 1993 GREENBOOK TRUMARKET Price Not Established	37.50
	7800—0	Town Crier	Current	37.50

* Originally part of the Lamplighter Series

WINTER SILHOUETTE

	Item #	Name	Status	Last or Current SRP
	7801—8	Jolly St. Nicholas	Current	$ 30.00
	7802—6	A Choir Of Angels Votive Holder	Current	18.00
	7803—4	A Choir Angel Candle Holder	Current	13.50
	7804—2	Carols Around The Spinet Set of 4	Current	100.00
	7805—0	Christmas Presents Set of 2	Current	35.00
	7807—7	The Marionette Performance Set of 3	Current	75.00
	7808—5	Cathedral Facade W/Switch, Cord & Bulb	Current	72.00

7835—2	Accompanying A Carol Set of 2	Current	55.00
7836—0	Winter Silhouette Church W/Switch, Cord & Bulb	Current	48.00
7837—9	Snowy White Deer Set of 2	Current	55.00
7838—7	Bedtime Stories Waterglobe, Music Box "Silent Night"	Current	30.00
7839—5	Decorating The Mantel Waterglobe, Music Box "Deck The Halls"	Current	35.00
7840—9	Hanging The Ornaments Waterglobe, Music Box "Oh, Christmas Tree"	Current	35.00
1993 ...			
7841—7	A Visit With Santa Set of 2	Current	$ 55.00
7842—5	Sharing A Christmas Moment Music Box "Brahms' Lullaby"	Current	36.00

* Originally part of the Lamplighter Series

WINTER SILHOUETTE

	Item #	Name	Status	Last or Current SRP ... 1993
	7843—3	A Bright Star On Christmas Eve Set of 2	Current	$ 48.00
	7844—1	Santa Lucia	Current	27.50
	7845—0	A Christmas Kiss Set of 2	Current	32.50

OTHER GUIDES FROM GREENBOOK

Published May 1994
Enesco Collectibles
(Includes Cherished Teddies, Memories Of Yesterday,
The Enesco Treasury Of Christmas Ornaments, Laura's Attic,
North Pole Village, Miss Martha's Collection, Maud Humphrey
Bogart and Lucy & Me)
First Edition
ISBN 0-923628-18-5

Published August 1994
The Enesco Precious Moments Collection
Ninth Edition
ISBN 0-923628-19-3

August 1994
Hallmark Collectibles
Second Edition
ISBN 0-923628-21-5

September 1994
Walt Disney Classics Collection
Premiere Edition
ISBN 0-923628-22-3

GLOSSARY

A CHRISTMAS CAROL

A Christmas story written in 1843 by Charles Dickens; a grouping within Dickens' Village, introduced in 1986

ACCESSORY

Any of the characters, animals, non-lit structures, etc. that are sold to compliment and complete any one of the villages

ADOBE

Sun-dried, unburned brick made of clay and straw; a building made with this type of brick; Adobe-SV

ALLOCATION

A specific number of goods, either in quantity or dollar amount, that a dealer is allowed to purchase

ALLOTMENT

Same as allocation

ALPINE VILLAGE

Third of the Heritage Villages, introduced in 1986; depicts villages found in the Alps

AMERICAN ARCHITECTURE SERIES

A series within the Original Snow Village introduced in 1990

AMISH

A Mennonite sect founded in the 17th century; a grouping of buildings and accessories in the New England Village

ANNUAL

A collectible issued for a single year - sometimes to commemorate an anniversary, holiday or other special date

ARTIST PROOF

Usually, the first piece in the production of an edition that has been reviewed and approved by the artist; most often with lithographs or prints

ATTACHMENTS

Any part of a building or accessory that has been molded separately and then added to the main body with liquid clay

BACHMAN'S

A Minneapolis-based floral supply company from which Department 56 was begun; was the parent company of Department 56 until 1992

BACHMAN'S HOMETOWN SERIES

Introduced in 1987, a short-lived series of three buildings produced exclusively for sale by Bachman's retail stores

BACHMAN'S VILLAGE GATHERING

An event held each summer in Minneapolis featuring Department 56 Villages and related items

BACKSTAMP

The information located on the back of a plate or other item that includes the manufacturer's name, name of the item, year of issue, etc.

BAS-RELIEF

A flat collectible with a raised design

BISQUE

A porcelain, generally white, that has no glaze or enamel applied to it

BOTTOM STAMP

Specific information embossed on the bottom of a piece containing D56 logo, year of introduction, etc.; became standard in 1988; previously could have been hand-carved or even non-existent

CCP

Acronym for Cold Cast Porcelain

CASE MOLD

Often referred to as the master mold, it is produced with a high density composite material that will not wear out as quickly as the more porous production molds

CASTING

The initial step in the production of a porcelain collectible, liquid clay is poured into a production mold and, after being allowed to dry, removed as a semi-firm piece

CERAMIC

A form of clay finished by firing at a high temperature

CERTIFICATE OF AUTHENTICITY

A document that attests to a piece being genuine and its place within a limited edition or production

CHINA

A high quality clay fired at a high temperature; also known as porcelain; the third country to produce Department 56 buildings

CHIP

The location on a piece where a small portion of porcelain has been broken off usually leaving a rough area

CHRISTMAS IN THE CITY

Fourth of the Heritage Villages, introduced in 1989; depicts a large city, possibly Manhattan

CLAY

Any of the earthen materials used to make ceramic items, it becomes hard when fired at high temperatures

COLD CAST PORCELAIN (AKA CCP)

A porcelain piece that is produced by mixing a resin with porcelain dust and forcing it into a mold under high pressure where it is allowed to harden; any of the 25 Dickens' Village and 13 New England Village CCP pieces

GLOSSARY CONTINUED

COMMEMORATIVE

An item specially made to mark an event, anniversary or holiday

DAVID COPPERFIELD

A story written by Charles Dickens; a grouping in Dickens' Village introduced in 1989 and retired in 1992

CHARLES DICKENS

English author born in 1812, died in 1870, he penned many well-known stories including *A Christmas Carol* and others referred to within the Dickens' Village; for whom Department 56's first porcelain village is named

CHARLES DICKENS HERITAGE COLLECTION

A portion of the royalties received by the Dickens Heritage Foundation from the sale of these items are donated for the benefit of the sick and needy in both England and the U.S.

CHARLES DICKENS HERITAGE FOUNDATION

Created in 1991 by the great-great grandson of Charles Dickens, Christopher Dickens, and his wife, Jeanne-Marie, to continue the charitable work of Dickens

CHARLES DICKENS SIGNATURE SERIES

Any of the various products displaying the Crest and Badge and "CD" emblem

JEANNE-MARIE DICKENS

Wife of Christopher Dickens, the great-great grandson of Charles Dickens; Founder and President of the Charles Dickens Heritage Foundation

DICKENS' VILLAGE

First of the Heritage Villages, introduced in 1984, depicts the England written about by Dickens

DISCONTINUED

Refers to an item that is no longer in production

EARTHENWARE

A form of porcelain usually glazed and fired

ERROR

Something that has been incorrectly done when producing a piece; this sometimes, but not always, adds to the value or collectibility of a piece; same as mistake

FACTORY FLAW

Any defect, usually a chip or crack, that happened when the piece was being produced

FIRE

To heat at high temperatures and harden a ceramic or clay material in a kiln

FIRING CRACK

A crack in a ceramic or porcelain product that occurred during the firing of the piece

FIRING PERIOD

The length of time in which a manufacturer produces a fired product

FIRST ISSUE

The first item in a series

GCC

Acronym for Gift Creation Concepts

GLAZE

A liquid material that is applied after firing and before decorating to create a shine

HERITAGE VILLAGE

Encompasses Dickens' Village, New England Village, Alpine Village, Christmas In The City, Little Town Of Bethlehem Collection, North Pole Collection and their accessories; introduced in 1984 with the Original Shops Of Dickens' Village

HISTORY LIST

The common reference for the Snow Village, Heritage Village and Snowbabies brochures that list the entire collections along with their issue date, SRP and retirement date

INCISED

A design that is cut into a piece to create a backstamp or decoration

INTERNATIONAL COLLECTIBLE EXPOSITION

The nation's largest collectible show that is held each summer in South Bend, IN and alternates each spring between Long Beach, CA and Secaucus, NJ

ISSUE PRICE

The suggested retail price of an item when it is first introduced

KNOCK-OFF

A copy of an original, usually crude in quality

LIMITED EDITION

An item that is restricted in quantity by an edition limit of a specific number

LIST PRICE

Usually the suggested retail price determined by the manufacturer

LITE-UPS

Small, porcelain replicas of 17 Dickens' Village and 13 New England Village buildings; each has a hole and clip on the bottom so that it may be clipped to a tree branch and a mini tree light inserted

MASTER MOLD

Often referred to as the case mold, it is produced with a high density composite material that will not wear out as quickly as the more porous production molds

MEADOWLAND SERIES

A ceramic "springtime" series introduced in 1979 and retired in 1980; consisting of two buildings and two sets of accessories, it resembles Snow Village pieces lacking snow

MID-YEAR INTRODUCTIONS

Announcements in May of the new pieces that will be available in the Fall

MINT CONDITION

Signifies that a piece is in its original, like-new condition with all documentation and box

MISTAKE

Something that has been incorrectly done when producing a piece; this sometimes, but not always, adds to the value or collectibility of a piece; same as error

MOLD

The form in which an item is created

MOTHER MOLD

This mold is taken from the clay model and is made with superfine plaster to allow fine details to be impressed into the mold

MS. LIT-TOWN

Department 56's pseudonym for their Public Relations person, Judith Price

NALED

Acronym for an organization for collectible retailers, the National Association Of Limited Edition Dealers

NEW ENGLAND VILLAGE

Second of the Heritage Villages, introduced in 1986, depicts New England, though it also represents the Hudson Valley and Pennsylvania

NICHOLAS NICKLEBY

A story written by Charles Dickens; a grouping in Dickens' Village introduced in 1988 and retired in 1991

NORTH POLE COLLECTION

A Department 56 Village introduced in 1990 depicting the fanciful world of Santa Claus and the North Pole

OLIVER TWIST

A story written by Charles Dickens; a grouping in Dickens' Village introduced in 1991

ORIGINAL SNOW VILLAGE

The first village marketed by Department 56, made of ceramic with a glazed finish, introduced in 1976, depicts "Anytown, USA"

OVERGLAZE

A decoration, usually painted by hand, that is applied after the original glazing and firing of a piece

PASTE

Porcelain in its raw form before shaping and firing

PRODIGY

The computer service used to gather or exchange information

PRODUCTION MOLD

A mold of porous plaster used to create the actual piece, the mold absorbs the moisture from the liquid clay during the firing process, these molds are replaced after 30 - 40 castings

PROOF

A piece produced to check the quality of the production; in a run of limited editions, proofs are marked as such and not numbered

PROTOTYPE

The original model created by hand by sculptors

QUARTERLY

The Department 56 magazine that is produced four times a year

RETIRED

Refers to a piece that is no longer being produced and will not be in the future

SECOND

Any item that is not of acceptable quality

SECONDARY MARKET

The market in which retired and limited pieces are purchased, sold or traded

SHRINKAGE

The amount of reduction in a piece when it is fired

SISAL

A hemplike fiber obtained from the agave plant

SLEEVE

The cardboard cover that slips over the styrofoam packing box

SLIP

Liquid clay that is poured in a mold or used to adhere two pieces together

SNOWBABIES

Department 56's version of children and animals frolicking in the snow; non-Department 56 Snowbabies were first popular about the turn of the century

SPECIAL EVENT PIECE

A piece that is produced to be sold only at a specific event or series of events

SWAP 'N SELL

An event organized so that collectors may sell or swap items with each other

TACKY WAX

A pliable wax used to secure accessories in place yet allows easy removal

TAIWAN

The first country to produce Department 56 villages

TOPIARY

Trees and bushes that are cut and trimmed into shapes

VARIATION

A change in form, mold or color of a piece from the first issue to subsequent issues

VILLAGE CCP MINIATURES

ITEM #	NAME/DESCRIPTION	YEAR ISSUED TO YEAR RETIRED	SRP AT ISSUE	GREENBOOK TRUMARKET PRICE
6558-7	DICKENS' VILLAGE ORIGINAL, SET OF 7	1987 - 1989	$ 72.00	--
•	Crowntree Inn	1987 - 1989	12.00	$ 35.00
•	Candle Shop	1987 - 1989	12.00	35.00
•	Green Grocer	1987 - 1989	12.00	35.00
•	Golden Swan Baker	1987 - 1989	12.00	28.00
•	Bean and Son Smithy Shop	1987 - 1989	12.00	35.00
•	Abel Beesley Butcher	1987 - 1989	12.00	30.00
•	Jones & Co. Brush & Basket Shop	1987 - 1989	12.00	70.00
6559-5	DICKENS' COTTAGES, SET OF 3	1987 - 1989	30.00	--
•	Thatched Cottage	1987 - 1989	10.00	100.00
•	Stone Cottage	1987 - 1989	10.00	115.00
•	Tudor Cottage	1987 - 1989	10.00	140.00
6560-9	DICKENS' VILLAGE, ASSORTED SET OF 3	1987 - 1989	48.00	--
•	Dickens' Village Church	1987 - 1989	16.00	45.00
•	Norman Church	1987 - 1989	16.00	125.00
•	Blythe Pond Mill House	1987 - 1989	16.00	45.00
6561-7	CHRISTMAS CAROL COTTAGES, SET OF 3	1987 - 1989	30.00	--
•	Fezziwig's Warehouse	1987 - 1989	10.00	30.00
•	Scrooge & Marley Counting House	1987 - 1989	10.00	30.00
•	The Cottage of Bob Cratchit & Tiny Tim	1987 - 1989	10.00	40.00
6562-5	DICKENS' VILLAGE, ASSORTED SET OF 4	1987 - 1989	60.00	--
•	The Old Curiosity Shop	1987 - 1989	15.00	55.00
•	Brick Abbey	1987 - 1989	15.00	115.00

Item	Name	Years		
•	Chesterton Manor House	1987-1989	$ 15.00	$ 125.00
•	Barley Bree Farmhouse	1987 - 1989	15.00	40.00
6565-0	DICKENS' KENILWORTH CASTLE	1988 - 1989	30.00	135.00
6591-9	DICKENS' LANE SHOPS, SET OF 3	1987 - 1989	30.00	--
•	Thomas Kersey Coffee House	1987 - 1989	10.00	65.00
•	Cottage Toy Shop	1987 - 1989	10.00	35.00
•	Tuttle's Pub	1987 - 1989	10.00	45.00
6592-7	DICKENS' CHADBURY STATION & TRAIN	1987 - 1989	27.50	70.00
5935-8	NEW ENGLAND VILLAGE ORIGINAL, SET OF 7	1988 - 1989	72.00	--
•	Apothecary Shop	1988 - 1989	10.50	40.00
•	General Store	1988 - 1989	10.50	60.00
•	Nathaniel Bingham Fabrics	1988 - 1989	10.50	30.00
•	Livery Stable & Boot Shop	1988 - 1989	10.50	45.00
•	Steeple Church	1988 - 1989	10.50	175.00
•	Brick Town Hall	1988 - 1989	10.50	45.00
•	Red Schoolhouse	1988 - 1989	10.50	95.00
5937-4	NEW ENGLAND VILLAGE, ASSORTED SET OF 6	1988 - 1989	85.00	--
•	Timber Knoll Log Cabin	1988 - 1989	14.50	40.00
•	Smythe Woolen Mill	1988 - 1989	14.50	145.00
•	Jacob Adams Farmhouse	1988 - 1989	14.50	50.00
•	Jacob Adams Barn	1988 - 1989	14.50	40.00
•	Craggy Cove Lighthouse	1988 - 1989	14.50	125.00
•	Maple Sugaring Shed	1988 - 1989	14.50	45.00
5976-5	LITTLE TOWN OF BETHLEHEM, SET OF 12	1987 - 1989	85.00	165.00
6564-1	VICTORIAN MINIATURES, SET OF 2	1986 - 1987	45.00	--
•	Estate	1986 - 1987	22.50	125.00
•	Church	1986 - 1987	22.50	150.00

VILLAGE RELATED ORNAMENTS

ITEM #	NAME/DESCRIPTION	YEAR ISSUED TO YEAR RETIRED	SRP AT ISSUE	GREENBOOK TRUMARKET PRICE
6504-8	CHRISTMAS CAROL CCP ORNAMENTS, SET OF 3 (flat)	1986 - 1989	$ 13.00	$ 40.00
•	Fezziwig's Warehouse	1986 - 1989	4.35	--
•	Scrooge & Marley Counting House	1986 - 1989	4.35	--
•	The Cottage of Bob Cratchit & Tiny Tim	1986 - 1989	4.35	--
6536-6	NEW ENGLAND VILLAGE CCP ORNS, SET OF 7 (flat)	1986 - 1989	25.00	--
•	Apothecary Shop	1986 - 1989	3.50	20.00
•	General Store	1986 - 1989	3.50	25.00
•	Nathaniel Bingham Fabrics	1986 - 1989	3.50	20.00
•	Livery Stable & Boot Shop	1986 - 1989	3.50	20.00
•	Steeple Church	1986 - 1989	3.50	50.00
•	Brick Town Hall	1986 - 1989	3.50	25.00
•	Red Schoolhouse	1986 - 1989	3.50	25.00
6505-6	CHRISTMAS CAROL CHARACTERS ORNS, SET OF 3 (flat)	1986 - 1987	13.00	40.00
•	Bob Cratchit & Tiny Tim	1986 - 1987	4.35	--
•	Scrooge	1986 - 1987	4.35	--
•	Poulterer	1986 - 1987	4.35	--
6521-8	DICKENS' VILLAGE LIT ORNS, SET OF 8	1985 - 1989	48.00	--
•	Crowntree Inn	1985 - 1989	6.00	40.00
•	Candle Shop	1985 - 1989	6.00	35.00
•	Green Grocer	1985 - 1989	6.00	30.00

	Item	Years		
•	Golden Swan Baker	1985 - 1989	$ 6.00	$ 20.00
•	Bean and Son Smithy Shop	1985 - 1989	6.00	25.00
•	Abel Beesley Butcher	1985 - 1989	6.00	20.00
•	Jones & Co. Brush & Basket Shop	1985 - 1989	6.00	35.00
•	Dickens' Village Church	1985 - 1989	6.00	45.00
6513-7	CHRISTMAS CAROL COTTAGES LIT ORNS, SET OF 3	1987 - 1989	16.95	60.00
•	Fezziwig's Warehouse	1987 - 1989	6.00	--
•	Scrooge & Marley Counting House	1987 - 1989	6.00	--
•	The Cottage of Bob Cratchit & Tiny Tim	1987 - 1989	6.00	--
6520-0	DICKENS' VILLAGE LIT ORNS, ASST SET OF 6	1987 - 1989	36.00	--
•	Blythe Pond Mill House	1987 - 1989	6.00	50.00
•	Barley Bree Farmhouse	1987 - 1989	6.00	25.00
•	The Old Curiosity Shop	1987 - 1989	6.00	35.00
•	Kenilworth Castle	1987 - 1989	6.00	60.00
•	Brick Abbey	1987 - 1989	6.00	100.00
•	Chesterton Manor House	1987 - 1989	6.00	45.00
6533-1	NEW ENGLAND VILLAGE LIT ORNS, SET OF 7	1986 - 1989	42.00	--
•	Apothecary Shop	1986 - 1989	6.00	25.00
•	General Store	1986 - 1989	6.00	50.00
•	Nathaniel Bingham Fabrics	1986 - 1989	6.00	40.00
•	Livery Stable & Boot Shop	1986 - 1989	6.00	30.00
•	Steeple Church	1986 - 1989	6.00	125.00
•	Brick Town Hall	1986 - 1989	6.00	45.00
•	Red Schoolhouse	1986 - 1989	6.00	80.00

VILLAGE RELATED ORNAMENTS

ITEM #	NAME/DESCRIPTION	YEAR ISSUED TO YEAR RETIRED	SRP AT ISSUE	GREENBOOK TRUMARKET PRICE
6534-0	NEW ENGLAND VILLAGE LIT ORNS, ASST SET OF 6	1987 - 1989	$ 36.00	--
•	Timber Knoll Log Cabin	1987 - 1989	6.00	$145.00
•	Smythe Woolen Mill	1987 - 1989	6.00	115.00
•	Jacob Adams Farmhouse	1987 - 1989	6.00	60.00
•	Jacob Adams Barn	1987 - 1989	6.00	66.00
•	Craggy Cove Lighthouse	1987 - 1989	6.00	150.00
•	Weston Train Station	1987 - 1989	6.00	55.00
6522-6	DICKENS' 2-SIDED TIN ORNS, SET OF 6	1984 - 1985	12.00	360.00
•	Crowntree Inn	1984 - 1985	2.00	--
•	Green Grocer	1984 - 1985	2.00	--
•	Golden Swan Baker	1984 - 1985	2.00	--
•	Bean and Son Smithy Shop	1984 - 1989	2.00	--
•	Abel Beesley Butcher	1984 - 1989	2.00	--
•	Jones & Co. Brush & Basket Shop	1984 - 1989	2.00	--
5099-7	ORIGINAL SNOW VILLAGE WOOD ORNS, SET OF 6	1983 - 1984	30.00	450.00
•	Gabled House	1983 - 1984	5.00	--
•	Swiss Chalet	1983 - 1984	5.00	--
•	Countryside Church	1983 - 1984	5.00	--
•	Carriage House	1983 - 1984	5.00	--
•	Centennial House	1983 - 1984	5.00	--
•	Pioneer Church	1983 - 1984	5.00	--